The HOLY S#!T of the BIBLE

A COUNTDOWN OF THE 75
BEST OBSCENITIES, ABSURDITIES, AND ATROCITIES
FROM THE BEST-SELLING BOOK OF ALL TIME

JERUEL W. SCHNEIDER

JERUEL SCHNEIDER

THE HOLY SHIT OF THE BIBLE

A Countdown of the 75 Best Obscenities, Absurdities, and Atrocities

From The Best-Selling Book Of All Time

JERUEL SCHNEIDER

Printed Worldwide

First Printing 2023

First Edition 2023

10 9 8 7 6 5 4 3 2 1

Book Cover by Jeruel Schneider

The HOLY SH!T of the BIBLE

CONTENTS

FOREWORD

The Bible is a text that has been revered, studied, and debated for centuries. It has inspired great works of art, literature, and philosophy, and it has shaped the beliefs and values of countless individuals and societies. But it is also a text that is steeped in historical and cultural contexts that can be difficult to understand, and it contains passages that are deeply problematic from a modern perspective.

In this book, the author takes a critical and incisive approach to deconstructing Bible passages, exposing the contradictions, biases, and problematic messages that lurk beneath the surface. The author's approach is both analytical and passionate, as they draw on a range of historical, literary, and social justice perspectives to unpack the meaning and implications of each passage.

This book is not a celebration of the Bible. It is a reckoning with the text and the ways in which it has been used to justify oppression, violence, and discrimination throughout history. The author does not shy away from confronting the problematic aspects of the text, delivering a fervent censuring with the occasional injection of satire and humor.

Of course, there are those who will disagree with the author's interpretations and conclusions. But that is part of the value of this book. It invites readers to engage in a critical dialogue with the text, to grapple with the complexities and contradictions of the Bible, and to question the assumptions and biases that underlie many traditional interpretations.

Whether you are a skeptic, a seeker, or a believer, this book offers a challenging and thought-provoking exploration of the Bible that is sure to stimulate discussion and reflection. It is a call to engage with the text in a new and critical way, to confront its problematic aspects, and to work towards a more just and inclusive understanding of the world. You may even enjoy a laugh or two.

Tom Jump
Philosopher

ACKNOWLEDGEMENTS

I would like to thank all those who have been an inspiration and an encouragement along the way in writing this book. First and foremost, I must thank my wife for her unending support, and for enduring my many rants pertaining to this book—many of which took place under the stars in the hot tub as we'd ponder all things unknown while enjoying our traditional champagne. *You're amazing and an amazing mom. I love you.*

My sincere gratitude goes out to my Dad, Tom Jump, Aron Ra, Matt Dillahunty, Seth Andrews, Dan Barker, Alex O'Connor, Bart Ehrman, Christopher DiCarlo, Joshua Bowen, Skylar Fiction, Peter Rollins, and the many others, including those who have passed on such as Robert Ingersoll, Christopher Hitchens, Bertrand Russell, Carl Sagan, Isaac Asimov, and Thomas Paine; whose force in continually expanding my horizon is of an incalculable magnitude. I love you all.

I thank my daughters that I love more than anything, and all children for the inspiration in grasping the importance of the responsibility that we all share in protecting your innocence, your freedom, your purity, your wonder, and all the beauty you are born with in your untainted nature; that we may forever stand in the way of anything that may promote fear and inadequacy. You bring me much joy. I'm here to support you and protect you in any way I can.

INTRODUCTION

In all affairs, it is a healthy thing now and then to hang a question mark on the things you've long taken for granted.
~ Bertrand Russell

Engaging in submitting my long-held sacred beliefs to a collision course with reality has been of indescribable enjoyment. Beginning as a child and through the years to follow, my incessant studying of the Bible, along with theological and philosophical matters, had always led me to naturally question—though never overstep my dearly treasured and hallowed foundation of Christianity. Upon reflection, I now realize, these questions and wonders, which were routinely met with age-old cliches, disdain, and shock, were but smoldering embers; those which would inevitably culminate and lead to a quenchless inferno—one that would finally scorch and devour much of all that I held sacred and lead to newfound freedom. Of utmost irony was the ensuing shedding of my old self; that *old man* in radical departure; dying a delightful death and being *reborn.* A metamorphosis that transcended any self-persuaded exhilaration from the compulsory prayer of salvation and baptism of my youth, had now renewed a happiness that I was promised would forever hide itself from me. Purification, that I was only promised through baptism and avowing the prayer of salvation as an innocent child (*though one having been born in sin; destitute of god's love, and in need of redemption),* had now truly cleansed my mind. Redemption, that I was promised in forsaking much of my fellow mankind by exercising an elitist, yet comfortably quiet judgment regarding the many walks of life other than my own—*had now become more real than anything I had ever felt before.* An overwhelming release; an extraordinary letting-go, and a massive weight being lifted, quickly became evident as I replaced the emphasis on a promise of a blissful life in eternity, with the one momentary life that I have here on Earth. The peace and tranquility I now feel in abandoning the lens of scrutiny, and embracing the lens of camaraderie with my fellow man, is unspeakably superior to that I had convinced myself of in my delusion. A new set of eyes, purely clear in blindness to the differences, those of which in signature self-righteous arrogance, had sadly established my unique and separate status in having been '*saved by a god.*'

I'm very grateful for the one source I can attribute to my personal transformation. Though there have been many inspirations along the way, this source entirely outweighs the fleeting words of any modern man; the self-aggrandizing sound bytes of any preacher; the doctrines, dogmas and religions of the world—including those found in any cathedral, temple, or Sunday clubhouse; current and prior friendships, whether good or indifferent, and all forms of academia, including every book in print...*except one.*

This one source is the Bible.

I've curated 75 of my favorite curiosities from the holy book, each of which if sacrilegiously eliminated, would make the Bible exponentially better in terms of morality and overall sensibility. (An improvement that should be impossible for the word of god.) After all, entrusting the affairs and eternity of my life into the hands of iron age scribes, whom promise calamitous repercussions if I merely disbelieve in whatever they penned, is a comical proposition in itself. As a father, I urge every parent to consider their children when reading the various passages inside. Though I don't think it will take much convincing, it's my *prayer* you find them as egregious and inflammatory as I do, and thus spare your innocent ones from such inanity.

In the words of Thomas Paine, *"Any system of religion that shocks the mind of a child cannot be true,"* and he concludes with the equally important, *"The world is my country, all mankind are my brethren, and to do good is my religion."*

With the focus on making this book an easy and quick read, the scriptural text and my personal commentary for each of the 75 passages is brief. I focused on using two translations when it was most necessary and two that indeed compliment each other, and most importantly, accurately corroborate with each other. The first is the NLT; the *New Living Translation,* and the second is the KJV; the *King James Version.* For many people, the New Living Translation is the easiest version of the Bible to read because it uses normal modern English. It is an accurate thought-for-thought translation of the original languages of the Bible and is widely accepted. (There may be other translations found throughout, including my personal translation as satire; the JST [Jeruel Schneider Translation]). Certain passages that needed to be paraphrased in order to keep things concise are marked with *'pp.'* Additional common abbreviations may be found throughout such as *'NT' (New Testament)* and *'OT' (Old Testament).* Full references are found in the back of the book.

With love,
Je Schneider

#75

Saint Paul the Scientist

Hebrews 11:3
NLT

3By faith we understand that the entire universe was formed at God's command, that what we now see did not come from anything that can be seen.

KJV

3Through faith we understand that the worlds were framed by the word of God, so that things which are seen were not made of things which do appear.

Romans 1:18-20
NLT

18But God shows his anger from heaven against all sinful, wicked people who suppress the truth by their wickedness.
19They know the truth about God because he has made it ob-
vious to them. 20For ever since the world was created, people
have seen the earth and sky. Through everything God made, they can clearly see his invisible qualities—his eternal power and divine nature. So they have no excuse for not knowing God.

Paul, within one verse, clearly illustrates the common archaic and fossilized mentality of nearly 2,000 years ago beginning with a logical fallacy in 'through faith—*we understand*' before proceeding to announce his revelatory debunking of basic science. The one thing that Paul most accurately states is 'through faith' as it takes a monumental amount of superhuman faith combined with utter disregard for science and the atomic structure of matter to believe his audacious, 'things which are seen were not made of things which do appear.' The origins of matter may never reach a perfectly unanimous consensus, though ancient declarations that purely defy science and mere logic, must stand the test of time and endure all trials by fire if we are to uphold Paul's scripture (and the entire Bible for that matter), as the inerrant word of god.

One must possess a profound wisdom in granting Paul's notion that god *spoke* all things into existence, thus implying matter was entirely non-existent prior to this. Consider the insurmountable odds one faces when making such drastic claims from a scientifically and technologically stymied era. If Paul were presented with not only the tools by which science has incomprehensibly advanced since his existence, but also the laws of science we have come to discover, I can only assume his faith and the scripture he penned would remain perfectly in tact out of sheer incredulity. Such an extreme leap into reality would be too overwhelming for the common man of antiquity when widely accepted legends and myths are forced to collide with empirical evidence as a result of the scientific method and other methodologies from an inestimably advanced human civilization in comparison. Contrarily, in the impossible scenario of a world made unaware of all venerated and *sacred* texts; free of all such myths, legends and presuppositions, and one solely dependent on the conclusive and verifiable evidence of our modern day; the inevitably high degree of incredulity would be astounding if newly presented with Paul's scientific theory. Nevertheless, in Romans 1:20, Paul boldly states that we are without excuse for not knowing god; in that 'through the observable world, we can clearly see his invisible qualities.' Paul even asserts that it's the wickedness and unrighteousness of those who may think otherwise and those who, in turn, must endure the wrath of god. Brazen, lofty, and sadly justifiable words when considering the age.

Those who fall prey to this essential and foundational threat of falling into the hands of a wrathful god for *thinking otherwise,* will forever remain the enemy of progress.

#74

One Way

Galatians 1:8-9
NLT

8Let God's curse fall on anyone, including us or even an angel from heaven, who preaches a different kind of Good News than the one we preached to you. 9I say again what we have said before: If anyone preaches any other Good News than the one you welcomed, let that person be cursed.

KJV

8But though we, or an angel from heaven, preach any other gospel unto you than that which we have preached unto you, let him be accursed. 9As we said before, so say I now again, If any man preach any other gospel unto you than that ye have received, let him be accursed.

Most commentaries on this passage will stress that Paul was specifically coming against the Judaizers who were still devoted to their uniquely bizarre fascination with the snipping of the foreskin. In all fairness, we can't exactly blame them as this sheering of the penis came from the top-down (pun intended) as god himself had commanded and declared this as a 'token of the covenant' in Genesis 17. (More on that later.) In any case, Paul begins by cursing anyone who may preach a different gospel than that of the apostles and casually skyrockets into another stratosphere to warn of the next most likely heretic: 'An angel from heaven.' We would let Paul off the hook a little here and allow for some inflationary prose if it weren't for his numerous mentions of angels throughout his writings including, *'Do you not know that we shall judge angels?'*[1] and *'Angels are merely spirits sent to serve people who are going to be saved.'*[2]

Nonetheless, most incendiary of the passage is Paul, twice reiterating his dire warning, and in one fell swoop, manages to reduce the billions to come within future generations and the thousands of religions to emerge throughout the world, to being accursed if they deviate from this gospel. (There is a nice buffet of adjectives from other translations in place of 'accursed' such as *'condemned to destruction,'* [AMP]; *'damned,'* [ABPE']; *'condemned to hell,'* [NET, GNT]; to name a few.)

We find countless examples of this throughout the entire Bible, so it shouldn't come as a surprise that Paul is simply reinforcing the doctrine of 'one way to god.' Again, this exclusivity eliminates all other religions, all other lines of thought, and certainly all who live by simply being 'a good person.'

1 I Corinthians 6:3 [NKJV]
2 Hebrews 1:14 [CEV]

#73

The Rich Man and Lazarus

Luke 16:19-31
NLT

19“There was a rich man who was clothed in purple and
fine linen and who feasted sumptuously every day. 20And at
his gate was laid a poor man named Lazarus, covered with
sores, 21who desired to be fed with what fell from the rich
man’s table. Moreover, even the dogs came and licked his
sores. 22The poor man died and was carried by the angels
to Abraham’s side. 23The rich man also died and was buried,
and in Hades, being in torment, he lifted up his eyes and saw
Abraham far off and Lazarus at his side. 24And he called out,
‘Father Abraham, have mercy on me, and send Lazarus to dip
the end of his finger in water and cool my tongue, for I am in
anguish in this flame.’ 25But Abraham said, ‘Child, remember that you in your lifetime received your good things, and
Lazarus in like manner bad things; but now he is comforted
here, and you are in anguish. 26And besides all this, between
us and you a great chasm has been fixed, in order that those
who would pass from here to you may not be able, and none
may cross from there to us.’ 27And he said, ‘Then I beg you,
father, to send him to my father’s house— 28for I have five
brothers—so that he may warn them, lest they also come into
this place of torment.’ 29But Abraham said, ‘They have Moses
and the Prophets; let them hear them.’ 30And he said, ‘No,

father Abraham, but if someone goes to them from the dead, they will repent.' 31He said to him, 'If they do not hear Moses and the Prophets, neither will they be convinced if someone should rise from the dead.'"

Aside from the long-standing debate over whether or not this well known parable of Jesus is an actual account or simply allegorical, there remain a plethora of exegetical commentaries on particular elements within the text. Exclusive to the Gospel of Luke, many find the passage to have a direct correlation with Abraham and Eliezer (variant of 'Eleazar'; Hebrew transliteration of the Greek name 'Lazarus') in Gen. 15:2. Additionally, symbolic associations and parallels are drawn between the rich man and Jacob's son Judah; the food scraps *('crumbs'; KJV)* in verse 21 as a possible reference to the gentiles (Matt. 15:22–28); and the valley between the highlands of Transjordan and the hill country of Ephraim in which the River Jordan flows as representing the chasm. Lastly, and most notably for those hell-bent on hell, we have Jesus speaking of the torment the rich man now endures in Hades. The interchangeability of the Greek mythological underworld of Hades and the Norse underworld of 'Helheim' (Hel, Hell) is a fun interactive feature of the Bible, and the subject matter is one of great importance to Jesus as he speaks of this abode of the damned more than any other character in the Bible. Jesus may have rather used the word 'Gehenna' (the English transliteration of the Hebrew word 'Hinnom') in place of Hades, figuratively referring to the Hinnom Valley (also called "The Valley of Slaughter") where child sacrifice had taken place and had become the city garbage dump. 'Sheol', a favorite of the Old Testament, is the least likely substitute as it wasn't spicy enough to compete with the rapidly evolving realm of eternal damnation. In keeping with the obvious overtones of Greek mythology throughout much of the Bible, let us yield to the most widely accepted among contemporary translations within this passage: *Hades.* Further support is found in Revelation 1:18, where we find Jesus holds the keys to Hades as does the Greek god of the underworld; the eponymous Hades himself.

We can now place the above mini-exegesis into the category of complete irrelevance. Of utmost importance is the colossal magnitude of the final verse, insomuch that it nearly renders the preceding verses meaningless. In concluding this parable, Jesus places enormous stature on the words of Moses and the prophets, immeasurably strengthening the supposed veracity of their writings.

The early-on placement of this commentary within this book is purely credited to this final verse 31. I *pray* the interspersed stories and memoirs of Moses to follow will serve as a stark reminder of this glaring verse.

#72

David's Sex Scandal Part I: Orgy as Divine Punishment

II Samuel 12:11-12
KJV

11Thus saith the LORD, Behold, I will raise up evil against
thee out of thine own house, and I will take thy wives before
thine eyes, and give them unto thy neighbor, and he shall lie
with thy wives in the sight of this sun. 12For thou didst it
secretly: but I will do this thing before all Israel, and before
the sun.

NLT

11"This is what the Lord says: Because of what you have done,
I will cause your own household to rebel against you. I will
give your wives to another man before your very eyes, and he
will go to bed with them in public view. 12You did it secretly,
but I will make this happen to you openly in the sight of all
Israel."

Before we get to the vengeance & voyeurism, let's recap the first half of the story of David, Uriah, and Bathsheba from the prior chapter; II Samuel 11. David, our first voyeur, sends his messengers[3] to retrieve this tantalizing woman 'Bathsheba' that he sees bathing from his roof. Despite her being married to Uriah, David impregnates her and then pursues a couple cheap attempts to cover things up. After failing, David then wastes no time and sends Uriah to the front lines of battle to be killed. Once Uriah is dead and out of the way, David fetches for Bathsheba, adds her to his list of wives, and she then gives birth to their son. The next chapter begins with the lord sending Nathan to deliver a clever parable to David before getting to the next act in verses 11 and 12. Our buddy Paul says it best in Romans 12:19 when he references Deuteronomy 32:35; *Dear friends, never take revenge. Leave that to the righteous anger of God. For the Scriptures say, "I will take revenge; I will pay them back," says the Lord. (NLT)* Well the lord certainly delivers here as he ups the ante and announces his vengeful plan of voyeurism in a grand orgy exposé; *"David did it secretly, but I'm putting this on full blast."* We can't exactly prove god watched (we wouldn't dare assume such a thing even though this whole exhibition was his idea), though it sounds like he wanted everybody else to watch? I wonder if the participants were guilty of sexual misconduct as this was a divinely inspired orgy?

Next up, don't miss the grand finale of David and the Housewives of Judah as something must be done about this newborn baby…

3 11:4Then David sent messengers to get her; and when she came to the palace, he slept with her. She had just completed the purification rites after having her menstrual period. [NLT]
11:4And David sent messengers, and took her; and she came in unto him, and he lay with her; for she was purified from her uncleanness. [KJV]

#71

David's Sex Scandal Part II: God Kills David's Baby

II Samuel 12:13-24
NLT

13Then David confessed to Nathan, "I have sinned against the Lord."

Nathan replied, "Yes, but the Lord has forgiven you, and you won't die for this sin. 14Nevertheless, because you have shown utter contempt for the word of the Lord by doing this, your child will die."[4]

15After Nathan returned to his home, the Lord sent a deadly illness to the child of David and Uriah's wife. 16David begged God to spare the child. He went without food and lay all night on the bare ground. 17The elders of his household pleaded with him to get up and eat with them, but he refused.

18Then on the seventh day the child died. David's advisers were afraid to tell him. "He wouldn't listen to reason while the child was ill," they said. "What drastic thing will he do when we tell him the child is dead?"

19When David saw them whispering, he realized what had happened. "Is the child dead?" he asked. "Yes," they replied, "he is dead."

4 Nevertheless, because by this deed you have given [a great] opportunity to the enemies of the LORD to blaspheme [Him], the son that is born to you shall certainly die." [AMP]

20Then David got up from the ground, washed himself, put on lotions, and changed his clothes. He went to the Tabernacle and worshiped the Lord. After that, he returned to the palace and was served food and ate. 21His advisers were amazed. "We don't understand you," they told him. "While the child was still living, you wept and refused to eat. But now that the child is dead, you have stopped your mourning and are eating again."

22David replied, "I fasted and wept while the child was alive, for I said, 'Perhaps the Lord will be gracious to me and let the child live.' 23But why should I fast when he is dead? Can I bring him back again? I will go to him one day, but he cannot return to me." 24Then David comforted Bathsheba, his wife, and slept with her. She became pregnant and gave birth to a son, and David named him Solomon. The Lord loved the child.

Apparently, the climax in our prior story wasn't gratifying enough. According to most of the translations,[5] god, within his infinite realms of wisdom, omniscience, and omnipotence, is also getting very concerned about the virality of David's sex scandal. He's met with a rush of questions spurred on by critical insecurity, sending high velocity shock waves through the universe;

"What will my enemies say!?"

"What will they think!??"

"Will they say bad things about me and my king!!??"

In today's terms, god is getting severe anxiety. He quickly contemplates his extra options for payback as the bang of the exposé in the first act of retribution has worn off:

1. *Shall I kill Bathsheba?...Eh..boring.*
2. *Shall I kill David?...Eh..too obvious..they'll guess that one.*
3. *A bigger orgy?...Eh..Already annihilated Sodom and Gomorrah for all that...boring..*
4. *Shall I kill some of David's wives?...Eh...How uneventful... unimportant...blah.*
5. *WAIT! I got it. Here's the most sensible idea. If David admits that he wronged me, I'll kill his newborn son! Bathsheba won't care and I don't care if she does, yet THIS will certainly affect David for some years to come.*

The coup de grace was not that #5 prevailed, but that it took seven days for the baby to die after being struck by god with a likely grueling and insufferable fatal illness. It's unfortunate this baby wasn't given one of the many swift executions god frequently dispensed, such as by the

5 Howbeit, because by this deed thou hast given great occasion to the enemies of the LORD to blaspheme, the child also *that is* born unto thee shall surely die. [KJV] Howbeit, because by this deed thou hast given great occasion to the enemies of Jehovah to blaspheme, the child also that is born unto thee shall surely die. [ASV]

sword, by drowning, by the earth swallowing it, or even by 'translation' as was the case with Enoch and Elijah.[6]

Upon hearing the news of his baby's death, David's ready to get his groove on. He cleans up, worships the lord, makes a snarky comment to his servants, and in one last climax, goes and makes a new baby with Bathsheba.

(And the lord loved this baby.)

6 Genesis 5:24 *{Enoch}* / II Kings 2:11 *{Elijah}*
Paul writes in Hebrews 11:5: Enoch was translated that he should not see death; and was not found, because God had translated him. [KJV]

#70

Achan for a Breakin'

Joshua 6-7
NLT, *pp*

6:2The Lord said to Joshua, "I have given you Jericho. 3You and your fighting men should march around the town once a day for six days. 4On the seventh day you are to march around the town seven times, with the priests blowing the horns. 5When you hear the priests give one long blast on the rams' horns, have all the people shout as loud as they can. Then the walls of the town will collapse, and the people can charge straight into the town. 18Do not take any of the things set apart for destruction, or you yourselves will be completely destroyed. 19Everything made from silver, gold, bronze, or iron is sacred to the Lord and must be brought into his treasury." 20When the people heard the sound of the rams' horns, they shouted as loud as they could. Suddenly, the walls of Jericho collapsed, and the Israelites charged into the town and captured it. 21They completely destroyed everything in it with their swords—men and women, young and old, cattle, sheep, goats, and donkeys.

7:1But Israel violated the instructions about the things set apart for the Lord. A man named Achan had stolen some of the sacred things, so the Lord was very angry. 2And Joshua sent some of his men to spy out the town of Ai. 3When they

returned, they told Joshua, "There's no need for all of us to go."
4So about 3,000 warriors were sent, but they were soundly
defeated 5and the men of Ai killed about thirty-six who were
retreating. The Israelites were paralyzed with fear, and their
courage melted away. 6Joshua and the elders tore their clothing, threw dust on their heads, and bowed face down to the
ground before the Ark of the Lord until evening. 10But the
Lord said to Joshua, "Get up! Why are you lying on your face
like this? 11"Israel has sinned and broken my covenant! They
have stolen some of the things that I commanded must be set
apart for me. 12Now Israel has been set apart for destruction.
13You will never defeat your enemies until you remove these
things from among you. 15The one who has stolen what was
set apart will be burned with fire, along with everything he
has." 16The next morning Joshua brought the tribes of Israel
before the Lord. 18and Achan was singled out. 19Joshua said
to Achan, "My son, give glory to the God of Israel, by telling
the truth." 20Achan replied, "It is true! I have sinned against
the God of Israel. 21Among the plunder I saw a beautiful robe
from Babylon, 200 silver coins, and a bar of gold. 21I wanted
them so much that I took them." 24Then Joshua and all the
Israelites took Achan, the sacred items, his sons, daughters,
livestock, and everything he had, and they brought them to
the valley of Achor. 25Then Joshua said to Achan, "Why have
you brought trouble on us? The Lord will now bring trouble
on you." And all the Israelites stoned Achan and his family
and burned their bodies. 26So the Lord was no longer angry.

Let's not overburden ourselves with the falling walls of Jericho by way of blasting ram horns and human shouting. Let's even grant it an absolute historical fact. We can then presume it factual that everything within the city was completely destroyed. (A routine mass genocide, and one found ubiquitously throughout these chronicles of the celestial conqueror.)

Joshua and his band of Israelites then proceed to burn the whole city, sparing only the silver, gold, and bronze for the treasury of the lord's house. He also spares Rahab, the prostitute and her family because Rahab had originally hid the spies Joshua sent to Jericho. (Of course there's no other motive here.) Joshua invokes a curse over the fallen Jericho and his fame spreads throughout the land. Joshua's conquest continues in a bid for the town of 'Ai', yet fails miserably. (The author divulges the embarrassing details of this battle: '*3,000 Israelite "warriors" were sent, 36 died and they ran away—paralyzed in fear.*'[7] *Joshua even joins in the snowflake jamboree in tearing his clothes in dismay and throws dust on his head.*) Ya....maybe stick to the horns and shouts next time.

God finally gets tired of watching these whiners rolling in the dirt and smacks down the ace card; *'Hey - get up! Don't you realize you only lost because someone stole some things from Jericho that I was supposed to have!? Seek and destroy him by fire!*'[8]

The next day, Achan admits he kept a robe, some coins, and gold from the scourge of Jericho. Joshua and all the Israelites then take Achan and all he has, including his sons and daughters, to the Valley of Achor where they are stoned to death and burned.

We're left thereafter with the comforting words of, *'So the Lord was no longer angry.'* Chapter eight then comes flying out of the gates with our reinvigorated god of war calling for an avenging in the destruction of Ai, and declares, *'This time I have given you Ai and this time you can keep the plunder and livestock for yourselves.'*

7 7:4-5 [NLT]
8 7:10-15 [NLT] pp

8:*25And so it was, that all that fell that day, both of men and women, were twelve thousand, even all the men of Ai. 26For Joshua drew not his hand back, wherewith he stretched out the spear, until he had utterly destroyed all the inhabitants of Ai. [KJV]*

#69

Parables, Riddles, and Other Secrets

Mark 4:10-13; 34
NLT

10Later, when Jesus was alone with the twelve disciples and
with the others who were gathered around, they asked him
what the parables meant.

11He replied, "You are permitted to understand the secret of
the Kingdom of God. But I use parables for everything I say
to outsiders, 12so that the Scriptures might be fulfilled:

'When they see what I do,

they will learn nothing.

When they hear what I say,

they will not understand.

Otherwise, they will turn to me

and be forgiven.'

13Then Jesus said to them, "If you can't understand the
meaning of this parable, how will you understand all the other
parables?

34In fact, in his public ministry he never taught without using
parables; but afterward, when he was alone with his disciples,
he explained everything to them.

KJV

10And when he was alone, they that were about him with the
twelve asked of him the parable. 11And he said unto them,
Unto you it is given to know the mystery of the kingdom of
God: but unto them that are without, all these things are done
in parables: 12that seeing they may see, and not perceive; and
hearing they may hear, and not understand; lest at any time
they should be converted, and their sins should be forgiven
them.

13And he said unto them, Know ye not this parable? and how
then will ye know all parables?

34But without a parable spake he not unto them: and when
they were alone, he expounded all things to his disciples.

The origin of our passage begins nearly 700 years prior when Isaiah[9] sees god and his accompaniment of seraphim angels.[10] Shocked by the scene and overcome with guilt, Isaiah admits he has filthy lips. Thankfully, one of the seraphim flies over with a burning coal he had taken from the altar with a pair of tongs and places it on Isaiah's mouth, absolving him of his guilt and his sins.

Isaiah was then charged by the lord to deliver a message to his people with a hint of sarcasm in Isaiah 6:9; *Say to this people, listen carefully, but do not understand. Watch closely, but learn nothing.* Things quickly turn paradoxical in verse 10 when god promotes one of his key weapons, 'the hardening of hearts'; *10Harden the hearts of these people. Plug their ears and shut their eyes. That way, they will not see with their eyes, nor hear with their ears, nor understand with their hearts and turn to me for healing. [NLT]* (This way, there isn't the slightest margin for error in accidental redemption.)

Many moons later, Jesus reveals his teachings in parable form are the fulfillment of what was spoken to Isaiah in Isaiah 6:9-10. He delivers the 'parable of the sower' to his disciples and the fun begins. Mark 4:10 shamelessly reveals the disciples responded to the parable with, 'Huh!? What's that mean?' Verse 11 keeps up the paradoxical momentum in Jesus responding to the disciples with, 'Because it is given unto you to know the mysteries *(alt. 'secrets')* of the kingdom of heaven, but to them, (*'outsiders' NLT*) it is not given.'[11]

Verse 13 would have been more fitting in place of Verse 11 as we can only imagine Jesus in this face palm moment replying with, 'You dingbats - you just ruined it! You're supposed to know the meaning of these stories! ~~GOD!!~~ DAD!!' Yet, in a relentless pursuit of exclusivity, verse 34 states he never taught without using parables, and that he would only decipher their cryptic nature in secret with his disciples.

---

9 Isaiah 6

10 John 12:41; 'Isaiah was referring to Jesus when he said this, because he saw the future and spoke of the Messiah's glory.' [NLT]

11 Matthew 13:11; Mark 4:11; Luke 8:10 parallel

Simply put, why? Unless one adheres to the Calvinistic approach of predestination, why not adapt the riddles so that all may understand?

Peter seemed to prefer the flip side of the paradox in his more all-inclusive message; *"The Lord is patient with you, not wanting anyone to perish, but everyone to come to repentance."* (*II Peter 3:9 NIV, pp*)

#68

Paul's Predestination

Romans 9:6-17
NLT

6Well then, has God failed to fulfill his promise to Israel?
No, for not all who are born into the nation of Israel are truly
members of God's people! 7Being descendants of Abraham
doesn't make them truly Abraham's children. For the Scriptures
say, "Isaac is the son through whom your descendants will be
counted," though Abraham had other children, too. 8This
means that Abraham's physical descendants are not necessarily
children of God. Only the children of the promise are considered to be Abraham's children. 9For God had promised,
"I will return about this time next year, and Sarah will have
a son." 10This son was our ancestor Isaac. When he married
Rebekah, she gave birth to twins. 11But before they were born,
before they had done anything good or bad, she received a
message from God. (This message shows that God chooses
people according to his own purposes; 12he calls people, but
not according to their good or bad works.) She was told, "Your
older son will serve your younger son." 13In the words of
the Scriptures, "I loved Jacob, but I rejected Esau." 14Are we
saying, then, that God was unfair? Of course not! 15For God
said to Moses, "I will show mercy to anyone I choose, and I
will show compassion to anyone I choose." 16So it is God

who decides to show mercy. We can neither choose it nor work for it.

17For the Scriptures say that God told Pharaoh, "I have appointed you for the very purpose of displaying my power in you and to spread my fame throughout the earth." 18So you see, God chooses to show mercy to some, and he chooses to harden the hearts of others so they refuse to listen.

KJV

11(for the children being not yet born, neither having done any good or evil, that the purpose of God according to election might stand, not of works, but of him that calleth;) 12it was said unto her, The elder shall serve the younger. 13As it is written, Jacob have I loved, but Esau have I hated.

Paul's arsenal of oddities never fail to entertain. He has the cunning ability of calling to remembrance the nonsensical obscenities of the old testament while attempting to write another happy unicorn-sparkles Sunday school message. In fact, being it is incumbent upon us to apply these ancient writings to our lives and the lives of our children, lest we fall into eternal hellfire, let us imagine Paul's modern-day version of this encouraging passage as if he were teaching Sunday school today:

'Ok gather 'round boys and girls. Boys in the first row, girls in the second—and you girls keep your mouths zipped; if you have ANY questions, ask your Daddy when you get home. Anyway boys, don't you realize god has a predetermined members-only club? Don't think you're all going to heaven just because—and that especially goes for any of you redheads. For example, there was once a couple boys named Joker and Redman. When they were in their mommy's belly, god hated Redman but he loved Joker, even though Joker would go on to play nasty tricks on his blind Daddy when he grew up. So you don't really get a choice. God decides who's in his members-only club. Some of you in here he may have loved when you were in your mommy's belly and some of you he may have hated. If you happen to be on the hated list, count it as a blessing! Remember the Pharaoh in our studies on Egypt? If you're as lucky as he was, you may get to show god's power and spread his fame throughout the world! Let's finish this lesson with something I jotted down: *When a potter makes jars out of clay, doesn't he have a right to use the same lump of clay to make one jar for decoration and another to throw garbage into?*[12] So, don't ask questions. Who are you to ask a question of god anyway?

Ok kids, in the future, I'll be working on unraveling this predestination mess I got myself into, but for now, I want you to study my prior chapter; specifically Romans 8:29-30, and also an important passage used for today's lesson: Malachi 1:2-3.

12 Romans 9:21 NLT

Lastly, if you have any issues understanding today's lesson, I want you to study a man named 'John Calvin'—at least he gets it.'

Romans 8:29-30: 29God knew his people in advance; he chose them to become like his Son, so that his Son would be the firstborn among many brethren 30Having chosen them, he called them to come to him; having called them, he gave them right standing with himself; through this, he gave them his glory. [NLT, pp]

Malachi 1:2-3: 2"I have always loved you," says the Lord. But you retort, "Really? How have you loved us?" And the Lord replies, "This is how I showed my love for you: I loved your ancestor Jacob, 3but I rejected his brother, Esau, and devastated his hill country. I turned Esau's inheritance into a desert for jackals." [NLT]

#67

Hit Me or Die *(by Lion Mutilation)*

I Kings 20:35-36
NLT

35Meanwhile, the Lord instructed one of the group of prophets to say to another man, "Hit me!" But the man refused to hit the prophet. 36Then the prophet told him, "Because you have not obeyed the voice of the Lord, a lion will kill you as soon as you leave me." And when he had gone, a lion did attack and kill him.

KJV

35And a certain man of the sons of the prophets said unto his neighbour in the word of the LORD, Smite me, I pray thee. And the man refused to smite him. 36Then said he unto him, Because thou hast not obeyed the voice of the LORD, behold, as soon as thou art departed from me, a lion shall slay thee. And as soon as he was departed from him, a lion found him, and slew him.

On numerous occasions, the book of Kings gets into some serious lion carnage, though as we learned in our prior lesson, who are we to question god? Why would any rational human being question such an enlightening story of the divine consequences for disobedience? Such gems of thought catapult the devout adherent into a critical juncture where they are forced to reconcile their position and their overall degree of fundamentalism. I find the more respectable, yet equally distasteful position affirms the words of Paul in II Timothy 3:16; declaring all scripture 'divine', 'inspired,' or 'god-breathed,' (depending on the translation) and profitable for teaching, rebuking, correcting, and training in righteousness. The dishonest and more common position is derived from a watered down concoction of self-serving biases—allowing for whatever manipulation and misinterpretation to advance one's justification in turning a blind eye to any borderline passage, and to appease any ambivalence.

I yield to the telling positions of these four renowned commentaries:

Jamieson-Fausset-Brown:

> The refusal of his neighbor to smite the prophet was manifestly wrong, as it was a withholding of necessary aid to a prophet in the discharge of a duty to which he had been called by God, and it was severely punished [1Ki 20:36], as a beacon to warn others.

Cambridge Bible for Schools and Colleges:

> Such a refusal was utterly at variance with the character of a prophet, who was to be prepared to obey at all costs a message which came as the word of the Lord.

Keil and Delitzsch:

> This occurrence shows with how severe a punishment all opposition to the commandments of God to the prophets was followed, as a warning for others.

Barnes:

> Said unto his neighbor - Rather, "to his friend" or "companion" - to one who was, like himself, "a prophet's son," and who ought therefore to have perceived that his colleague spoke "in the word of the Lord."

#66

Ananias and Sapphira

Acts 4:32-37; 5:1-10
NLT, *pp*

4:32All the believers were united in heart and mind. They felt that what they owned was not their own, so they shared everything they had. 34There were no needy people among them, because those who owned land or houses would sell them 35and bring the money to the apostles to give to those in need. 36For instance, Joseph, 37sold a field he owned and brought the money to the apostles.

NLT

5:1But there was a certain man named Ananias who, with his wife, Sapphira, sold some property 2and kept back part of the price,[13] his wife also being privy to it, and brought a certain part, and laid it at the apostles' feet.

3Then Peter said, "Ananias, why have you let Satan fill your heart? You lied to the Holy Spirit, and you kept some of the money for yourself. 4The property was yours to sell or not sell, as you wished. And after selling it, the money was also yours to give away. How could you do a thing like this? You weren't lying to us but to God!"

5As soon as Ananias heard these words, he fell to the floor and

13 [KJV]

died. Everyone who heard about it was terrified. 6Then some young men got up, wrapped him in a sheet, and took him out and buried him.

7About three hours later his wife came in, not knowing what had happened. 8Peter asked her, "Was this the price you and your husband received for your land?" "Yes," she replied, "that was the price."

9And Peter said, "How could the two of you even think of conspiring to test the Spirit of the Lord like this? The young men who buried your husband are just outside the door, and they will carry you out, too."

10Instantly, she fell to the floor and died. When the young men came in and saw that she was dead, they carried her out and buried her beside her husband.

My, the ill-fated destiny that rewarded such altruism. Of all peculiarities, what manner of a black magic death spell assisted by some otherworldly agency is this? In other words, what in god's name happened here!? For s#!ts & giggles, let's assume this entire story to be true; what supernatural force ripped the life right out of these two in a matter of seconds? By what spirit did these acts of deadly sorcery occur? Peter has pinpointed satan to be in the heart of Ananias and we can assume the same goes for Sapphira—leaving us one less likely source. I'll leave the rest to your imagination.

Anyway, the author (likely Luke), found it quite necessary to insert this magical story; disregarding an optional jump from 4:37 to 5:11—which would have resulted in a harmless segue. He also, as the legend goes, was a doctor and should have been thoroughly perplexed at such a highly potent life-sucking vacuum. Nevertheless, let's continue in throwing logic and sensibility out the window and look at a couple highlights:

A) "There were no needy people among them" (4:34)

Wow. Well in that case, I think the proper response to Ananias and Sapphira for their kind donation would be: "Thank you."

Extended Version: "We don't need it, but thank you."

B) "The property was yours to sell or not sell, as you wished. And after selling it, the money was also yours to give away." (5:4)

Is this glimmer of coherency the predecessor of the Freudian slip? One we may dub a Lukan slip? I'm sure one will slice & dice this scripture as they wish and whip it into a smooth Sunday cocktail, though I prefer to take this one at face value by honoring exactly what it says: Ananias was under no obligation to sell, nor was he obligated to donate any proceeds. Is this scripture implying their lives would have been spared if they donated nothing? I guess we'll never know as Ananias wasn't given a spare moment to respond to Peter before his demise.

For anyone that may be on edge in a tizzy of a cringe; just dying to reveal the REAL and truly justified reason this happened, don't worry…I hear you…*"They lied about how much they sold it for and therefore deserved to die."*

#65

David's Evil Census

II Samuel 24:1-17;[14] 25
NLT

1Once again the anger of the Lord burned against Israel, and
he caused David to harm them by taking a census. "Go and
count the people of Israel and Judah," the Lord told him. 2So
the king said to Joab and the commanders of the army, "Take
a census of all the tribes of Israel—from Dan in the north to
Beersheba in the south—so I may know how many people
there are." 3But Joab replied to the king, "May the Lord your
God let you live to see a hundred times as many people as there
are now! But why, my lord the king, do you want to do this?"
4But the king insisted that they take the census, so Joab and
the commanders of the army went out to count the people of
Israel. 8Having gone through the entire land for nine months
and twenty days, they returned to Jerusalem. 9Joab reported
the number of people to the king. There were 800,000 capable
warriors in Israel who could handle a sword, and 500,000 in
Judah. 10But after he had taken the census, David's conscience
began to bother him. And he said to the Lord, "I have sinned
greatly by taking this census. Please forgive my guilt, Lord, for
doing this foolish thing."

11The next morning the word of the Lord came to the prophet

14 *(:5-:7 omitted)*

Gad, who was David's seer. This was the message: 12"Go and say to David, 'This is what the Lord says: I will give you three choices. Choose one of these punishments, and I will inflict it on you.'" 13So Gad came to David and asked him, "Will you choose three years of famine throughout your land, three months of fleeing from your enemies, or three days of severe plague throughout your land? Think this over and decide what answer I should give the Lord who sent me." 14"I'm in a desperate situation!" David replied to Gad. "But let us fall into the hands of the Lord, for his mercy is great. Do not let me fall into human hands." 15So the Lord sent a plague upon Israel that morning, and it lasted for three days. A total of 70,000 people died throughout the nation, from Dan in the north to Beersheba in the south. 16But as the angel was preparing to destroy Jerusalem, the Lord relented and said to the death angel, "Stop! That is enough!" At that moment the angel of the Lord was by the threshing floor of Araunah the Jebusite. 25David built an altar there to the Lord and sacrificed burnt offerings and peace offerings. And the Lord answered his prayer for the land, and the plague on Israel was stopped.

As baffling as this story is, leaving most scholars and renown commentators with unanswered questions, it apparently was sacred enough to earn another seat; a parallel version—in Chronicles 21. The parallel wastes no time in launching with the notorious contradiction of 'Satan did it,' versus Samuel's version in verse 1; 'God did it.' Theological acrobatic aces will of course funnel into the same pool and wash this away with *'well obviously there was a dual agency here as there was in the book of Job.'* Though convenient, let's grant it.

Taking 24:1 into consideration, one may expect yet another Israelite rebellion is underway. Maybe some leaven seeped into some bread? Maybe a particular tribe had become fond of oysters or shrimp? Maybe someone stacked some wood on a Saturday? Oddly enough, in a testament that is largely dominated with human err, usually resulting in catastrophic devastation from above; we get no such exciting buildup. In fact, two chapters prior, in chapter 22, is a signature psalm of David as he exalts himself and sings praise to god for helping him crush, trample, and grind down his enemies as the dust of the earth; even those enemies who cried to god for help. Chapter 23 follows with a continuation of praise and an accounting of David's warriors and their accomplishments. We then find ourselves confronted with this most egregious act of David counting the people in chapter 24, having been swooned by one of the celestial foes as stated above. A shockingly savage counting rampage ensues, resulting in a deeply troubled and remorseful David. The vast kingdom among the arid plains, teeming with a once unnumbered people, now must face the utter devastation and demoralization of being numbered. Imagine the victims along the way…Screaming…Shrieking…Wailing in agony—*'Don't count me! Don't Count Me!!'* as they try to take cover. Thankfully, god offers David a multiple choice sentencing to get out of this absolute mess. David just happens to choose (C); likely the least harmful to him and his people. Obviously, a just god must deliver a just punishment and so it cost 70,000 people their lives.

Let's break this down:

God is angry again—god gets David to harm the people by counting them—David then repents for sinning in doing what god caused him to do—and god then punishes David by killing 70,000 of his people.

Sounds logical to me.

Moral of the story: Don't count people.

(Even if god tells you to.)

#64

Angelic Muting

Luke 1:5-20
NLT, *pp*

5There was a priest named Zechariah and his wife's name was Elizabeth. 7They had no children because Elizabeth was unable to conceive, and they were both very old. 11While Zechariah was in the sanctuary, an angel of the Lord appeared to him, standing to the right of the incense altar. 12Zechariah was shaken and overwhelmed with fear when he saw him. 13But the angel said, "Don't be afraid, Zechariah! God has heard your prayer. Your wife, Elizabeth, will give you a son, and you are to name him John." 18Zechariah said to the angel, "How can I be sure this will happen? I'm an old man now, and my wife is also well along in years." 19Then the angel said, "I am Gabriel! I stand in the very presence of God. It was he who sent me to bring you this good news! 20But now, since you didn't believe what I said, you will be silent and unable to speak until the child is born. For my words will certainly be fulfilled at the proper time."

KJV, *pp*

5There was a certain priest named Zacharias and his wife's name was Elizabeth. 7And they had no child, because that Elisabeth was barren, and they both were now well stricken in years.

11And there appeared unto him an angel of the Lord standing
on the right side of the altar of incense. 12And when Zacharias
saw him, he was troubled, and fear fell upon him. 13But the
angel said unto him, Fear not, Zacharias: for thy prayer is
heard; and thy wife Elisabeth shall bear thee a son, and thou
shalt call his name John.

18And Zacharias said unto the angel, Whereby shall I know
this? For I am an old man, and my wife well stricken in years.
19And the angel answering said unto him, I am Gabriel, that
stand in the presence of God; and am sent to speak unto thee,
and to shew thee these glad tidings. 20And, behold, thou shalt
be dumb, and not able to speak, until the day that these things
shall be performed, because thou believest not my words,
which shall be fulfilled in their season.

In the prototype version of this story,[15] we have Abraham at 100 years old and Sarah at 90, both laughing in unbelief when god tells them they will conceive Isaac. Somehow their doubt goes unpunished, though the archangel Gabriel, in his saintly wizardry, would prove unmerciful in this dramatic remake starring Zechariah and Elizabeth.

If we follow the crumbs, we find Zechariah must clearly suffer from DPS (Delusional Prayer Syndrome), as he supposedly is praying for a child well into he and his wife's old age. (First red flag for any parents out there.) Suspicions of this psychosis (among others) are greatly bolstered by the degree of shock he apparently displays toward Gabriel when he is told his prayer has been answered; truly revealing this is the last thing (or wish) on his mind.

Zechariah's response stirs an unimaginable tumultuous storm of fury within the archangel; 'How dare this old man of the human race doubt me! He is having this child whether he believes it or not and whether he likes it or not! In fact, last time this happened, god let those humans laugh and get away with it! NOT THIS TIME. YOU SIR ARE MUTED until the day your baby comes screaming into the world!' Unbeknownst to Gabriel, his veneration for millennia to come would be at little risk regardless of his magical muting escapade. The saint-making machine of Rome likely found consolation in Gabriel giving Mary a pass when she too responded in unbelief at the news of her immaculate conception.[16]

Thankfully, our story has a happy ending—and circumcision[17]… Go figure.

15 Gen 17:17; Gen 18:12
16 Luke 1:34
17 Luke 1:59-64

Ol' zip-lipped Zechariah finally has his tongue freed at the baby's 8-day bash with friends & family, better known as the "circumcision ceremony." The party must've been a kosher dandy, filled with laughter, joy, bagels & baby blood, and a mantra for the ages ~

'Snip the tip
Unzip the lip
For now & forever
Gabriel's hip!'

#63

You Will Know My Opposition

Numbers 13-14
NLT, *pp*

13:1The Lord said to Moses, 2"Send men to explore the land of Canaan, the land I am giving to the Israelites." 25After exploring the land for forty days, the men returned 26to Moses, Aaron, and the whole community of Israel. 27This was their report to Moses: 28"The people living there are powerful, and their towns are large and fortified. We even saw giants there, the descendants of Anak!" 30But Caleb tried to quiet the people as they stood before Moses. "Let's go at once to take the land," he said. "We can conquer it!" 31But the other men who had explored the land disagreed. 32So they spread this bad report about the land among the Israelites: "The land we explored will devour all who goes to live there. The people we saw were huge."

14:1Then the whole community wept aloud, and they cried all night. 3"Our wives and little ones will be carried off as plunder!" 11And the Lord said to Moses, "How long will these people treat me with contempt? 12I will disown them and destroy them with a plague." 13But Moses objected. "What will the Egyptians think when they hear about it?" 19In keeping with your magnificent, unfailing love, please pardon the sins of this people." 20Then the Lord said, "I will pardon them as you have requested. 22But not one of these people will ever enter that land. 28Tell them this: 29Because you complained against me, every one of you who is twenty years old or older and was included in the registration will die. 31You said your children would be carried off as plunder. Well, I will bring them safely into the land. 32But you will drop dead in this wilderness. 33And your children will wander in the wilderness for forty years. They will pay for your faithlessness, until the last of you lies dead in the wilderness. 34Because your men explored the land for forty days, you must wander in the wilderness for forty years—a year for each day, suffering the consequences of your sins. Then you will discover what it is like to have me for an enemy. 35I, the Lord, have spoken! I will surely do these things to every member of the community who has conspired against me. They will be destroyed here in this wilderness, and here they will die!"

God unfolds his ingenious plan by having Moses send spies to explore a special unconquerable land he wants to give to the Israelites. Upon returning with the message of 'Umm...We're gonna get smoked if we dare attempt to fight these guys'; little do they know their caution has sealed their fate. God, in his omniscience, is already well aware of the heavenly weaponry this battle will require in light of the insurmountable odds his people face, yet he prepares to rain down his wrath on the tribe for not attacking.

First, he and Moses have a little chat:

'These dumb desert nomads, though ridiculously outnumbered, keep crying and are worried for the lives of their wives and children. Like sooo annoying!! Ya...I will destroy them with a plague. By not attending the suicide mission, they've already killed themselves. Oh wait, except that one hyper pipsqueak, 'Caleb' and his buddy 'Joshua.' They're cool. Regardless of the other spies trying to protect the tribe and all that, these two at least get it.'

'No, God,' says Moses. 'Don't forget...The Egyptians will talk trash about you if you destroy your people. Plus...Remember...You have unfailing love. Stop it.'

'Hmm...Guess you're right,' replies god. 'Ok. I'll pardon them for skipping out on the suicide mission. BUT, come a place called 'Hell' or high-water, they are NEVER going to see that land, let alone enter it.'

We then reach the climax of this masterpiece when god, soon after shootin' the breeze with Moses, breaches his pardon and capriciously flies into a rage. In signature bloody prose, we find the death hammer of god in full vigor. God will 'show them what it's like to have him as an enemy'[18] and begins by decreeing the execution of all that are 20 years and older (600,000+) who are in the registration.[19] He then follows it with a dash of sass: 'You thought about your kids' safety!? Haha, well, tell ya what...They'll be safe...Oh, but they will pay for

18 :34;You will know my: *opposition*, NASB/*rejection*, NKJV/*alienation*, ASV/*displeasure*, ESV/ *what it is like to have me against you*, NIV

19 Numbers 1:45-46

your sins. They will wander in this desert as your carcasses waste away. By wander, I mean some serious wandering. I'm talking one year for every day those wimps explored Canaan. Just so happens to add up to one of my favorite numbers. Hmm that's odd.

Anyway, future generations will spin this into an iconic story and debate why a two to three-week journey would take 40 years for the two to three-million of you, and why there would be zero evidence of this Exodus. I, the Lord, have spoken!'

#62

Numbers Compilation: Divine Paranoia

Numbers Compilation; NLT, *pp*

1:51 *(The Lord had said to Moses):* When it is time for the Tabernacle to move, the Levites will take it down. When it is time to stop, they will set it up. Any unauthorized person who goes too near the Tabernacle must be put to death.

3:10 *(The Lord had said to Moses):* Appoint Aaron and his sons to carry out the duties. But any unauthorized person who goes too near the sanctuary must be put to death.

3:38 The area of the Tabernacle, in the east toward the sunrise, was reserved for the tents of Moses and of Aaron and his sons. Anyone other than a priest or Levite who went too near the sanctuary was to be put to death.

4:15 *(The Lord said to Moses and Aaron):* The camp will be ready to move when Aaron and his sons have finished covering the sanctuary and all the sacred articles. The Kohathites will carry these things to the next destination. But they must not touch the sacred objects, or they will die.

4:20 *(The Lord said to Moses and Aaron):* The Kohathites must never enter the sanctuary to look at the sacred objects for even a moment, or they will die.

17:12 The people of Israel said to Moses, "Look, we are

doomed! We are dead! 13Everyone who even comes close to the Tabernacle of the Lord dies."

18:3 *(The Lord said to Aaron):* But as the Levites go about all their assigned duties at the Tabernacle, they must be careful not to go near any of the sacred objects or the altar. If they do, both you and they will die.

18:22 *(The Lord said to Aaron):* No Israelites except priests or Levites may approach the Tabernacle. If they come too near, they will be judged and will die.

18:5;7 *(The Lord said to Aaron):* If you follow these instructions, the Lord's anger will never again blaze against the people of Israel. Any unauthorized person who comes too near the sanctuary will be put to death.

di·vine par·a·noi·a

• *{of a deity or spirit};* maximally unwarranted anxiety, distrust and suspicion; exclusively characterized as exceeding the bounds of that which is humanly capable, often leading to fanatical irrationality and the inflicting of severe consequences such as capital punishment.

As mentioned in Exodus,[20] these people are indeed a peculiar treasure, who wallow in endless oppression, yet continually attempt to please the ever dissatisfied oppressor. The tiresome and overbearing fixation with this tent ("tabernacle") and its furnishings, leaves any sensible reader of the 21st century wishing for Toto to run up and pull back the curtain. Unfortunately, the threat of death for anyone who may dare cross into the forbidden proximity of the tent, had established a paralyzing fear throughout the camp. They understood an ever watchful eye beams forth from a highly classified cockpit of calamity; a phantom marksman, gunning down any contestants—resulting in a bloody game of Curiosity Killed the ~~Cat~~ Israelite. Sorry Dorothy, this Ozian force, who suffers from a severe case of divine paranoia, wishes to remain anonymous. I'm afraid at the end of the blood stained road, a tug and a pull on the curtain will reveal absolutely nothing—not a being, not a spirit, nor even a presence.

When in doubt of the mind-bending degree of barbarism throughout countless stories in the Bible, do recall what is laid out right here before us. Here's a "chosen" people who are thoroughly warned with lethal action if they approach where this 'god' supposedly hangs out from time to time. Additionally, every man-made object within this tent carries a death sentence with it if merely seen with the naked eye—even for just an instant. Of course, 'specially' chosen people within the "chosen people" were given a unique security clearance to play around and conjure god. (Cut, slaughter, and burn up animals and their organs, light secret incenses, play with candles, pour out wine, perform blood rituals, create special aromas that god likes—just

20 Exodus 19:5

to name a handful.) They must have been outfitted with some sort of advanced resistor device that would deflect the highly sophisticated motion detection IR rays that monitored the rest of the camp.

All this in the name of a god who demands a perfect adoration and worship in the form of idolatrous preparations, rituals, and man-made objects. All this in the name of a god who's volatility spasmodically flies all over the spectrum with this "chosen" people; at one moment, vowing eternal love, and in another, vowing to disown and destroy them.

#61

The Primordial Jigsaw Plays a Lion Game

I Kings 13:11-26
NLT

11As it happened, there was an old prophet living in Bethel,
and his sons came home and told him what the man of God
had done in Bethel that day. They also told their father what
the man had said to the king. 12The old prophet asked them,
"Which way did he go?" So they showed their father which
road the man of God had taken. 13"Quick, saddle the donkey,"
the old man said. So they saddled the donkey for him, and he
mounted it. 14Then he rode after the man of God and found
him sitting under a great tree. The old prophet asked him,

"Are you the man of God who came from Judah?"

"Yes, I am," he replied.

15Then he said to the man of God,

"Come home with me and eat some food."

16"No, I cannot," he replied. "I am not allowed to eat or
drink anything here in this place. 17For the Lord gave me this
command: 'You must not eat or drink anything while you are
there, and do not return to Judah by the same way you came.'"
18But the old prophet answered,

"I am a prophet, too, just as you are. And an angel gave me
this command from the Lord: 'Bring him home with you so

he can have something to eat and drink.'" But the old man was lying to him.

19So they went back together, and the man of God ate and drank at the prophet's home. 20Then while they were sitting at the table, a command from the Lord came to the old prophet. 21He cried out to the man of God from Judah, "This is what the Lord says: You have defied the word of the Lord and have disobeyed the command the Lord your God gave you. 22You came back to this place and ate and drank where he told you not to eat or drink. Because of this, your body will not be buried in the grave of your ancestors." 23After the man of God had finished eating and drinking, the old prophet saddled his own donkey for him, 24and the man of God started off again. But as he was traveling along, a lion came out and killed him. His body lay there on the road, with the donkey and the lion standing beside it. 25People who passed by saw the body lying in the road and the lion standing beside it, and they went and reported it in Bethel, where the old prophet lived.

26When the prophet heard the report, he said, "It is the man of God who disobeyed the Lord's command. The Lord has fulfilled his word by causing the lion to attack and kill him."

Our illustrious story features a nameless "man." Earlier in the episode, this undisclosed operative and his invisible counterpart prove proficiency in the art of Jedi Force stasis; displaying a magical dominance over Jeroboam's hand. In a bloody twist of fate, Force fatigue will render this *handy* hocus-pocus useless when he needs it most.

Let us regard the renowned Matthew Henry's Commentary in light of this story:

> '*What shall we make of this? The judgments of God are beyond our power to fathom; and there is a judgment to come. Nothing can excuse any act of willful disobedience. This shows what they must expect who hearken to the great deceiver. They that yield to him as a tempter, will be terrified by him as a tormentor.*'

What shall we make of this? Matthew Henry makes a flowery bouquet of hellish delights in his unsurprising case for the fundamentalist in summing up this OG OT brutality as 'disobedience.' In this widely accepted theory (nauseatingly considered by plenty an objective fact), where the cosmic boss of earth waste management gets to create any set of rules and even attach 'disobedience is punishable by death' as the overarching scare tactic, then any scenario means open season. Above all, is this hilarious, yet sickening notion of disobedience when considering the omniscient antagonist, *god*, in his divine foreknowledge, is playing with an impossibly loaded deck. (Any alternative position regarding god's possessing of these properties is a defeater for the god of the Bible.)

In the case of our passage, any usage of the usual trickery or deceit is fair game—even if it's used on one of his own 'men of god.' A wickedly crafted premeditated path of doom begins with the man of god exhibiting his elite level of supernatural power. Next, a 'prophet' lies to him and entices him to eat some food. God apparently doesn't mind a lying prophet, and rather, commands him to prophecy damnation over the man of god for disobeying and partaking of the food. Next up on the checklist is some entertainment the Romans would eventually become fond of; *Damnatio ad bestias.* Yes indeed, it's time for a lion to kill the man of god for his disobedience.

Although we may have a killer ending to this story, if "don't eat or drink anything on your journey," and "don't return home the same way you came" is too boring, then you're in luck. This primordial Jigsaw hybrid and his more glorious games of death have been extensively documented throughout the Bible and here within this book for your reading pleasure.

#60

The Adultery Wing

Deuteronomy 24:1; KJV

When a man hath taken a wife, and married her, and it come to pass that she find no favour in his eyes, because he hath found some uncleanness in her; then let him write her a bill of divorcement, and give it her in her hand, and send her out of his house.

Matthew 5:18; KJV

18For verily I say unto you, Till heaven and earth pass, one jot or one tittle shall in no wise pass from the law, till all be fulfilled.

Matthew 5:31-32; NLT

31"You have heard the law that says, 'A man can divorce his wife by merely giving her a written notice of divorce.' 32But I say that a man who divorces his wife, unless she has been unfaithful, causes her to commit adultery. And anyone who marries a divorced woman also commits adultery.

Matthew 19:9; KJV, *pp*

9I say unto you, whosoever put away his wife, except it be for fornication, and shall marry another, commits adultery: and whoso marrieth her which is put away doth commit adultery.

Mark 10:10-12; KJV

> 11And he saith unto them, Whosoever shall put away his wife, and marry another, committeth adultery against her. 12And if a woman shall put away her husband, and be married to another, she committeth adultery.

Luke 16:17-18; KJV

> 17It is easier for heaven and earth to pass, than one tittle of the law to fail. 18Whosoever putteth away his wife, and marrieth another, committeth adultery: and whosoever marrieth her that is put away from her husband committeth adultery.

Romans 7:2-3; KJV, *pp*

> 2The woman which hath a husband is bound by the law to him so long as he lives. If her husband dies, she is loosed from the law of her husband. 3So then if, while her husband is alive, she marries another man, she shall be called an adulteress:

I Corinthians 6:9-10; KJV, *pp*

> 9Be not deceived: adulterers 10shall not inherit the kingdom of God.

I Corinthians 7:11; KJV

> 10And unto the married I command, yet not I, but the Lord, Let not the wife depart from her husband: 11but and if she depart, let her remain unmarried, or be reconciled to her husband: and let not the husband put away his wife.

For those who would gouge their eyes out before daring to read 3/4 of their own holy Bible, and for those who conveniently claim the majority of the volume is nullified under the guise of 'fulfillment' and through the psychologically supportive wording of "old" testament and "new" testament, Jesus and Paul have a little reminder. An appalling reminder insomuch that it shocked the hell out of hell. What once was a manageable habitat for Satan & Co., would immediately turn catastrophically chaotic; forcing a boundless expansion of the adultery wing to house the continuous flood of new tenants for all generations to come.

This all begins in the synoptic gospels with Jesus strengthening the significance of the law in Matthew 5:18.[21] The modern believer will of course pull the twitch, wiggle, & twist move on this one—and especially in regard to Jesus' teaching on divorce. Jesus continues by recalling the law of divorce in Deuteronomy and proceeds to greatly tighten the noose by instituting new rules. (As one would expect from the divine torah, a man was allowed to divorce his wife for basically anything,[22] and, lest we forget, impose death by stoning for committing adultery.) In contrast with Mark and Luke, Matthew contains the famed 'exception clause'; allowing for divorce only on the grounds of adultery and fornication. Of course this clause gives a preferred means of justification compared to Mark and Luke where there is no such exception.

This newly implemented lockdown after the mere uttering of

21 Pulpit Commentary, *pp*: Luke 16:17
"See," he said, "the new state of things I now teach, instead of loosening the cords of the old Law, will rather tighten them. My law of divorce is a severer one than that written by Moses."
Matthew Poole's Commentary, *pp*: Matthew 5:18
The law is the certain, unchangeable will of God concerning and shall never be altered in the least, nor abolished; therefore know that I come into the world upon no such errand.

22 Benson Commentary: Some uncleanness; hateful thing, distemper of body, or quality of mind, but not amounting to adultery which was not punished with divorce, but with death. Jamieson Commentary adds: shamefulness; some filthy or hateful thing; loathsome distemper of body.

wedding vows is simply outrageous. Other than the convenient exception clause, Jesus leaves no room for ambiguity in cause for divorce and quickly hands down the sin of adultery; even onto those who look or think upon a woman in lust, or those who marry a divorcee; thereby erecting a giant contradiction to the essence of his message of peace, joy, love, and forgiveness—to name a handful. It's almost comical to think on the statistics of all, who for countless good reasons outside of adultery—have split, and regardless of their newfound happiness, are on their way to burn in hell.[23] Saint Paulradox, in his saintly wisdom, nearly topples Jesus with not only his call to celibacy, but his command *('according to the law')*, that a woman is bound to her husband as long as he is alive. Let us resign and get out of this mess with the simple razor of Malachi: God hates divorce. *{Malachi 2:16}*

23 Revelation 21:8; I Corinthians 6:9-10

#59

The Scapeman

Leviticus 24:10-17; 23
NLT
"An Example of Just Punishment"

10One day a man who had an Israelite mother and an Egyptian father came out of his tent and got into a fight with one of the Israelite men. 11During the fight, this son of an Israelite woman blasphemed the Name of the Lord with a curse. So the man was brought to Moses for judgment. His mother was Shelomith, the daughter of Dibri of the tribe of Dan. 12They kept the man in custody until the Lord's will in the matter should become clear to them. 13Then the Lord said to Moses, 14"Take the blasphemer outside the camp, and tell all those who heard the curse to lay their hands on his head. Then let the entire community stone him to death. 15Say to the people of Israel: Those who curse their God will be punished for their sin. 16Anyone who blasphemes the Name of the Lord must be stoned to death by the whole community of Israel. Any native-born Israelite or foreigner among you who blasphemes the Name of the Lord must be put to death. 17Anyone who takes another person's life must be put to death."

23After Moses gave all these instructions to the Israelites, they took the blasphemer outside the camp and stoned him to death. The Israelites did just as the Lord had commanded Moses.

KJV (11-16; 23), *pp*

11the Israelitish woman's son blasphemed the name of the
LORD, and cursed. They brought him unto Moses: 12and put
him in ward, that the mind of the LORD might be shewed
them. 13And the LORD spake unto Moses, saying, 14Bring
forth him that cursed without the camp; and let all that heard
him lay their hands on his head, and let all the congregation
stone him. 15And say to the children of Israel, Whoever
curseth his God shall bear his sin; 16he that blasphemes the
name of the LORD shall be put to death, and the congregation
shall certainly stone him: and the stranger born in the land,
when he blasphemes the name of the LORD, shall be put to
death. 17And he that kill any man shall surely be put to death.

23And Moses spake to the children of Israel, that they should
bring forth him that had cursed out of the camp, and stone
him with stones. And the children of Israel did as the LORD
commanded Moses.

Our engagement begins by paying tribute to the author behind the literary prowess of the NLT (New Living Translation) section heading: 'An example of just punishment.' Presumably this biblically 'good idea' (to break down the heading even further), should be applicable and necessary for all time, especially if it happens to directly violate one of the ten commandments. Let's find out what in god's name happened here.

We're presented with two belligerent bedouins getting scrappy. One, who happens to be half-Egyptian, unleashes a forbidden sure-kill fatality move by blaspheming and cursing the name of the lord. Little does he know, by this utterance, he has sealed his own fate. The spectators are appalled at the man's outburst, so they take him to Moses for judgment. Moses is an excellent fit for the job. Not only is he the leader of the entire desert detention camp, but he is also quite skilled in the art of slaughtering those of Egyptian descent. Overcome by the terrifying report, he locks the man away in high security isolation and ponders a *just punishment.* Fortunately, the lord steps in, and for the sake of utmost clarity, speaks directly to Moses and extends the law of stoning to all blasphemers, regardless of nationality. It appears Moses had forgotten this *just punishment* that was gaining traction, and one the lord was growing fond of.

He delivers the execution instructions to the Israelites and proceeds to his box seat. (A far cry from the skybox seats where the lord has year-round passes in perpetuity.) In preparation, they emulated their new god-given invention of the scapegoat [24] and created the first scapeman. The witnesses had become unclean just by hearing the man's treacherous words, so they laid their hands on his head to put that guilt back on him. Upon the completion of the magical cleansing of their sorely defiled ears and mind, it was then time for the whole congregation to join in stoning the man to death.

It's no wonder why this disgusting and detestable murderous act of brutality on behalf of the lord would lead to great measures in avoiding

24 Passage #48; *'The Scapegoat'*

saying or writing the name of God. In time, the Jews would write Adonai ("Lord") instead of Yahweh. Instead of "God," they would write "G-d." They would refer to *God* with names like "the Name" instead of saying "God."

If you're anything like me and in need of some serious comic relief after this serious insanity, just read the brilliant insertion of verse 17:

17And he that kill any man shall surely be put to death. [KJV]

(Of course this scripture does not apply to g/d or anyone 'killing for g/d.')

Well dear brethren, let's conclude our devotional by kindly adjusting the NLT section heading: *'Divine Insecurity Illness'* or *'BS (broad statements) of Bloodthirsty Barbarians?'*

#58

~~The Story of Samson~~ The Myth of Hercules

Judges 13-16; NLT, *pp*

13:3An angel appeared to Manoah's wife and said, "Though you are barren, you will soon become pregnant and give birth to a son. 13:24When he was born, she named him Samson. 14:5When Samson went to Timnah, a lion attacked him. 6The Spirit of the Lord came upon him, and he easily ripped the lion's jaws apart with his bare hands as if it were a young goat. 14:8Later, he found a swarm of bees had made honey in the carcass of the lion. 9and he ate some of it.

(Samson challenges 30 men to a riddle. They extort the answer from his wife.)

14:19Then the Spirit of the Lord came powerfully upon him. He went to Ashkelon, killed thirty men and gave their clothing to the men who had solved his riddle. 15:4Samson caught 300 foxes. He tied their tails together in pairs, and fastened a torch to each pair. 5He lit the torches and let the foxes run through the grain fields of the Philistines and they burnt them to the ground. 15:6"Who did this?" the Philistines demanded. "Samson," was the reply. So the Philistines went and got the woman *(Samson was originally supposed to marry)* and her father and burned them to death. 15:8So Samson then attacked the Philistines; killing many of them. 15:11 3,000 men of Judah went to get Samson 15:14But Samson snapped the ropes on his arms and broke free. 15Then he found the jawbone of a donkey and killed 1,000 Philistines with it. 15:18Samson was now very thirsty 19So God caused water to gush out of the ground and Samson drank. 16:1One day Samson spent the night with a prostitute. 3Then he got up, took the doors of the town gate, including the two posts, and lifted them up. He put them on his shoulders and carried them to the top of the hill across from Hebron. 16:4Samson then fell in love with a woman named Delilah. 16:5The Philistines went to her and said, "Entice Samson to tell you what makes him so strong." 17*(After three attempts)* Samson shared his secret with her; "My hair has never been cut. If it were cut, my strength would leave me." 19Delilah lulled Samson to sleep and had a man shave off the seven locks of his hair. In this way she began to bring him down and he grew weak. When he awoke, the Lord had left him. 21The Philistines captured him and gouged out his eyes. 22Before long, his hair began to grow back. 23The Philistine rulers held a great festival 25they brought Samson from the prison to amuse them, and had him stand between the pillars supporting the roof. 27the Philistine rulers were there with about 3,000 men and women. 28Then Samson prayed, "strengthen me just one more time." 29Then Samson put his hands on the two center pillars that held up the temple, pushing against them with both hands, 30and the temple crashed down on the Philistine rulers and all the people. So he killed more people when he died than he had during his entire lifetime.

Along with the three citations below and the comparison table, it's worth noting that Paul inducted Samson into his *Hall of Faith.*[25]

> *'Without enumerating them, we can safely say, that there was not a nation of antiquity, from the remotest East to the furthest West, that did not have its mighty hero, and counterpart of Hercules and Samson.'* -George W. Cox

> *'The most complete and rounded-off Solar myth extant in Hebrew, is that of Shimshon (Samson), a cycle of mythical conceptions fully comparable with the Greek myth of Hercules.'* -Ignaz Goldziher

> *'...the atmosphere of mythology enveloping the story is so oppressive, that no one, who has the least susceptibility to its influence can resist it for a moment. Only such as cannot distinguish between accurate history and mythology at all, or are completely stunted by theological preconceptions, will fail to respond to such an overwhelming case as this.'* -Terry Vanderheyden

25 Hebrews 11:32-34

Solar Imagery	*Samson*
'Shemesh' (sun)/'Shamash' (sun god)	Sun child, little sun, man of the sun
'Beth Shemesh' (Temple of the sun)	Born in nearby town of 'Zorah'
Delilah *('lilah' - Night/Dark/ Moon)*	Sun/Adversary of the moon
7 rays of sun gods (Helios/ Apollo)	7 locks of hair/strength
Zodiac & constellation symbolism	Allegory of the sun's path
Fox: Sun symbolism/Pagan rituals	300 foxes tied together & lit on fire
Setting of sun/'death' of the sun	Dies between two pillars

Hercules	*Samson*
1st exploit/'labor': slays lion	1st exploit: slays lion
Pillars of Hercules/Strait of Gibraltar	The two pillars/Temple of Dagon
Supernatural/Demigod Strength	Supernatural/Demigod Strength
Solar Imagery and Symbology	Solar Imagery and Symbology
Kills with Club	Kills with Jawbone
Water conjuring exploit	Water conjuring exploit
Deception/Betrayal by Woman	Deception/Betrayal by Woman
Birth via Zeus and mortal woman	Divinely ordained birth
Breaks loose of bonds	Breaks loose of bonds
Carries the columns/gates of Cadiz	Carries the gates/posts of Gaza
From the Danaans	From the Tribe of Dan
Died by sacrifice/suicide	Died by sacrifice/suicide

Mythological Origins	*Samson*
Aristaeus captures bees from carcass	Swarm of bees/honey in lion carcass
Ra the sun god of Egyptian mythology fights darkness daily	Delilah (night) tries to defeat Samson (sun); Cuts his locks (sun-rays)
Superhero w/solar imagery and symbolism is common in ancient mythology	

#57

Divine Retribution: *Lashing with Leprosy*

Leviticus 13:45-46; 14:1-2; NLT

13:45Anyone with such a defiling disease (leprosy) must wear torn clothes, let their hair be unkempt, cover the lower part of their face and cry out, 'Unclean! Unclean!' 46As long as they have the disease they remain unclean. They must live alone; they must live outside the camp.

'Cleansing from Skin Diseases'

14:1And the LORD spake unto Moses, saying, 2This shall be the law of the leper in the day of his cleansing: He shall be brought unto the priest 3who will examine them at a place outside the camp. If the priest finds that someone has been healed of a serious skin disease, 4he will perform a purification ceremony, using two live birds that are ceremonially clean, a stick of cedar, some scarlet yarn, and a hyssop branch. 5The priest will order that one bird be slaughtered over a clay pot filled with fresh water. 6He will take the live bird, the cedar stick, the scarlet yarn, and the hyssop branch, and dip them into the blood of the bird that was slaughtered over the fresh water. 7The priest will then sprinkle the blood of the dead bird seven times on the person being purified of the skin disease. When the priest has purified the person, he will release the live bird in the open field to fly away. 8The persons being purified must then wash their clothes, shave off all their hair, and bathe themselves in water. Then they will be ceremonially clean and may return to the camp. However, they must remain outside their tents for seven days. 9On the seventh day they must again shave all the hair from their heads, including the hair of the beard and eyebrows. They must also wash their clothes and bathe themselves in water. Then they will be ceremonially clean. 10On the eighth day each person being purified must bring two male lambs and a one-year-old female lamb, all with no defects, along with a grain offering of six quarts of choice flour moistened with olive oil, and a cup of olive oil. 11Then the officiating priest will present that person for purification, along with the offerings, before the Lord at the entrance of the Tabernacle. 12The priest will take one of the male lambs and the olive oil and present them as a guilt offering, lifting them up as a special offering before the Lord. 13He will then slaughter the male lamb in the sacred area where sin offerings and burnt offerings are slaughtered. As with the sin offering, the guilt offering belongs to the priest. It is a most holy offering. 14The priest will then take some of the blood of the guilt offering and apply it to the lobe of the right ear, the thumb of the right hand, and the big toe of the right foot of the person being purified. 15Then the priest will pour some of the olive oil into the palm of his own left hand. 16He will dip his right finger into the oil in his palm and sprinkle some of it with his finger seven times before the Lord. 17The priest will then apply some of the oil in his palm over the blood from the guilt offering that is on the lobe of the right ear, the thumb of the right hand, and the big toe of the right foot of the person being purified. 18The priest will apply the oil remaining in his hand to the head of the person being purified. Through this process, the priest will purify the person before the Lord. 19Then the priest must present the sin offering to purify the person who was cured of the skin disease. After that, the priest will slaughter the burnt offering 20and offer it on the altar along with the grain offering. Through this process, the priest will purify the person who was healed, and the person will be ceremonially clean.

If you're able to read this, I will assume you did not contract a sudden onset of ocular leprosy after submitting your eyes to a page of atrocious and primitive blood ritual savagery. If such is the case, (and I hope it is), then take into account the entire passage and humor me in redirecting your attention to what becomes the most atrocious verse of all; Verse 1…'And the LORD spake unto Moses, saying…' Of the staggering 72 times this phrase pops up between Exodus, Leviticus, and Numbers, this particular message delivered to god's conduit as a 'law,' is certainly isolated in a league of its own for its largely impure insanity.

It must first be understood that among Rabbinical and biblical scholars of the Tanakh, the Bible, and the Talmud; along with modern medical academia, and all other associated fields; the general consensus acknowledges the word 'leprosy', *(greek; 'lepra')* as a mistranslation of the original Hebrew word, *'tzaraath,'* which stands for any of various disfigurements of a person's skin, hair, clothing or home. The Talmud states tzaraath generally refers to any disease that produces sores and eruptions on the skin. The Talmudical and Rabbinical *(and obvious)* explanation is that tzaraath serves as a 'divine punishment' or 'spiritual affliction' for sin, of which requires special rituals of atonement. Dr. Jay Schamberg, eponymous with Schamberg's disease, gives an explanation in his chapter; 'The Nature of the Leprosy of the Bible from a Medical and Biblical Point of View' from *'The Biblical World'- [circa 1899]:*

> 'Leprosy was a disease inflicted by God upon those who transgressed his laws. It was a divine retribution, a visitation of providence for evil thoughts and evil deeds. It was called the "finger of God." Every leper mentioned in the Old Testament was smitten with this disease because of some transgression (e.g., Miriam, Joab and family, Gehazi and family and King Uzziah). The Talmud declared that leprosy should be looked upon by the sufferer as an "altar of atonement," since it was only sent for great transgressions, such as idolatry, incest, calumny, and perjury. It was only natural, therefore, that the people

> by a posteriori reasoning should have looked upon persons afflicted with tsaraath as transgressors. They had violated the laws of God, and their transgression had been great, else they would not have been so afflicted. Their presence, therefore, in the community was likely to contaminate, to morally infect others: hence were they ostracized. And so long as the signs of the disease, or, metaphorically speaking, the finger of God, remained upon them, so long were they obliged to remain without the camp. When the leper was cured, the priest was to make an atonement before the Lord, and expiatory sacrifices in the form of a sin-offering and a trespass-offering were to be made. There is absolutely nothing in the Greek description of lepra that suggests, even in a remote manner, the modern leprosy. The Greeks in speaking of true leprosy did not use the term lepra, but elephantiasis. It is evident that they meant by lepra an affection distinct and apart from our modern disease of leprosy.'

Leprosy is a completely different disease. The skin does not turn white as we find in Chapter 13 and it cannot be cured in 7 days.

If this 'treatment' for those with a skin disease, handed down by the supposed infallible, omniscient, omnipotent, omnibenevolent, eternal, and infinitely wise god and creator of the universe, does not utterly reek of pure and unadulterated barbaric nonsense at its finest, then I don't know what does.

#56

Generational Hexes

Exodus 34:5-7
NLT

5Then the Lord came down in a cloud and stood there with
him; and he called out his own name, Yahweh. 6The Lord
passed in front of Moses, calling out,

"Yahweh! The Lord!
The God of compassion and mercy! I am slow to anger
and filled with unfailing love and faithfulness.

7I lavish unfailing love to a thousand generations.

I forgive iniquity, rebellion, and sin.
But I do not excuse the guilty.
I lay the sins of the parents upon their children and
grandchildren; the entire family is affected—
even children in the third and fourth generations."

KJV

5And the LORD descended in the cloud, and stood with
him there, and proclaimed the name of the LORD. 6And the
LORD passed by before him, and proclaimed, The LORD,
The LORD God, merciful and gracious, long-suffering, and
abundant in goodness and truth, 7keeping mercy for thousands, forgiving iniquity and transgression and sin, and that
will by no means clear the guilty; visiting the iniquity of the

fathers upon the children, and upon the children's children, unto the third and to the fourth generation.

As much as these people have already proven their stunted way of life and underdeveloped intellect within these first two books of the Bible, it would be expected of them to attribute their ignorance of inherited traits, such as basic characteristics and genetic disorders from chromosomal abnormalities—to that of a vengeful god at the helm of a complex hierarchical system of divine hexes.

That said, we commence in our legends of sandlore with Moses scaling the mountain again for the re-inscribing of the ten commandments. Moses has some seriously supernatural reserves as he neither eats nor drinks anything for the forty days and nights that he's up there. Before the lightning of letters hits any stone, god begins with a litany of praises to himself. He gloriously declares his many attributes such as his name, his compassion and mercy, his slowness to anger, his unfailing love, his faithfulness, and his forgiveness. Oh and one more thing within the same lines of affection: he "lays the sins of the parents upon their children and grandchildren; the entire family is affected—even children in the third and fourth generations."

One can attempt to somehow apply logic to this antiquated and hyperbolic 'inheritance of sin' by posing valid questions such as,

"Is it my fault my great grandma always cheated on bingo night?"

"Is it my fault gramps had those secret magazines under his bed?"

—and entirely unhumorous: *"Is it my fault my dad beat my mom?"*

"Is it my fault my mom is an alcoholic?"

The answer is NO, but that doesn't matter to god, and in fact, according to the Bible, the overarching curse over all of humanity was brought into the world by Adam and Eve.

Therefore, in following the traditional biblical ideology, we are all born in sin, having been accursed. This of course leads us to the treasured accoutrement of the ancients, and the sacred crowning jewel when endeavoring to obtain atonement: Blood. Paul even goes so far as to say, *"In fact, according to the law of Moses, nearly everything was purified with blood. For without the shedding of blood, there is no forgiveness." (Hebrews 9:22)*

In Duane Vander Klok's article, "Breaking Generational Curses," he gives us two ingredients after his motivational slogan:

'The good news is that generational curses can be stopped today!"

1. A generational curse comes through the blood line.
2. A generational curse can only be cancelled by blood and that one can only cancel the generational curse by appropriating the blood of Jesus for deliverance.

If you're still unsure of how to 'cancel' these generational curses, may you be blessed with 'Michael Bradley's' 6-step system, allowing "total deliverance from any demons who may have followed you into your adult life as a result of any severe transgressions made by one or both of your natural parents":

1. The full surrender.
2. Confess the sins of your sinning parent to God the Father.
3. Be willing to fully forgive your sinning parent.
4. Break any ungodly soul ties with the sinning parent.
5. Break the curse line of the demons.
6. Verbally command the demons to leave you in the name of Jesus Christ.

#55

Deuteronomy Compilation:
Highlights of the ~~10~~ 613 Commandments

7:2...and when the LORD thy God shall deliver them before thee; thou shalt smite them, and utterly destroy them; thou shalt make no covenant with them, nor shew mercy unto them: 3neither shalt thou intermarry with them. *[KJV, pp]*

13:12-16 When you begin living in the towns the Lord your God is giving you, you may hear 13that scoundrels among you have led fellow citizens astray by saying, 'Let us worship other gods you have not known before.' If you find the report is true and such a detestable act has been committed, 15you must attack that town and completely destroy all its inhabitants, as well as all the livestock. 16Then you must pile all the plunder in the middle of the open square and burn it. Burn the entire town as a burnt offering to the Lord your God. *[NLT, pp]*

15:19 You must set aside for the Lord your God the firstborn males from your flocks & herds. Don't use the firstborn of your herds to work, or shear the firstborn of your flocks. *[NLT, pp]*

20:10-16 As you approach a town to attack it, first offer its people terms for peace. 11If they accept your terms then its people will serve you in forced labor. 12If they refuse to make peace and prepare to fight, you must attack the town. 13When the Lord your God hands the town over to you, use your swords to kill every man. 14But you may keep all the women, children, livestock, and other plunder. You may enjoy the plunder. 15These instructions apply only to distant towns, not to the towns of the nations in the land you will enter. 16In those towns that the Lord your God is giving you as a special possession, destroy every living thing. *[NLT, pp]*

21:1 If one be found murdered in the land the Lord your God is giving you and you don't know who committed the murder 2your elders and judges must measure the distance from the site of the crime to the nearby towns. 3Upon determining the town, that town's elders must select from the herd a heifer 4They must lead it down to a valley that has a stream. There they must break the heifer's neck. 5The Levitical priests must step forward; they are to decide all legal cases. 6The elders of the town must wash their hands over the heifer whose neck was broken. 7They must say, 'Our hands did not shed this person's blood, nor did we see it happen. 8Lord, forgive your people Israel whom you've redeemed. Do not charge your people with the guilt of murdering an innocent person.' Then they will be absolved of the guilt of this person's blood. 9In this, you will cleanse the guilt of murder from the community. *[NLT, pp]*

22:8 When you build a new house, you must build a railing around the edge of its flat roof. That way you will not be considered guilty of murder if someone falls from the roof. *[NLT]*

22:10 You must not plow with an ox and a donkey harnessed together. *[NLT]*

22:11 You must not wear clothing made of wool and linen woven together. *[NLT]*

22:12 You must put four tassels on the hem of your cloak; the front, back, and sides. *[NLT, pp]*

22:23 If a man meets a young virgin woman who is engaged to be married, and he has sexual intercourse with her 24you must take both of them to the gates of that town and stone them to death. The woman is guilty because she did not scream for help. The man must die because he violated another man's wife. In this way, you will purge this evil from among you. *[NLT, pp]*

23:1 He that is wounded in the stones, or hath his privy member cut off, shall not enter into the congregation of the LORD. *[KJV]*

25:5 If two brothers live on the same property and one dies without a son, his widow may not marry outside the family. Her husband's brother shall marry her and have intercourse with her to fulfill the duties of a brother-in-law. 6The first son she bears will be the son of the dead brother, that his name remain in Israel. *[NLT, pp]*

25:11 If two Israelite men get into a fight and the wife of one tries to rescue her husband by grabbing the testicles of the other man, 12you must cut off her hand. Show her no pity. *[NLT]*

25:19 You must destroy the Amalekites and erase their memory from under heaven. *[NLT, pp]*

It is unquestionably a foundational principle of the Bible that the Torah was dictated by God to Moses, letter-for-letter. According to the Ohr Somayach International yeshiva (*yeshiva* being a Jewish academy focusing on Rabbinic literature, the Talmud, the Torah, biblical exegesis, and Jewish philosophy), 'G-d gave the Torah to Moses and the Jewish people at Mount Sinai 3,316 years ago.' (3,335 as of now.) Such precision and literalism merits a spotlight on some of the special commandments that came out of this wonderfully enigmatic rendezvous, and more importantly, these again being those that came directly from god.

Chronologically curated & condensed curiosities of Deuteronomy:

1) 7:2-3: "This relentless doom of extermination which God denounced against those tribes of Canaan cannot be reconciled with the attributes of the divine character, except on the assumption that their gross idolatry and enormous wickedness left no reasonable hope of their repentance and amendment."-*Jamieson-Fausset-Brown Bible Commentary.* (Well said. I'm convinced.)

2) 13:12-16: More relentless doom! Down with the infidels! (...and apparently it was equally important to murder the livestock too.) One of MANY examples where that whole 'thou shalt not kill' thing—doesn't apply.

3) 15:19: You guessed it. Kill your firstborn male animals (cattle, sheep, goats, etc.) for god. It's amazing how animal sacrifice is so vile, wicked, and unthinkable outside of the Bible.

4) 20:10-16: Cool. The peace treaty actually means forced labor for the townsfolk. Great. Now if they decide, *'nah - we like our town that YOU'VE APPROACHED TO ATTACK,'* then annihilate them! Oh and you can keep the women and the other stuff...Oh sorry, one more thing—this only applies to distant towns don't ya know! The others...ya...Kill. Every. Thing.

5) 21:1-9: This unspeakably repulsive absurdity of a ritual sheds a great light on 'the chosen.' Their attempted ingenuity considerably

discredits god's omniscience as he's naturally all-informed in cases of whodunit. We can safely say this is rather a case of a nomadic people plagued by a severe obsession with zoosadism.

6) 22:8: Yeah, because people falling off roofs and dying must've been a common thing.

7) 22:10: Thanks.

8) 22:11: Brilliant.

9) 22:12: Thus we have the law of the 'Tzitzit'—the specially knotted ritual fringes or tassels.

> Numbers 15:39: When you see the tassels, you will remember & obey all the commands of the Lord instead of following your own desires and defiling yourselves, as you're prone to do. 40The tassels will help you recall that you must obey my commands and be holy to your God. *[NLT, pp]*

10) 22:23-24: In *'because she did not scream for help,'* we'll kindly grant the typical explanation of 'she consented to it.' Though we find yet another 'law' of 'purging' by stoning. Another gem in the vast ocean of merciless edicts on behalf of divine thuggery.

11) 23:1: This chapter wastes no time in coming right out with it. The NLT bluntly states,

> *'If a man's testicles are crushed or his penis is cut off.'* (Although I enjoy the 'privy member' of the KJV.) Anyway, I think we found the origin of Lorena's generational curses.

12) 25:5-9: Isn't that lovely. We mustn't forget the coup de grace in verse 9 in the event the brother in law happens to say 'no': 9the widow must walk over to him in the presence of the elders, pull his sandal from his foot, and spit in his face. Then she must declare, 'This is what happens to a man who refuses to provide his brother with children.' Quite sassy aye!?

13) 25:11-12: The KJV reads, *'and taketh him by the secrets.'* Not much more to be said here. Oh the hand thing?? Eh...what's the loss of a hand...This poor man had his secrets squeezed!

14) 25:19: Plot: No getting even with these fellow barbarians.

Only an absolute genocidal massacre resulting in pure eradication will be accepted.

#54

Mosaissism

Exodus 32:9-14
NLT

9Then the Lord said, "I have seen how stubborn and rebellious
these people are. 10Now leave me alone so my fierce anger can
blaze against them, and I will destroy them. Then I will make
you, Moses, into a great nation."

11But Moses tried to pacify the Lord his God. "O Lord!" he
said. "Why are you so angry with your own people whom you
brought from the land of Egypt with such great power and
such a strong hand? 12Why let the Egyptians say, 'Their God
rescued them with the evil intention of slaughtering them in
the mountains and wiping them from the face of the earth'?
Turn away from your fierce anger. Change your mind about
this terrible disaster you have threatened against your people!
13Remember your servants Abraham, Isaac, and Jacob. You
bound yourself with an oath to them, saying, 'I will make your
descendants as numerous as the stars of heaven. And I will give
them all of this land that I have promised to your descendants,
and they will possess it forever.'"

14So the Lord changed his mind about the terrible disaster he
had threatened to bring on his people.

KJV

9And the LORD said unto Moses, I have seen this people,
and, behold, it is a stiffnecked people: 10now therefore let
me alone, that my wrath may wax hot against them, and that
I may consume them: and I will make of thee a great nation.
11And Moses besought the LORD his God, and said, LORD,
why doth thy wrath wax hot against thy people, which thou
hast brought forth out of the land of Egypt with great power,
and with a mighty hand? 12Wherefore should the Egyptians
speak, and say, For mischief did he bring them out, to slay
them in the mountains, and to consume them from the face
of the earth? Turn from thy fierce wrath, and repent of this
evil against thy people. 13Remember Abraham, Isaac, and
Israel, thy servants, to whom thou swarest by thine own self,
and saidst unto them, I will multiply your seed as the stars of
heaven, and all this land that I have spoken of will I give unto
your seed, and they shall inherit it for ever. 14And the LORD
repented of the evil which he thought to do unto his people.

The finger of god had just finished engraving the tablets, when suddenly, all heaven was about to break loose. Thankfully, Moses is a master crisis negotiator and saves his people from the destroyer. We all can use a good therapist like Moses now and then—one that just so happens to be similarly skilled in Cognitive Behavioral Therapy for gods (CBTg). Often times, root cause analysis will lead the therapist to a common diagnosis of intermittent explosive disorder of the gods (IEDg), which manifests itself in the form of impulsive outbursts of rage or aggression; resulting in the desiring of, or achieving of mass murder. As is the case in the traditional IED, the same applies for that of the gods in that the episodes are out of proportion to the situation that triggered them. In the case of our passage, this trigger would be a golden calf that Aaron and the Israelites made from melted earrings. To make things worse, they declare, "O Israel, these are the gods who brought you out of the land of Egypt!"

In dealing with this particular deity of the Bible in whom the author(s) have already embarrassingly intertwined with numerous clinical psychoses, such as those covered in prior segments (divine insecurity illness; [*DII*] and divine paranoia; [*DPI*]), one must understand the severe trauma it places on the fragile self esteem of the deity when discrediting any conquests. Of all accomplishments this grand wizard of decimation is most proud of is his intervention and deliverance of his people from Egyptian bondage. The exhaustingly redundant reminder of "('*I, the god,*' or '*he*') who brought you out of the land of Egypt, out of the land of slavery," appears 125+ times in the Old Testament, and is certainly off limits for any other gods to lay claim.

Allow me to pose an extraordinarily heretical hypothetical that many may find entirely unfathomable. Let's imagine this very warm and redeeming story is simply an all-out fabrication and myth. This of course finds Moses, our heroic negotiator, in the unfortunate state of also requiring urgent diagnosis and treatment. As the purported author of the book of Exodus among the other four of the Torah, what manner of psyche must one suffer when penning memoirs of not only speaking and negotiating with a god, but changing the mind of a god? Reconciling this with a shameless plug from Moses in the notorious Numbers 12:3 gets us one step closer in our assessment. It reads: 'Now Moses was very humble—more humble than any other person on earth.' *[NLT]*

Narcissism? Nah. Too trendy and we're already overburdened with excessive similarities between the stories of Greek and ancient mythology and those of the Bible. Although a tinge of parallelism is tolerable and thus we celebrate Moses as the progenitor of Mosaissism; classified as a highly delusional disorder for those in positions of power, in which one claims exclusivity in communicating with a deity or supernatural being to the point of possessing influential power over said deity or supernatural being in order to advance ideologies of ethnocentrism to the members of its society. *Fortunately for Moses, Moses likely never existed.*

#53

Solunar Siege and Homing Hailstones

Joshua 10:11-14
KJV

11And it came to pass, as they *(the Amorites)* fled from before Israel, and were in the going down to Beth-horon, that the LORD cast down great stones from heaven upon them unto Azekah, and they died: they were more which died with hailstones than they whom the children of Israel slew with the sword. 12Then spake Joshua to the LORD in the day when the LORD delivered up the Amorites before the children of Israel, and he said in the sight of Israel, Sun, stand thou still upon Gibeon; And thou, Moon, in the valley of Aijalon. 13And the sun stood still, and the moon stayed, until the people had avenged themselves upon their enemies.

NLT

11As the Amorites retreated down the road from Beth-horon, the Lord destroyed them with a terrible hailstorm from heaven that continued until they reached Azekah. The hail killed more of the enemy than the Israelites killed with the sword. 12On the day the Lord gave the Israelites victory over the Amorites, Joshua prayed to the Lord in front of all the people of Israel. He said, "Let the sun stand still over Gibeon, and the moon over the valley of Aijalon." 13So the sun stood still and the moon stayed in place until the nation of Israel had defeated its enemies. Is this event not recorded in The Book of Jashar? The sun stayed in the middle of the sky, and it did not set as on a normal day. 14There has never been a day like this one before or since, when the Lord answered such a prayer. Surely the Lord fought for Israel that day!

Proudly inducted into the Hall of Fables and one of resounding acclaim is the fantastical story of the solunar siege of Joshua. Celestial weaponry is on full display with heaven unleashing the storehouse of its coveted homing hailstones. Soon thereafter, the sun and the moon stop in their tracks, allowing for as much light as possible in order to slaughter as many as possible.

> *'...it is distinctly stated that more were destroyed by hail than were slain by the sword, that there might be no doubt of the victory having been obtained from heaven.'* -John Calvin

Joshua and his partner in crime had the perfect opportunity to revolutionize, modernize, and shake the very core of geocentrism by alternatively and correctly commanding the *Earth* (rather than the sun and the moon) to stand still and thus introduce the reality of heliocentrism. (Though even this impossibility would result in catastrophic consequences.) Nevertheless, and yet again, iron clad proof of the archaic and underdeveloped range of the ancients is right before our eyes. For Joshua to suspend the light of the sun (in order to continue the annihilation), Earth would have to stop its approximate 1,000mph constant rotation, resulting in unimaginable devastation. Naturally, these were a people, like all of the known world, who knew little to nothing about the fundamental mechanics of the universe, and rather, relied on legends and myths. Joshua and the Israelites were followers of the Genesis creation account, which speaks of the sun and moon being attached to the firmament above an expanse of land. They undoubtedly envisioned a flat-earth model with god directing the simple trajectory of the sun and moon as mere 'lights,' and to stop them in their tracks would be plausible and of little impact.

Let us yield to the contrary, more fundamental view, as it's too good to pass up:

> *'Since God is all-powerful, we conclude that He can stop the sun and moon, freeze the laws of physics and still maintain the universe. Any other view is a very low, illogical and dishonoring view of an all-powerful, omniscient, self-existing God. He does not*

need our help to explain away a divine miracle with a humanistic and rationalistic explanation.' -Jean L. Calahan Jr.

You're spot on Jean. I do have a very low and dishonoring view of this god in that case. In all his omnipotence, wouldn't body snatching be more efficient and sanitary versus raining down hail bombs? Either this god is unable to perform a mass *zap & dissolve move* upon his 'enemies' or he simply wants to display his divine butchery and elimination of an entire tribe. I will assume the latter.

We conclude with gems from the Liberty University article of which there could be no greater title: '100-Pound Hailstones'; written by Dr. Thomas Ice:

> *'This is a clear example of the implementation of the purpose stated in Job, that the Lord has a storehouse of hail for the very purpose of "the time of distress" and "for the day of war and battle." Here God fights with divinely directed hailstones during a time of distress and on the day of war and battle on behalf of Israel.'*
>
> *'...secondly, had not God darted it directly, part would have fallen on the heads of the Israelites.'*
>
> *'...To the same effect it is said that God threw down great stones of hail from heaven: for the meaning is that they fell with extraordinary force, and were far above the ordinary size.'* (Approximately 50lbs here compared to Revelation 16:21; 'talent'=75/100lbs.)
> *'...The Egyptian plague of hail was literal, so this one must be too.'*

#52

Saint Korah

Numbers 16-17
NLT, *pp*

1Now Korah took men 2chosen from the assembly, chiefs of the congregation, well known men, 250 altogether. 3They assembled against Moses and Aaron and said to them, "You have gone too far! For all in the congregation are holy, and the Lord is among them. Why then do you exalt yourselves above the assembly of the Lord?" 4When Moses heard it, he fell on his face, 5and said to Korah and his company, "In the morning the Lord will show who is his, and who is holy 6Do this: take censers, Korah you and your company; 7put fire and incense in them before the Lord tomorrow, and the man whom the Lord chooses shall be the holy one. 3You have gone too far, sons of Levi!"

18So every man took his censer and put fire and incense in them and stood at the entrance of the tent of meeting with Moses and Aaron. 20And the Lord spoke to Moses and Aaron, saying, "Separate yourselves that I may consume them in a moment." 27And *[those of Korah, Dathan and Abiram]* stood at the door of their tents, together with their wives, their sons, and their little ones.

32And the earth opened its mouth and swallowed them up, with their households and all the people who belonged to

Korah and all their goods. 33So they and all that belonged to them went down alive into Sheol, and the earth closed over them, and they perished from the midst of the assembly. 35And fire came out from the Lord and consumed the 250 men offering the incense.

41But the next day the people of Israel grumbled against Moses and against Aaron, saying, "You have killed the people of the Lord." 44and the Lord spoke to Moses, saying, 45"Get away from this congregation, that I may consume them in a moment." 46And Moses said to Aaron, "Take your censer, and put fire on it from off the altar and lay incense on it and make atonement for them, for wrath has gone out from the Lord; the plague has begun." 48And he stood between the dead and the living, and the plague was stopped. 49Those who died in the plague were 14,700, besides those who died in the affair of Korah.

17:1The Lord spoke to Moses, saying, 2"Speak to the people of Israel, and get twelve staffs, one from all their chiefs according to their fathers' houses. Write each man's name on his staff, 3and write Aaron's name on the staff of Levi. 4Then place them in the tent of meeting before the testimony, where I meet with you. 5And the staff of the man whom I choose shall sprout. 7And Moses placed the staffs before the Lord in the tent of the testimony. 8The next day Moses went into the tent of the testimony, and behold, the staff of Aaron had sprouted and put forth buds and produced blossoms, and ripe almonds.

Thanks to Saint Jude, we have an improperly titled story, known throughout the ages as 'Korah's Rebellion.' In a stroke of irreverence, I would rename this long-trending tale into something more fitting such as *'Tremors - The Prequel'* or *'Dune 3 - Korah and the Sandworms,'* though *'Saint Korah'* will suffice.

According to the Midrash, which includes early rabbinic exegesis of the Tanakh, Korah is unintentionally portrayed as a levelheaded semicivilized leader of the Levites. What becomes known as a harrowing revolt is prompted by his questioning of the illogic of various mitzvah's such as the tzitzit, which commands four strings be attached to the corners of the men's garments. In defiance, he and his 250 followers adorn themselves in garments without the tzitzit. Korah then challenges Moses on the law of the mezuzah. This 81st law of the Mitzvot commands a scroll be inscribed with the scriptures of Deuteronomy 6:4-9 and 11:13-21, and be affixed to every doorpost within a special case.

He asks Moses, "Does a house filled with Torah scrolls require a mezuzah?" "Yes, it does," Moses replies. "If an entire Torah scroll does not suffice," Korah taunts, "how can a single paragraph be enough?! You did not receive these commandments from god; you devised them on your own!"

Fun Fact: There are 4,649 separate instructions that govern the preparation and inscription of a proper mezuzah scroll and it remains an observed law within Judaism to this day.

"You devised them on your own..." In this single statement, it is likely we have discovered one of the few grains of truth pertaining to the words and stories of Moses. Unfortunately Korah, there are those who still uphold this saga as absolute truth and prefer the divine killing spree as due recompense for your questioning of Moses. The wrath of god begins with the newly developed tectonic terra-kill move, devouring Korah and a portion of his camp, including his little ones. After the earth closes back up, high velocity precision fire-beams strike and kill the chosen 250 of his assembly. The following day, the people

of Israel share their grief and contempt concerning the latest sci-fi massacre by confronting Moses in disapproval. Yet another instance where challenging illogic will not go unpunished. God takes this personally and begins his third wave of mass execution in releasing a plague from the arsenal. Thankfully, Aaron's magic incense calms god down, yet not before he kills 14,700 Israelites.

We finally conclude yet another memoir of Moses & mayhem and it's time to lighten things up with the magic staff contest in chapter 17. Our grand event will stop the 'grumbling' of the Israelites and give the winner exclusive rights to the priesthood of the Levites. Aaron's staff is the top seed having garnered an array of accolades for impressive wizardry, including turning the waters of Egypt into blood and mutating into a lethal snake. The following day, the judges declared Aaron as the decisive winner as his staff had sprouted and produced flowers and almonds. Aaron even gets a shout-out in Hebrews 9:4 from Paul, who memorializes the induction of Aaron's staff into the Ark of the Covenant. Glory!

#51

Snakes on a Desert Plain

Numbers 21:4-9
NLT

4From Mount Hor they *(the Israelites)* set out by the way to the Red Sea, to go around the land of Edom. And the people became impatient on the way. 5And the people spoke against God and against Moses, "Why have you brought us up out of Egypt to die in the wilderness? For there is no food and no water, and we loathe this worthless food." Then the Lord sent fiery serpents among the people, and they bit the people, so that many people of Israel died. And the people came to Moses and said, "We have sinned, for we have spoken against the Lord and against you. Pray to the Lord, that he take away the serpents from us." So Moses prayed for the people. 8And the Lord said to Moses, "Make a fiery serpent and set it on a pole, and everyone who is bitten, when he sees it, shall live."
9So Moses made a bronze serpent and set it on a pole. And if a serpent bit anyone, he would look at the bronze serpent and live.

KJV

4And they *(the Israelites)* journeyed from mount Hor by the way of the Red sea, to compass the land of Edom: and the soul of the people was much discouraged because of the way. 5And the people spake against God, and against Moses, Wherefore

have ye brought us up out of Egypt to die in the wilderness?
for there is no bread, neither is there any water; and our soul
loatheth this light bread. 6And the LORD sent fiery serpents
among the people, and they bit the people; and much people
of Israel died. 7Therefore the people came to Moses, and said,
We have sinned, for we have spoken against the LORD, and
against thee; pray unto the LORD, that he take away the
serpents from us. And Moses prayed for the people. 8And the
LORD said unto Moses, Make thee a fiery serpent, and set
it upon a pole: and it shall come to pass, that every one that
is bitten, when he looketh upon it, shall live. 9And Moses
made a serpent of brass, and put it upon a pole, and it came
to pass, that if a serpent had bitten any man, when he beheld
the serpent of brass, he lived.

This is unequivocally and undisputedly, a wildly preposterous gem of a story.

Equally outlandish is the lesser-known absurdity of Jesus hearkening back to this passage within the same breath of what is sometimes referred to as 'the golden text of the Bible.' Martin Luther called it "the gospel in miniature"; author Max Lucado described it as the "hope diamond of the Bible"; William Barclay noted, "this text has been called 'Everybody's text'", and it is easily one of the most recognized and beloved scriptures of the entire Bible. This scripture, is of course, John 3:16. A justifiably common footnote regarding the prior verse, John 3:15, reads, "some interpreters hold that the quotation ends at verse 15." Nevertheless, John 3:14-16 reads:

> *'14As Moses lifted up the serpent in the wilderness, even so must the Son of Man be lifted up; 15that whosoever believeth in him should not perish, but have eternal life. 16For God so loved the world, that he gave his only begotten Son, that whosoever believeth in him should not perish, but have everlasting life.'* Thus, for this exercise and in utmost sacrilege, we can eliminate the repetitious verse 16 and further isolate the bizarre adjoining of these verses.

A choice defense among adherents is the constant usage of *'context.'* Usually, one will try a feeble attempt in bolstering the veracity of a Bible verse or story by profusely using the trendy fallback of, *'You have to consider the context.'* Yes, for those that haven't read the Bible in its entirety, nor have read even half of the stories within its pages and usually abstain from the old testament due to the indescribably horrific and immoral nature of god (which many attempt to defend), nor can quote the books and the alleged authorship of the Bible, nor simply cite the 10 commandments among many other laughable irregularities when considering the gravity one places upon its contents; the *'context'* fallback remains a safe haven and a favorite. Putting 'context' to bed, the one word answer is: 'obviously'; though only 'obviously' for when it obviously applies.

If I were Nicodemus, or a nearby disciple listening in on this teaching of Jesus in John 3, I would've enjoyed asking him to expound on the *context* of his obscure citation in verse 14. Something like, "Jesus, since you and the father are one (to quote only one of many references of Jesus being equal to god; the son of god; part of the trinity, preexistent, etc.), you either aided or advocated the acts of what every jot and tittle records in the old testament, including the demented snake story you just referenced. Call me stupid, or that of a reprobate mind, or maybe demonically possessed, but why did you send snakes to bite and kill? Also, why the idolatrous command to make a magically healing bronze serpent? Sorry, lastly, why are you quoting this insane story? Context please?"

Yes, one will attempt to draw parallels between the snake on the pole and Jesus on the cross, inferring symbols of atonement, yet I refuse to accept this convenient narrative to water down this senseless snake story. How entertaining it may be if all Sunday school teachers required a more contextual memory verse drill with the inclusion of this 14th verse of John. Parents would *unfortunately* have to think twice when their children recite it?

#50

Rules for a Goring Ox

Exodus 21:28-29
NLT

28If an ox gores a man or woman to death, the ox must be stoned, and its flesh may not be eaten. In such a case, however, the owner will not be held liable. 29But suppose the ox had a reputation for goring, and the owner had been informed but failed to keep it under control. If the ox then kills someone, it must be stoned, and the owner must also be put to death.

KJV

28If an ox gore a man or a woman, that they die: then the ox shall be surely stoned, and his flesh shall not be eaten; but the owner of the ox shall be quit. 29But if the ox were wont to push with his horn in time past, and it hath been testified to his owner, and he hath not kept him in, but that he hath killed a man or a woman; the ox shall be stoned, and his owner also shall be put to death.

If you haven't already been laughing through much, if not all of the divine masterpieces of stories and wisdom we have covered up to this point, then you may fancy some sadistic comic relief in the 'rules for a goring ox.'

First and foremost of laughable irrationalities is the purported progenitor of this law. As a continuation of the commandments beginning in Exodus 20, this most certainly is not the brainchild of Moses, nor his brother Aaron, nor simply a concept or principal fabricated by the mind of man. This law is brought to you by god himself amidst the fire and smoke atop Mount Sinai, having been signed, sealed, and delivered to Moses, and it remains one of the 613 laws of the Mitzvot with the convenient omission of verse 29. Interestingly, though unsurprisingly, both the codes of Hammurabi and Eshnunna, which long predate the alleged writings of Moses containing 'god's laws,' bear striking similarities to these biblical rules regarding the ox. It certainly couldn't be the distinct Mesopotamian roots and relationships these early civilizations shared that may have inspired this law and many other stories, could it? *(I.e., The Epic of Gilgamesh and Noah's Flood; the ancient Sumerian myth of the Garden of Edin and the biblical Garden of Eden; the ancient Mesopotamian myth of Enkidu—the hairy man who fights with Gilgamesh, being likened to Cain and Abel and Jacob and Esau; the prominence of cattle within much of the regional ancient mythology such as the Mesopotamian 'Bull of Heaven,' Aaron's golden calf and the Egyptian divine bull of Apis; and the ancient Mesopotamian legend of Enki's rib and Ninti, which is thought to have inspired the story of Adam's rib and the creation of Eve—just to name a handful.)*

Needless to say, throughout the centuries, rabbis and scholars have attempted to make sense of this bovine balderdash. Berakhot 61a of the Talmud lends credence to the idea of an animal possessing a conscience and thus is equally liable and tried as a human for acting upon its 'evil inclination.' The Pulpit Commentary reinforces this by stating, 'He shall suffer the same death that would have been the portion of a human murderer.' The precise and swift clean kill of the matador is far too civilized (and likely requires too much skill), so as expected, this 1500lb-2500lb beast is executed by way of stoning. The Cambridge Bible for Schools and Colleges expounds on verse 28; the prohibiting of eating the flesh of the ox, by reminding us that 'blood-guilt would be resting upon it, which would be transferred to any one partaking of it.' Author and Theologian, James B. Jordan, seeks to remove all doubt for those of little faith who may question the substance of this law by declaring, "Animals are created to be submissive to human beings, and animals that rebel are like the serpent. The ox is an incorrigible rebel against human authority, a demonized beast. To this, we might add that bovines are particularly associated with the Mosaic period of Israel's history and with the priesthood. An incorrigible ox is an incorrigible priesthood." In closing, be encouraged! Talmudic rabbis saw it fit to adjust things a little by revising the very words of god in verse 29 and thereby provided a path of restitution for the owner of the ox in lieu of a death sentence.

#49

New Testament Slaves

NLT

Ephesians 6:5-7

5Slaves, obey your earthly masters with deep respect and fear. Serve them sincerely as you would serve Christ. 6Try to please them all the time, not just when they are watching you. As slaves of Christ, do the will of God with all your heart. 7Work with enthusiasm, as though you were working for the Lord rather than for people.

Colossians 3:22-24

22Slaves, obey your earthly masters in everything you do. Try to please them all the time, not just when they are watching you. Serve them sincerely because of your reverent fear of the Lord. 23Work willingly at whatever you do, as though you were working for the Lord rather than for people. 24Remember that the Lord will give you an inheritance as your reward, and that the Master you are serving is Christ.

I Timothy 6:1-2

1All slaves should show full respect for their masters so they will not bring shame on the name of God and his teaching. 2If the masters are believers, that is no excuse for being disrespectful. Those slaves should work all the harder because their efforts are helping other believers who are well loved.

Titus 2:9-10

9Slaves must always obey their masters and do their best to please them. They must not talk back 10or steal, but must show themselves to be entirely trustworthy and good. Then they will make the teaching about God our Savior attractive in every way.

I Peter 2:18-21

18You who are slaves must submit to your masters with all respect. Do what they tell you—not only if they are kind and reasonable, but even if they are cruel. 19For God is pleased when, conscious of his will, you patiently endure unjust treatment. 20Of course, you get no credit for being patient if you are beaten for doing wrong. But if you suffer for doing good and endure it patiently, God is pleased with you. 21For God called you to do good, even if it means suffering, just as Christ suffered for you. He is your example, and you must follow in his steps.

Imagine how proud these two celebrated saints must be right now, peering down from the pearly gates to find the elect in continued defense of these enlightening utterances from nearly 2,000 years ago. Beyond that, I expect that up in the click, those in their ripe old age of immortality are simply flabbergasted at how long this whole thing has continued on Earth. Well, needless to say, maybe Paul is right in his II Timothy 3:16 declaration, that 'all scripture is inspired by god and god-breathed.' Such a monumental tidal wave of a claim should certainly require we pay attention to what he and his fellow best-selling author have to say.

If you would like to submit yourself to a masochistic stomach turning exercise of putridity, engage in the subject of biblical slavery with a fan of the Bible. It's a fantastic indicator of just how morally depraved and unsympathetic one may be by the manner in which they attempt to water down and wash away this entire subject. In this particular commentary, I've already removed the infamous and appalling advocating of slavery throughout the Old Testament, yet let us also eliminate Peter's passage and stack the deck even more in favor of the devotee.

Supremely favored, supremely infantile, and the undisputed champion of fallbacks regarding critical matters of the Bible is the 'time period' crutch. In simple terms, for one to continue in caressing their personalized narrative and make this thing work, they will often respond with *'You need to consider the time period of when this was all written.'* This fallacious knee-jerk response presumes their own omnipotent and omniscient god; creator of the universe and one of infinite wisdom, possesses about a millimeter of the mentality of a millipede. It also indirectly places an expiration date on most of what we read throughout the Bible and clearly implies there is a better way. A way, such as an unmistakable abolishment that apparently god refused to deliver to his conduits for publication within the Bible. An abolishment that Jesus and his disciples could go on to preach with extreme conviction and vigor, fiercely condemning the destructive nature of slavery; sending shockwaves through the known world; this *'time period when this was all written,'* providing a definitive termination of this injustice and a revolutionary axiom for all generations to come. Yet no such declaration of abolishment would ever come.

Fortunately, one man among many would eventually arise in a land where such a revolution would forever change the course of its history. One whose opposition and resistance to the norm of 'the time period' would ultimately lead to his untimely death, though not before leaving us many shining examples of what Paul and company might have said. One simple array of words, and one set among his vast library that I find superior to those of Paul's:

"I am naturally anti-slavery.
If slavery is not wrong, nothing is wrong."
~Abraham Lincoln

#48

The Scapegoat

Leviticus 16
NLT

1The Lord spoke to Moses after the death of Aaron's two sons, who died after they entered the Lord's presence and burned the wrong kind of fire before him.

5Aaron must take from the community of Israel two male goats for a sin offering and a ram for a burnt offering. 8He is to cast sacred lots to determine which goat will be reserved as an offering to the Lord and which will carry the sins of the people to the wilderness of Azazel.

20When Aaron has finished purifying the Most Holy Place and the Tabernacle and the altar, he must present the live goat. 21He will lay both of his hands on the goat's head and confess over it all the wickedness, rebellion, and sins of the people of Israel. In this way, he will transfer the people's sins to the head of the goat. Then a man specially chosen for the task will drive the goat into the wilderness. 22As the goat goes into the wilderness, it will carry all the people's sins upon itself into a desolate land.

34This is a permanent law for you, to purify the people of Israel from their sins, making them right with the Lord once each year.

KJV

1And the LORD spake unto Moses after the death of the two
sons of Aaron, when they offered before the LORD, and died.
5Aaron shall take of the congregation of the children of Israel
two kids of the goats for a sin offering, and one ram for a burnt
offering. 8And he shall cast lots upon the two goats; one lot
for the LORD, and the other lot for the scapegoat.

20And when he hath made an end of reconciling the holy
place, and the tabernacle of the congregation, and the altar, he
shall bring the live goat: 21and Aaron shall lay both his hands
upon the head of the live goat, and confess over him all the
iniquities of the children of Israel, and all their transgressions
in all their sins, putting them upon the head of the goat, and
shall send him away by the hand of a fit man into the wilderness: 22and the goat shall bear upon him all their iniquities
unto a land not inhabited: and he shall let go the goat in the
wilderness.

34And this shall be an everlasting statute unto you, to make
an atonement for the children of Israel for all their sins once a
year. And he did as the LORD commanded Moses.

Aaron's slaughterhouse is about to make some serious history in paving the way for what will become the holiest day in Judaism: Yom Kippur; *(Day of Atonement.)* This 'Sabbath of all Sabbaths' is a day of focusing on individual 'spiritual well-being' and requires a fivefold abstaining from pleasures such as eating and drinking, wearing leather, bathing, shaving, brushing one's teeth, and having sex. Failure to rest and abide by the rules of what is otherwise known as 'the five afflictions,' risks one being destroyed, compliments of the destroyer.[26]

Verse 1 is a two-pronged treat. Firstly, it establishes who the mastermind is behind the forthcoming derangement. (Make no mistake, this is another divine ordinance 'spoken' by god himself to his conduit—*Moses.*) Secondly, it gives a teaser for the upcoming passage and commentary on Nadab and Abihu.

The chapter proceeds in leading up to the grand finale of fatuousness by meticulously detailing the animal slaughters and blood rituals Aaron must perform while cloaked in sacred garments. Mystical rites are enforced, specifying the locations of where and how many times to sprinkle the blood of the sacrificial bull and goat. This sacrificial goat is one of the two chosen by way of casting lots, or casting bones, which is better described as 'rolling dice to reveal god's will.' (Essentially a means of divination, also known as 'cleromancy,' of which was a common practice among pagans, and many other cultures—including you-know-who. Oh and it was also common among witches. *You know...those that are to be murdered according to Exodus 22:18.)*

It's finally happy-magic-hour at the tent of ~~beating~~ meeting, which means it's time for Aaron to convert the sins of the Israelites into electromagnetic waves and transfer them to the head of the goat. The goat is then sent to the wilderness.

In addition to a whopping four reminders that this specific entire process of atonement be an everlasting statute, or a permanent law[27]; the rabbis of the Talmud decided to alter things a little and spice up the

26 Leviticus 23:29-30

27 Leviticus 16:29, 16:31, 16:34, 23:3

magic. In Mishnah Yoma 6 of the Talmud, a newly introduced strip of scarlet-dyed wool was tied to the head of the goat and to the door of the temple. When the goat reached the wilderness the thread would turn white, as it is written, *"Though your sins be as scarlet they shall be as white as snow" (Isaiah 1:18).* This color changing phenomenon was the indication that god had forgiven the sins of the people. Sadly, they also felt it necessary to revise the fate of the goat by adding some carnage. Yoma 6:6 says, *'What did the one designated to dispatch the goat do there? He divided a strip of crimson into two parts, half he tied to the rock, and half he tied between the two horns of the goat. And he pushed the goat backward, and it rolls and descends. And it would not reach halfway down the mountain until it was torn limb from limb.'* Whereas before, the innocent goat was sent to merely wander, the Talmudic version calls for its launch off a cliff. This practice, later coined as the 'scapegoat,' fell out of favor within Judaism.

#47

Saint Paulradox on the Joys of Circumcision and Exclusivity

Romans 3:1-2
NLT

1Then what's the advantage of being a Jew? Is there any value in the ceremony of circumcision? 2Yes, there are great benefits! First of all, the Jews were entrusted with the whole revelation of God.

KJV

1What advantage then hath the Jew? or what profit is there of circumcision? 2Much every way: chiefly, because that unto them were committed the oracles of God.

[Additional References; NLT]
Romans 2:25

The Jewish ceremony of circumcision has value only if you obey God's law. But if you don't obey God's law, you are no better off than an uncircumcised Gentile.

Romans 2:28-29 NLT

28For he is not a Jew, which is one outwardly; neither is that circumcision, which is outward in the flesh: 29but he is a Jew, which is one inwardly; and circumcision is that of the heart, in the spirit, and not in the letter; whose praise is not of men, but of God.

Romans 9:4

> *4They are the people of Israel, chosen to be God's adopted children. God revealed his glory to them. He made covenants with them and gave them his law. He gave them the privilege of worshiping him and receiving his wonderful promises.*

Saint Paulradox returns with another savory befuddlement on the subject of an ol' time favorite: Circumcision. Among a variety of commentaries, theologians attempt to bridge the mystification between the concluding verses of chapter 2 and these opening verses of chapter 3, by presenting the potential 'objection' that Paul faces.

Meyers NT Commentary states, *'Romans 3:1-2, as an inference from Romans 2:28-29, the objection might now be made from the Jewish standpoint against the Apostle, that he quite does away with the advantage of Judaism and the benefit of circumcision. This objection he therefore raises in his own person, in order to remove it himself immediately, Romans 3:2.'*

The Pulpit commentary on 'the objection' reads:

> *'Objection 1 (verse 1). If being a Jew, if circumcision itself, gives one no advantage over the Gentile, what was the use of the old covenant at all? It is thus shown to have been illusory; and God's own truth and faithfulness are impugned, if he is supposed to have given, as conveying advantages, what really conveyed none.* Answer (verses 2-4): *(1) It was not illusory; it did convey great advantages in the way of privilege and opportunity; this advantage first, that "the oracles of God" were entrusted to the Jew. (2) if some (more or fewer, it matters not) have failed to realize these advantages, it has been their fault, not God's. It is man's unfaithfulness, not his, that has been the cause of the failure.'*

Well there we have it. In Romans 3:1-2, Paul circumvents an explosive trial by commencing in dichotomous prose after his glimmer of poetic wisdom in 2:28-29, which additionally, is in clear contrast to 2:25. Now Peter, as he writes in his 2nd epistle (3:16), may be right regarding my impending destruction due to my ignorance, instability, and twisting of Paul's words. Though a curious and rather short revision to the beginning of chapter 3, especially one to assist in consistency and reinforce the 'neither Jew nor Gentile,' may read as such:

> *1Then what's the advantage of being a Jew? Nothing. Is there any value in the ceremony of circumcision? 2No, there are no benefits!*

The problem is, the commentaries above, and my dooming sacrilegious mockery of a revision, prove Paul's 'lukewarm' state of mind on these issues as he couldn't markedly deny and terminate the ubiquitous message of the exclusivity of the Jews. Numerous examples of Paul's ambiguity and fluctuations are riddled throughout his epistles, such as this aforementioned exclusivity. For instance, as a Jew himself, his stance in 3:2 and Romans 9:4 is quite convenient in their tremendous claims. Above all, is the great paradox right before us in verse 2. If 'unto them were committed the oracles *(the whole revelation, NLT)* of God' (especially of how and when to razor the penis), then it's obviously settled.

#46

Abrascam and his ~~Sister~~ Wife

Genesis 12:10-19; Genesis 20
NLT, *pp*

10A famine had struck Canaan, forcing Abram to go to
Egypt. 11As he was approaching Egypt, Abram said to his
wife, Sarai, "You are very beautiful. 12When the Egyptians
see you, they will say, 'Let's kill him; then we can have her!'
13So tell them you are my sister. Then they will spare my
life." 14When Abram arrived in Egypt, 15The palace officials
sang her praises to Pharaoh and she was taken to his palace.
16And Pharaoh gave Abram many gifts—sheep, goats, cattle,
donkeys, servants, and camels. 17But the Lord sent terrible
plagues upon Pharaoh and his household because of Sarai.
18So Pharaoh summoned Abram and accused him. "What
have you done to me? Why didn't you tell me she was your
wife? 19Why did you say, 'She is my sister,' and allow me to
take her as my wife? Now, here is your wife. Take her and get
out of here!"

Genesis 20
NLT, *pp*

1In Gerar, 2Abraham introduced his wife, Sarah, as his sister.
So King Abimelech of Gerar sent for Sarah and brought her
to his palace. 3That night God came to Abimelech in a dream
and said, "You are a dead man. That woman you have taken is

already married!" 4Abimelech had not slept with her and said, "Lord, will you destroy an innocent nation? 5Abraham told me, 'She is my sister' and she said, 'He is my brother.' I am innocent!" 6God responded, "I know you are innocent. That's why I did not let you touch her. 7Return her to Abraham, and he will pray for you and you will live. If you don't return her, you and your people will die." 9Then Abimelech sent for Abraham. "What have you done to us? What crime have I committed to be treated like this, making me and my kingdom guilty of this great sin? 10What possessed you to do such a thing?" 11Abraham replied, "I thought, 'This is a godless place. They will want my wife and will kill me to get her.' 12And she really is my sister for we have the same father, but different mothers and I married her. 13I told her, 'Wherever we go, tell the people that I am your brother.'" 14Then Abimelech gave Abraham sheep, goats, cattle, servants, and returned Sarah. 15Then Abimelech said, "Look over my land and choose where you would like to live." 16And he said to Sarah, "I am giving your 'brother' 1,000 pieces of silver to compensate you for any wrong I may have done to you." 17Then Abraham prayed to God, and God healed Abimelech, his wife, and his female servants, so they could have children. 18For the Lord had caused all the women to be infertile because of what happened with Abraham's wife, Sarah.

Moses, if he indeed wrote the book of Genesis, must have felt compelled to pen two very similar accounts of Abraham's rascally escapades with his ~~sister~~ wife. Two bone-chilling tales from the mystical roots of the desert, tell of ravishing beauty, deceit, pranking, pimping, and incest. We can't exactly blame the inbred tender heart of Moses for venerating his distant great gramps and grams by telling their story, and for that, we are much obliged.

Building up to the first saga in the earlier verses of chapter 12, we find the renowned 'Abrahamic Covenant.' This is the crucial moment where we learn of the racially motivated god of exclusivity; the great segregationist, isolating a people unto himself, and as a bonus, later earns Abram ("high father") a name change to 'Abraham' ("father of a multitude") in chapter 17. (Sarai also receives the new name of Sarah.) It's only a handful of verses later that Abram and Sarai pull off their first successfully executed sleight of hand.

The great Abram, who has just been promised the world by the god of the universe, approaches Egypt with Sarai and begins to fear for his own life. As a loving brother and husband, he rather decides to risk the life of Sarai and anyone else who may get caught up in this bronze age soap. Here, Moses spices up the story with some fun plot twists. Firstly, Abram's selfish motivations are clearly revealed as his obvious intent was not in protecting Sarai. She inevitably ends up at Pharaoh's palace regardless of his own paranoia in verse 12. Abram's life is then not only spared, but he also reaps the rewards for exploiting Sarai in receiving a nice bounty from Pharaoh. Great gramps couldn't possibly be at fault, so who gets punished? Pharaoh and his household are thereby plagued by the lord 'because of Sarai' as we read in verse 17. The final kicker is the news leak and climax of verse 19: Abram was the one who passed off Sarai as his sister and Pharaoh is the hero of the story; displaying the utmost honor and integrity. (Abram gets his wife back; keeps the riches; leaves unharmed = Win!)

The new and improved 'Abraham' is rather fond of this trickery in representing Sarah as free for the taking and tries it out again in

Genesis 20. God, Abraham's biggest fan, doesn't seem to mind either and unleashes death threats on the victims of Abraham's prank, rather than finally telling him to shut up. Instead of visiting Abraham with a haunting nightmare for yet another act of deception, misrepresentation, and instigation, god visits King Abimelech in a dream and kindly threatens the eradication of him and his family if he doesn't return Sarah. Fortunately, as was the case with Pharaoh, there are those with much more integrity than Abraham. Abimelech returns Sarah untouched and unharmed, and like Pharaoh, showers Abraham with gifts. Abimelech's innocence now earns him *a prayer* from Abraham and god decides to withdraw his curse of infertility by *'healing Abimelech, his wife, and his female servants because of what happened with Abraham's wife, Sarah.'* (Abraham gets his wife back; keeps the riches; leaves unharmed = Double Win!!)

#45

Parable of the 10 Servants

Luke 19:12-27
NLT

12He said, "A nobleman was called away to a distant empire
to be crowned king and then return. 13Before he left, he
called together ten of his servants and divided among them
ten pounds of silver, saying, 'Invest this for me while I am
gone.' 14But his people hated him and sent a delegation after
him to say, 'We do not want him to be our king.' 15 "After
he was crowned king, he returned and called in the servants
to whom he had given the money. He wanted to find out
what their profits were. 16The first servant reported, 'Master, I
invested your money and made ten times the original amount!'
17 "'Well done!' the king exclaimed. 'You are a good servant.
You have been faithful with the little I entrusted to you, so you
will be governor of ten cities as your reward.'

18 "The next servant reported, 'Master, I invested your money
and made five times the original amount.' 19 "'Well done!'
the king said. 'You will be governor over five cities.' 20 "But
the third servant brought back only the original amount
of money and said, 'Master, I hid your money and kept it
safe. 21I was afraid because you are a hard man to deal with,
taking what isn't yours and harvesting crops you didn't plant.'
22 "'You wicked servant!' the king roared. 'Your own words

condemn you. If you knew that I'm a hard man who takes what isn't mine and harvests crops I didn't plant, 23why didn't you deposit my money in the bank? At least I could have gotten some interest on it.' 24 "Then, turning to the others standing nearby, the king ordered, 'Take the money from this servant, and give it to the one who has ten pounds.' 25 "'But, master,' they said, 'he already has ten pounds!' 26 "'Yes,' the king replied, 'and to those who use well what they are given, even more will be given. But from those who do nothing, even what little they have will be taken away. 27And as for these enemies of mine who didn't want me to be their king—bring them in and execute them right here in front of me.'"

This parable is widely accepted to be analogous with the return of Jesus and the ensuing judgment in the final days. With this in mind, and as we find in the very similar parable of the talents in Matthew 25, the overarching and continued theme of 'one way to salvation' (and destruction), remains a key element. The two parables of Jesus in Luke 19 and Matthew 25 include severe consequences. We read of the wicked servant in the parable of the talents being cast into 'outer darkness, where there shall be weeping and gnashing of teeth'; commonly known as hell, or the lake of fire. In Luke 19, the parable concludes with a more immediate 'execution' ('slaughter,' 'slay,' and 'kill' being among the more popular terms of the translations) for those who do not want the nobleman (Jesus) to be king. We can assume the third servant of this parable and those of whom are executed are also tossed into hell thereafter.

Oddly enough, both teachings are void of a particular 'sin.' Other than an allusion to the first commandment, we find no direct violation of any specific commandment and yet it appears that Jesus hands down the same punishment to those in the parables as he does to those who commit the sinful acts of murder, stealing, adultery, etc. What Jesus is obviously implying as sin within these passages, is along the lines of his teaching in Luke 12:48: '*To whom much is given, much will be required.*' Contrary to the popularized easy-way-out method of simply being 'saved' (with many scriptural reinforcements from Saint Paul), Jesus appears to place a strong emphasis on the 'works' aspect of salvation. The third servant in each parable didn't necessarily wrong anyone, but rather, freely received salvation and chose not to harvest it. Although these 'bad stewards' are condemned as they 'hid their talents' and did nothing with them, they are innocent of charges such as disavowment and mockery, and by no means inflicted harm on anyone. As burying ones cash may be regarded as selfish and may result in missing out on interest and possible investment opportunities, it still remains safe and intact. One can even choose whether or not to talk about it, or remain silent until questioned. According to Jesus, this burial process with his gift of salvation will result in a first-class ticket to Gnashville.

Satan's morning roll call seems to lose its luster as hell continues to veer toward an all-are-welcome torture resort:

'Mornin. State your damned name and why in hell you're here.'

'Hi everyone, I'm Mao and I recently murdered 70M people.'

'Hi everyone, I'm Adolf and I recently murdered 6M of god's people and 50M+ in total.'

'Hi everyone, I'm Joe and I recently murdered an undecided amount of people. 9M+ for now.'

'Hi everyone, I'm Ted and I'm a serial rapist and murderer.'

'Hi everyone, I'm Andrea and I drowned five of my children.'

'Hi everyone, I'm Jordan and I'm a multi-commandment-offender; a thief, a cheat and a liar+.'

'Hi everyone, I'm Edna and I divorced my husband and remarried. I'm an adulteress.'

'Hi everyone, I'm Hank and I married Edna! I'm an adulterer.'

'Hi everyone, I'm Dorothy and I called Hank a fool.'

'Hi everyone, I'm Leo and I'm a salvation hider.'

#44

Top Picks of Petey the Rock

II Peter 2:4-16
NLT

4For God did not spare even the angels who sinned. He threw them into hell, in gloomy pits of darkness, where they are being held until the day of judgment. 5And God did not spare the ancient world—except for Noah and the seven others in his family. Noah warned the world of God's righteous judgment. So God protected Noah when he destroyed the world of ungodly people with a vast flood. 6Later, God condemned the cities of Sodom and Gomorrah and turned them into heaps of ashes. He made them an example of what will happen to ungodly people. 7But God also rescued Lot out of Sodom because he was a righteous man who was sick of the shameful immorality of the wicked people around him. 8Yes, Lot was a righteous man who was tormented in his soul by the wickedness he saw and heard day after day. 9So you see, the Lord knows how to rescue godly people from their trials, even while keeping the wicked under punishment until the day of final judgment. 10He is especially hard on those who follow their own twisted sexual desire, and who despise authority. These people are proud and arrogant, daring even to scoff at supernatural beings without so much as trembling. 11But the angels, who are far greater in power and strength, do not dare to bring from the Lord a charge of blasphemy against those supernatural beings. 12These false teachers are like unthinking animals, creatures of instinct, born to be caught and destroyed. They scoff at things they do not understand, and like animals, they will be destroyed. 13Their destruction is their reward for the harm they have done. They love to indulge in evil pleasures in broad daylight. They are a disgrace and a stain among you. They delight in deception even as they eat with you in your fellowship meals. 14They commit adultery with their eyes, and their desire for sin is never satisfied. They lure unstable people into sin, and they are well trained in greed. They live under God's curse. 15They have wandered off the right road and followed the footsteps of Balaam son of Beor, who loved to earn money by doing wrong. 16But Balaam was stopped from his mad course when his donkey rebuked him with a human voice.

Peter's blast from the past manages to splatter a wide array of obscurities in merely 13 verses. As the 61st book of the Bible; 22nd book of the New Testament, and with only 5 books left in the entire volume, it's a significant call to remembrance on Peter's part, and one that likely receives a blind eye. When taking the whole of I and II Peter into consideration, this entire passage may almost seem like a random insertion from a fantasy novel.

'Petey the Rock' throws a few warm-up lobs and then suddenly delivers a nasty screwball in verse 4: '*...the angels who sinned.*' The upcoming 1-chapter book of Jude, bearing a striking similarity to II Peter 2, expounds on this in Jude 1:6: *'And the angels which kept not their first estate, but left their own habitation, he hath reserved in everlasting chains under darkness unto the judgment of the great day.' [KJV]* Both KJV accounts in II Peter 2 and Jude speak of the 'chains of/under darkness' which we are told are restraining these angels in the holding tanks of hell at this very moment. Both mentions of these 'fallen angels,' along with Jude's honoring of 'Enoch' in verse 14, point us directly to Genesis 6:2 and 6:4; '2*that the sons of God saw the daughters of men that they were fair; and they took them wives of all which they chose'; 4'...when the sons of God came in unto the daughters of men, and they bare children to them'* (the 'Nephilim'). The apocryphal Book of Enoch corroborates this in stating that certain angels sinned by having intercourse with women. The sinning angels, along with the story of Satan's fall from heaven, further suggests that not all was perfect before man supposedly ruined everything. Assuming these supernatural celestial beings were created by god and resided in heaven, this would confirm the suspicion that free will and the possibility of sin, are indeed, realistic properties of heaven and predate man. (Yes, this would also include the peculiar ability of an angel to anthropomorphically grow a male appendage and impregnate women on Earth.)

Next up, for the fans of divine global domination by way of flooding and drowning, ol' Pete proceeds to further cement the story of Noah and the flood as a literal and undeniably true account. Directly after, he then reminds us of the destruction of Sodom and Gomorrah, having been reduced to ashes by the vehement raining down of fire and sulfur balls. Verses 7 and 8 thereafter are personal favorites in extolling the 'righteousness of Lot.' Our righteous friend earned (2) well-deserved inductions into the top 10 of this book, so I mustn't expound on his gloriousness just yet. Saint Pete decides to return to the supernatural beings in verse 10 and 11, condemning anyone who may dare 'scoff'; or simply mock & talk trash about these celestial entities. We find another near identical parallel to this in Jude 1:8 and a bonus obscurity in 1:9, which speaks of Michael the archangel contending with the devil over the body of Moses, and how even he didn't accuse or judge the devil.

As if that wasn't an overly sufficient mashup of wdafuq's, Peter throws a heater from way out in left field, presenting us with a beautiful prelude to the talking donkey of #43 up next!

#43

Saved by the Ass

Numbers 22
NLT, *pp*

1Then the people of Israel traveled to the plains of Moab.
4Balak, the king of Moab, said "They will devour everything
in sight." So he 5sent messengers to Balaam and said: "A vast
horde has arrived and they are threatening me. 6Come and
curse these people." 9That night God came to Balaam and
asked, "Who are these men visiting you?" 10Balaam said,
"Balak sent me this message: 11'Come and curse these people
for me.'" 12But God told Balaam, "Do not go with them. You
are not to curse these people." 13That morning Balaam told
the officials, "The Lord will not let me go." 14So the officials
returned and said, "Balaam refused to come." 15Balak tried
again. 16They delivered this message to Balaam: "Don't let
anything stop you from helping me. 17I will pay you well.
Come and curse these people!" 18Balaam responded with, "If
Balak gave me his palace, I would be powerless against the
will of the Lord." 20That night God came to Balaam and
said, "Go with these men but do only what I tell you to do."
21That morning Balaam saddled his donkey, and went with
the officials. 22But God was angry that Balaam was going,
so he sent the angel of the Lord to stand in the road to block
his way. As Balaam was riding along, 23his donkey saw the
angel standing in the road with a drawn sword. The donkey

bolted off the road, but Balaam beat it and turned it back onto the road. 24Then the angel stood where the road narrowed between two walls. 25When the donkey saw the angel, it tried to squeeze by and crushed Balaam's foot against the wall. So Balaam beat the donkey again. 26Then the angel went further down the road and stood in a place too narrow for the donkey to pass. 27When the donkey saw the angel, it lay down under Balaam. In a rage, Balaam beat the animal again with his staff. 28Then the Lord gave the donkey the ability to speak. "What have I done to you that deserves your beating me three times?" it asked Balaam. 29"You have made me look like a fool!" Balaam shouted. "If I had a sword, I would kill you!" 30"But I am the same donkey you have ridden all your life," the donkey answered. "Have I done anything like this before?" "No," Balaam said. 31Then the Lord opened Balaam's eyes, and he saw the angel standing in the roadway. Balaam fell face down before him. 32"Why did you beat your donkey those three times?" the angel asked. "I've come to block your way because you are resisting me. 33Three times the donkey saw me and shied away; otherwise, I would have killed you by now and spared the donkey." 34Then Balaam said to the angel, "I have sinned. I didn't realize you were standing in the road to block my way. I will return home if you are against my going." 35But the angel told Balaam, "Go with these men, but say only what I tell you to say." So Balaam went on.

Fresh off the heels of Peter's honorable mention in the prior passage of #44, the story of Balaam and his talking ass is well worth commemorating.

Balaam is a non-Israelite prophet who seems to have a good working relationship with god and is known for his success in blessings and curses. Somehow he gets entangled in this whole mess and is eventually killed by the sword for his role in leading the Israelites to worship 'Baal of Peor'; or 'Lord of the Opening.' Ya...Let's get back on track before I cause anyone to stumble.

Balaam is first mentioned here in Numbers 22 when King Balak requests that he curse the threatening encampment of the Israelites. Balaam tells the official messengers to stay overnight so that he may hear from god regarding this request. That night, god and Balaam get together and have a little talk. God tells Balaam to not go with the messengers and to not curse these people. Balaam obeys and sends the messengers on their way. They return with yet another request from Balak, and this time, god changes his mind and tells Balaam to go with them. The next morning, he saddles his donkey and is on his way. Balaam has been entirely obedient to god up to this point, even leading him to deny the first request of the king. In Balaam's obedience to god, we find that god becomes angry. This is where the fun and games begin.

In verse 22, only a mere two verses after god now tells Balaam to go with the men, god's anger is kindled, and he sends a sword-wielding angel to block his path. This presumably astute prophet whom converses with god and is sought out by a king to save his nation, is unable to see the angel. Unfortunately, the donkey can see the angel and suffers abuse in return. Twice, the donkey tries to get around the angel, and in turn is beaten by the oblivious Balaam. The third time around, the donkey finally surrenders to the angel, earning a beating severe enough to get it to talk:

"What are you doing!?" the donkey asked.

"You're such an ass!!" Balaam replied. "If I had a sword I'd cut your head off right now!"

"What!?? Why?? It's me! Your buddy! Have I ever done this before?" replied the donkey.

"Hmm…No, that's true…You've never done this before," said Balaam.

It was only then, after a few donkey beatings and an angry dialogue between the two, that god decided to open Balaam's eyes and reveal the angel. As a smart-ass himself, the angel pops off with, *"Hey, why'd you beat your donkey those three times? Ya know, you're lucky. If it weren't for that donkey of yours, I would've already killed you."* Balaam somehow feels he has sinned by not seeing the invisible angel and humbly tells the angel, *"I'll return home if that's what you want."*

Let's see. God is angry Balaam is on his way after telling him to go. The angel is blocking the path with a sword which results in multiple ass-beatings. Balaam then asks if he should turn around. The answer? No! Of course not. Even though god sent the angel to block the path, the sensible ending is: "Keep going."

#42

Woman, Thou Art Not Loosed

I Corinthians 14:34-35
NLT

34Women should be silent during the church meetings. It is not proper for them to speak. They should be submissive, just as the law says. 35If they have any questions, they should ask their husbands at home, for it is improper for women to speak in church meetings.

KJV

34Let your women keep silence in the churches: for it is not permitted unto them to speak; but they are commanded to be under obedience, as also saith the law. 35And if they will learn any thing, let them ask their husbands at home: for it is a shame for women to speak in the church.

I Timothy 2:11-15
NLT

11Women should learn quietly and submissively. 12I do not let women teach men or have authority over them. Let them listen quietly. 13For God made Adam first, and afterward he made Eve. 14And it was not Adam who was deceived by Satan. The woman was deceived, and sin was the result. 15But women will be saved through childbearing,[28] assuming they continue to live in faith, love, holiness, and modesty.

KJV

11Let the woman learn in silence with all subjection. 12But I suffer not a woman to teach, nor to usurp authority over the man, but to be in silence. 13For Adam was first formed, then Eve. 14And Adam was not deceived, but the woman being deceived was in the transgression. 15Notwithstanding she shall be saved in childbearing, if they continue in faith and charity and holiness with sobriety.

---

28 *2:15 Or will be saved by accepting their role as mothers, or will be saved by the birth of the child.*

Saint Paul, the proud celibate who wishes all could be like him,[29] is charitable enough to offer sage advice on how to handle this seemingly feeble organism of the human race. Although, Paul would find great injury in stamping this as mere advice. In 14:37, he reassures us of the divine nature of the chapter:

'...the things that I write unto you are the commandments of the Lord.'

Matthew Poole's Commentary: (14:37)

> If there be any amongst you who hath a conceit that he is inspired by God, and from that inspiration understandeth the mind and will of God, he must acknowledge, that I also am an apostle, and know the mind and will of God as well as he; and being so, that what I tell you are the commandments of the Lord.

This end-of-chapter spoiler is simply provided as an aid to the reader who may irreverently laugh or sneer at the contents of the chapter. Tread carefully as you can be certain that Paul has received these words directly from god.

Now that Paul had finished all the mushy love stuff in the prior chapter 13, ending with 'the greatest of these is love,' it was time to get some things straight. In chapter 14, Paul lays down these 'commandments of the Lord' regarding orderly worship; calling for strict adherence to the guidelines of who, where, and how many concerning singing, prophesying, and the speaking and translating of tongues, and caps it off by calling for the silence of women. This is but a warmup compared to what we read of in the included passage of I Timothy 2,

29 For I wish that all men were even as I myself (having the gift of continence/celibacy.) But each one has his own gift from God, one in this manner and another in that. I Corinthians 7:7 [KJV]
but he that is married cares for the things of the world, how he may please his wife. 7: 33 [KJV]
And you should imitate me, just as I imitate Christ. I Corinthians 11:1 [NLT]

and one of many throughout the writings of Paul that speak of the inferiority of women.[30]

Barnes Commentary: (14:34)

> Let your women keep silence…This rule is positive, explicit, and universal. There is no ambiguity in the expressions; and there can be no difference of opinion, one would suppose, in regard to their meaning. No rule in the New Testament is more positive than this; and however plausible may be the reasons which may be urged for disregarding it, and for suffering women to take part in conducting public worship, yet the authority of the apostle Paul is positive, and his meaning cannot be mistaken.

Gill's Exposition of the Entire Bible: (14:34)

> But they are commanded to be under obedience, as also saith the law. In Genesis 3:16, "thy desire shall be to thy husband, and he shall rule over thee." By this the apostle would signify, that the reason why women are not to speak in the church, or to preach and teach publicly, or be concerned in the ministerial function, is, because this is an act of power, and authority; of rule and government, and so contrary to that subjection which God in his law requires of women unto men. The extraordinary instances of Deborah, Huldah, and Anna, must not be drawn into a rule or example in such cases.

Cambridge Bible for Schools and Colleges: (14:34)

> 34. Let your women keep silence in the churches. The position of women in Christian assemblies is now decided on the principles laid down in ch. 1 Cor. 11:3; 7-9. [as also saith the law] in Genesis 3:16.

30 But I would have you know, that the head of every man is Christ; and the head of the woman is the man; and the head of Christ is God. 1 Corinthians 11:3 [KJV]

#41

Killing vs Injuring a Slave

Exodus 21:20-21
NLT

> 20If a man beats his male or female slave with a club and the slave dies as a result, the owner must be punished. 21But if the slave recovers within a day or two, then the owner shall not be punished, since the slave is his property.

KJV

> 20And if a man smite his servant, or his maid, with a rod, and he die under his hand; he shall be surely punished.
> 21Notwithstanding, if he continue a day or two, he shall not be punished: for he is his money.

Just before god and Moses are really about to get their lawmaking groove on and churn out the covenant code beginning in Chapter 21, god squeezes in one last bit of godly advice in the last verse of Chapter 20:

20:26And do not approach my altar by going up steps. If you do, someone might look up under your clothing and see your ~~#!$%@~~ nakedness. [NLT]

Oh god, you ol' silly rascal you! Were you really reminding your elect, sophisticated, high society of the upper echelon dunes-people to mind their virtuous manners? Certainly a people willing to accept and enforce your overabundance of truly divine commandments, rules, ordinances, and laws, such as that of Exodus 21:20-21, need no reminding! Their state of mental destitution in comprehending a shred of the humane is far too great to facilitate even the slightest reminder of ethics.

On the subject of ethics and morality overall, let's investigate yet another fine example handed down as an edict from the alleged source of morality itself. This is after the Decalogue *(the Ten Commandments)* of chapter 20, and begins the next and major leg of the Mitzvot (the 613 laws of the Torah). Exodus 21:1:

'Now these are the judgments (laws) which thou shalt set before them.'

Soon we find ourselves at verses 20-21, where god reveals another ray of his character and morality by outlining the treatment of slaves. Many commentaries pronounce the death of the slave by way of beating, is in itself, the just punishment the owner bears as the slave is his own property; his money.

Cambridge Bible for Schools and Colleges Commentary:

> 21. If the slave survives a day or two, his master escapes even the comparatively light penalty of v. 20; for then it is clear that he did not intend to kill him, but only to correct him. He is his money; i.e. his master's property, purchased by his master's

money. His master is considered to have sufficiently punished himself by the loss of his property.

Keil and Delitzsch Biblical Commentary on the Old Testament:

'The case was different with regard to a slave. The master had always the right to punish or "chasten" him with a stick (Proverbs 10:13; Proverbs 13:24); this right was involved in the paternal authority of the master over the servants in his possession...."Notwithstanding, if he continue a day or two (i.e., remain alive), it shall not be avenged, for he is his money." By the continuance of his life, if only for a day or two, it would become perfectly evident that the master did not wish to kill his servant; and if nevertheless he died after this, the loss of the slave was punishment enough for the master.'

Pulpit Commentary:

'...he is his money. The slave had been purchased for a stun of money, or was at any rate money' s worth; and the master would suffer a pecuniary loss by his death.'

It's quite the exhibition (and one of many) when theological acrobatic aces attempt to maneuver around this one. The usual round of blanks include embarrassingly juvenile blabber blunders such as:

"You have to consider the era and the culture."

Got it. God is cultural and wickedly barbaric.

"Lots of people had slaves. Slaves were normal."

Got it. It's ok to own people (and beat them).

"There are slaves in the world today."

Got it. That must make it ok. Maybe god likes it. Ok.

What clearly surfaces here, is the unspeakable amount of pride and utter lack of empathy on the part of anyone who will not condemn passages such as this.

#40

The Last Triumph of Moses

Numbers 31:1-2; 7-18
NLT

1Then the Lord said to Moses, 2"On behalf of the people of
Israel, take revenge on the Midianites for leading them into
idolatry. After that, you will die and join your ancestors."

7They attacked Midian as the Lord had commanded Moses,
and they killed all the men. 9Then the Israelite army captured
the Midianite women and children and seized their cattle and
flocks and all their wealth as plunder. 10They burned all the
towns and villages where the Midianites had lived. 11After
they had gathered the plunder and captives, both people
and animals, 12they brought them all to Moses and Eleazar
the priest, and to the whole community of Israel, which was
camped on the plains of Moab beside the Jordan River, across
from Jericho. 13Moses, Eleazar the priest, and all the leaders
of the community went to meet them outside the camp.

14But Moses was furious with all the generals and captains
who had returned from the battle. 15"Why have you let all
the women live?" he demanded. 16"These are the very ones
who followed Balaam's advice and caused the people of Israel
to rebel against the Lord at Mount Peor. They are the ones
who caused the plague to strike the Lord's people. 17So kill
all the boys and all the women who have had intercourse with

a man. 18Only the young girls who are virgins may live; you
may keep them for yourselves."

KJV

14And Moses was wroth with the officers of the host, with the
captains over thousands, and captains over hundreds, which
came from the battle. 15And Moses said unto them, Have
ye saved all the women alive? 16Behold, these caused the
children of Israel, through the counsel of Balaam, to commit
trespass against the LORD in the matter of Peor, and there
was a plague among the congregation of the LORD. 17Now
therefore kill every male among the little ones, and kill every
woman that hath known man by lying with him. 18But all
the women children, that have not known a man by lying with
him, keep alive for yourselves.

Sadly, it's time for Moses to die, but not before one last hurrah. Before the cupids carry Moses to heaven, he leaves us this comforting anecdote of his final exploit. Allow me to paint the scene with the accompaniment of the JS Translation as we can presume these interactions were hardly that of a nice renaissance painting. I'll conveniently skip to verse 12 rather than illustrate the vengeful gore that god requested of Moses; making it yet another instance where the omnipotent god of all things mighty, miraculous, and magical, prefers bloodshed over harmless soul-zapping, mass-vanishment, or insta-death by disappearance—to name a few.

Numbers 31:12-18 [JST] *[Jeruel Schneider Translation]*

> 12Moses and Eleazar had finished eating the hind of a blemished disfigured goat and were enjoying some joy plant, better known as Sumerian Hul Gil. The serenity of the distant horizon soon became overly cluttered with what appeared to be an excessive amount of captive women. 13Moses and Eleazar quickly left the bonfire to confirm their suspicions. 14Upon arriving and beholding an inordinate amount of used women, Moses flew into a hysterical rage and began to berate his generals and captains. 15"You dingbats! Why have you let this scum live!? 16These are the very women who are responsible for introducing our people to the Lord of the Opening! They are the reason god killed 24,000 of our people! 17So I'll tell ya what. See all these little boys you kept from killing? Kill every one of them. See all these women you also kept from killing? Kill them too, but only kill the used ones; those who have had sex with a man. I leave that to you to figure out." 18Moses then walked up to a young girl who was visibly shaken and distraught from the ravages of war. He knelt down closely in front of her and wiped the tears from her eyes. He arose and said, "But spare these young girls and keep them for yourselves. They too must be virgins and I also leave that to you to figure out."

One easy way to 'figure this out' is by sparing those that look the youngest and appear the most undeveloped. I'm sure the permissive act of Moses equated to a very minimal amount of time spent selecting and filtering. Though I wonder, in the case of the Israelite gentleman, what a 9-year-old girl would say if she were kindly asked if she's a virgin or not. Traumatized by the death of her father and mother of which she likely witnessed, I wonder how she would answer in this moment of life or death.

Thus, other than calling for a purification ritual and divvying up the plunder, we have Moses's final act of war here in Numbers 31. Certainly, this man should forever be immortalized as a true hero. George Washington led the Continental Army to victory over a nearly insurmountable foe; forever altering history. Patton's final act delivered a deathblow to the nazis in the Battle of the Bulge. Lincoln lost his life due to his final Emancipation Proclamation. Moses nobly retired by extending the slaughter and gifting the remaining virgins to his men.

#39

Jeremiah's Rotten Underwear

Jeremiah 13:1-14
NLT

1This is what the Lord said to me: "Go and buy a linen loincloth and put it on, but do not wash it." 2So I bought the loincloth as the Lord directed me, and I put it on. 3Then the Lord gave me another message: 4"Take the linen loincloth you are wearing, and go to the Euphrates River. Hide it there in a hole in the rocks." 5So I went and hid it by the Euphrates as the Lord had instructed me. 6A long time afterward the Lord said to me, "Go back to the Euphrates and get the loincloth I told you to hide there." 7So I went to the Euphrates and dug it out of the hole where I had hidden it. But now it was rotting and falling apart. The loincloth was good for nothing. 8Then I received this message from the Lord: 9"This is what the Lord says: This shows how I will rot away the pride of Judah and Jerusalem. 10These wicked people refuse to listen to me. They stubbornly follow their own desires and worship other gods. Therefore, they will become like this loincloth—good for nothing! 11As a loincloth clings to a man's waist, so I created Judah and Israel to cling to me, says the Lord. They were to be my people, my pride, my glory—an honor to my name. But they would not listen to me. 12So tell them, 'This is what the Lord, the God of Israel, says: May all your jars be filled with wine.' And they will reply, 'Of course! Jars are made to be filled with wine!' 13Then tell them, 'No, this is what the Lord means: I will fill everyone in this land with drunkenness—from the king sitting on David's throne to the priests and the prophets, right down to the common people of Jerusalem. 14I will smash them against each other, even parents against children, says the Lord. I will not let my pity or mercy or compassion keep me from destroying them.'"

Ironically enough, chapter 13 continues with god warning his chosen people of arrogance and pride; demanding glory and worship 'before it is too late,' where he is then forced to 'turn the light into the shadow of death,' among other threats. Additionally, if the people remain rebellious, they will make god cry.

Though let us return to the grand feature passage.

Somehow, radically ridiculous stories such as this in Jeremiah 13, managed to find their way into this 'holy book.' Furthermore, this story, being one of many that in complete erasure would be of no consequence, finds its way to pulpits today. One may even have the fortunate experience of sitting in the pew with his prepubescent daughter as the preacher proceeds in borrowing from a reminiscent passage on loins and blood: *Isaiah 64:6: But we are all as an unclean thing, and all our righteousnesses are as filthy rags. [KJV]*

Jamieson-Fausset-Brown: (Isaiah 64:6)

> filthy rags—literally, a "menstruous rag" (Lev. 15:33; 20:18; Lam. 1:17).

Barnes: (Isaiah 64:6)

> As filthy rags...No language could convey deeper abhorrence of their deeds of righteousness than this reference, as it is undoubtedly to the vestis menstruis polluta (soiled menstrual clothes).

Jeremiah takes a slightly different direction, although, in comparison to Isaiah's cute analogy, Jeremiah's story bears far greater importance as it's directly from god. A simple logical deduction leads us to conclude that either *(a),* indeed, god spoke these very words to Jeremiah and felt it necessary to draw inferences between a nasty loincloth *(undergarment/underwear)* and his chosen people, or *(b),* this is entirely fabricated by the mind of a man and it's he who possesses a twisted imagination of men's rotten loin-wear being analogous to god and his chosen people. In any event, both conclusions lead us to believe that either god or Jeremiah, or possibly both as coconspirators, are severely starved of more realistic and reasonable metaphors.

Benson Commentary: (Jeremiah 13:11)

> "'For as the girdle cleaveth to the loins of a man' — Here God shows the prophet why he commanded him to put the girdle about his loins. 'So have I caused' — Rather, 'had I caused; to cleave unto me the house of Israel' — I had betrothed them to myself in righteousness, and entered into a marriage covenant with them, that they might cleave to me as a wife cleaveth to her husband. By the laws I gave them, the prophets I sent among them, and the favours which, in my providence, I showed them, I brought them near to myself, and allowed them access to me, and intercourse with me, above every other nation. 'That they might be unto me for a people' — A peculiar people; that they might have the honour of being called by my name; 'and for a praise and a glory' — That I might be glorified by their showing forth my power, goodness, and faithfulness, and all my other glorious perfections to the world, so that I might be honoured and praised through them."

Finally pulling ourselves away from moldy decomposing underwear, we read of god's warning of an interesting curse of drunkenness that will sweep the land.

He goes on to state that he will pit people against people, and family against family, and that no amount of his boundless love, mercy, and compassion will keep him from destroying them. Magnificent.

#38

Staffshifting

Exodus 7:1-13
NLT

1Then the Lord said to Moses, "Pay close attention to this. I
will make you seem like God to Pharaoh, and your brother,
Aaron, will be your prophet. 2Tell Aaron everything I command you, and Aaron must command Pharaoh to let the
people of Israel leave his country. 3But I will make Pharaoh's
heart stubborn so I can multiply my miraculous signs and
wonders in the land of Egypt. 4Even then Pharaoh will refuse
to listen to you. So I will bring down my fist on Egypt. Then
I will rescue my forces—my people, the Israelites—from the
land of Egypt with great acts of judgment. 5When I raise my
powerful hand and bring out the Israelites, the Egyptians will
know that I am the Lord." 6So Moses and Aaron did just as
the Lord had commanded them. 7Moses was eighty years old,
and Aaron was eighty-three when they made their demands to
Pharaoh. 8Then the Lord said to Moses and Aaron, 9"Pharaoh
will demand, 'Show me a miracle.' When he does this, say
to Aaron, 'Take your staff and throw it down in front of
Pharaoh, and it will become a serpent. *[7:9 Hebrew tannin,
which elsewhere refers to a sea monster. Greek version translates it
"dragon."]*" 10So Moses and Aaron went to Pharaoh and did
what the Lord had commanded them. Aaron threw down his
staff before Pharaoh and his officials, and it became a serpent!

11Then Pharaoh called in his own wise men and sorcerers, and
these Egyptian magicians did the same thing with their magic.
12They threw down their staffs, which also became serpents!
But then Aaron's staff swallowed up their staffs. 13Pharaoh's
heart, however, remained hard. He still refused to listen, just
as the Lord had predicted.

Just before the ten plagues rain doom over the land of Egypt, we're served an appetizer in the form of these slithering snacks. The talking bush and Moses had practiced this stunt in Exodus 4 and now it was time for the grand finale; the metamorphosis of an inanimate walking stick—mutating into a reptilian predator; better known as the process of 'Staffshifting.'

It's a showdown of wizardry in the courts of Pharaoh as Aaron and the sorcerers of Egypt throw down in a game of magic staffs. What seems providential, quickly turns humiliating as Pharaoh's magicians immediately respond by performing the same staff-to-serpent trick with ease. However, Aaron's mutated staff is a hungry critter and takes the win by stunningly swallowing all of the opposing staffshifted serpents. *(I prefer the more entertaining translations we read of in the in-text reference of 7:9: 'sea monster' or 'dragon'.)* As outlined in passage #52, our friend Paul celebrates the enigmatic magical staff of Aaron by affirming its final resting place inside the Ark of the Covenant. The ark, being under 4 feet long and just over 2 feet tall and wide, would've made for a uniquely small staff. Nevertheless, we of course mustn't assume the staffshifted serpent was limited to such a small size, especially when considering its profound ability to swallow numerous serpents in one sitting. Thankfully, Moses left out the digestion visual, and only a handful of verses later, we read of the re-petrified walking stick, magically turning the Nile river into blood to kick off the series of plagues.

Sadly, this most wonderful feat of sorcery never reached the height of remembrance and celebration as those of the plagues, such as *'The Passover.'* Rarely do we hear the plagues argued as an allegorical set of disasters, yet the first course snake-snacks tend to get spewed out, watered down, and washed away, or conveniently tossed aside and left unaddressed.

Again, we owe it to Paul. Not only does the saint bless us in recalling Aaron's staff in Hebrews 9:4, but in the most pure and literal sense, he additionally mentions its magical sprouting of buds, which produced blossoms and almonds.

This triumphant staffshifting talisman of doom, known for its skills in mutating into a reptile, turning water into blood, and growing flowers and almonds, was, and is still considered by many, to be a very real and divinely charged walking stick.

With regard to the lives of Moses and Aaron and the miracles attributed to them, especially those involving their magic staffs; any cherry-picking to preserve a smooth narrative will prove to be a slippery slope.

#37

Goodness Gracious, Great Cloven Tongues of Fire!

Acts 2:1-4
NLT

1On the day of Pentecost all the believers were meeting together in one place. 2Suddenly, there was a sound from heaven like the roaring of a mighty windstorm, and it filled the house where they were sitting. 3Then, what looked like flames or tongues of fire appeared and settled on each of them. 4And everyone present was filled with the Holy Spirit and began speaking in other languages, as the Holy Spirit gave them this ability.

KJV

1And when the day of Pentecost was fully come, they were all with one accord in one place. 2And suddenly there came a sound from heaven as of a rushing mighty wind, and it filled all the house where they were sitting. 3And there appeared unto them cloven tongues like as of fire, and it sat upon each of them. 4And they were all filled with the Holy Ghost, and began to speak with other tongues, as the Spirit gave them utterance.

In observance and in strict accordance with the ordinances and rituals originally laid out in Exodus 23 and Leviticus 23, Jesus stays perfectly on queue before and after his crucifixion.

It's the week of the Feast of Unleavened Bread, better known as Passover. It's the most wonderful time of the year when the Israelites observe the command of god to forever memorialize and celebrate his killing spree of every firstborn of Egypt. Jesus and his crucifixion are timed accordingly, and thus, ecumenically, he becomes the sacrificial lamb of the passover. He then resurrects the day after the sabbath on the day of the 'Feast of First Fruits;' another day that god commanded be permanently observed. The next god-ordained and required observance is celebrated exactly 7 weeks after the Feast of First Fruits *(7 sabbaths and one day from the first sabbath, totaling 50 days),* and is called 'the Feast of Weeks' or 'Festival of the Weeks'; better known as 'Shavuot' or 'Pentecost' *(from the Greek 'pentekoste,' meaning fifty.)* It originally marked the beginning of the wheat harvest, and to this day, it commemorates the day god gave Moses the ten commandments and the Torah on Mount Sinai. These festivals are all directly correlated and intertwined with the day of Pentecost spoken of in Acts 2, placing an even greater emphasis on their origin and the expectation of celebrating them in perpetuity.

With all this in mind, it is clearly no accident that on this very day of Pentecost; an exact 50 days after the resurrection, we read of the invasion of the great cloven tongues of fire. The immeasurably tall tale of Moses and his many escapades had just been one-upped on the very anniversary of his remembrance.

The new flavor of the unquestionably non-psychoactive kosher kool-aid was an immediate hit. Mysterious tongues set aflame were reportedly seen landing on people and were even activating the new ability of fluency in diverse languages.

Christian tradition maintains the location of this event to be that of the 'upper room' we read of in Acts 1. Here, we have the 11 disciples gathered together, and in order to replace Judas, they say a prayer and throw dice, which leads to the selection of Matthias. This closes out chapter 1 and it's an approximate 10 days later that our main event occurs. In the prior book of John, we read of Jesus breathing the holy spirit onto 10 of these disciples on the day of his resurrection, which raises the question of just what, if any, the possible relationship is between the holy spirit of Acts 2:4.

The mysterious orphaned firetongues are still many millennia ahead of their time. We are blessed to read of the first wireless heat-seeking body organs that come pre-installed with human languages and dialects. Peter takes it a step further by declaring that Joel is the actual inventor, pushing the date of invention further into antiquity.

Today, Pentecost remains as a multi-faceted celebration and largely commemorates this descent of the holy spirit.

#36

The Voyeur of Sperm Spillage

Gen 38:1-10
NLT

> 1About this time, Judah left home and moved to Adullam, where he stayed with a man named Hirah. 2There he saw a Canaanite woman, the daughter of Shua, and he married her. When he slept with her, 3she became pregnant and gave birth to a son, and he named the boy Er. 4Then she became pregnant again and gave birth to another son, and she named him Onan. 5And when she gave birth to a third son, she named him Shelah. At the time of Shelah's birth, they were living at Kezib. 6In the course of time, Judah arranged for his firstborn son, Er, to marry a young woman named Tamar. 7But Er was a wicked man in the Lord's sight, so the Lord took his life. 8Then Judah said to Er's brother Onan, "Go and marry Tamar, as our law requires of the brother of a man who has died. You must produce an heir for your brother." 9But Onan was not willing to have a child who would not be his own heir. So whenever he had intercourse with his brother's wife, he spilled the semen on the ground. This prevented her from having a child who would belong to his brother. 10But the Lord considered it evil for Onan to deny a child to his dead brother. So the Lord took Onan's life, too.

KJV

1And it came to pass at that time, that Judah went down
from his brethren, and turned in to a certain Adullamite,
whose name was Hirah. 2And Judah saw there a daughter
of a certain Canaanite, whose name was Shuah; and he took
her, and went in unto her. 3And she conceived, and bare a
son; and he called his name Er. 4And she conceived again,
and bare a son; and she called his name Onan. 5And she yet
again conceived, and bare a son; and called his name Shelah:
and he was at Chezib, when she bare him. 6And Judah took
a wife for Er his firstborn, whose name was Tamar. 7And Er,
Judah's firstborn, was wicked in the sight of the LORD; and
the LORD slew him. 8And Judah said unto Onan, Go in
unto thy brother's wife, and marry her, and raise up seed to
thy brother. 9And Onan knew that the seed should not be his;
and it came to pass, when he went in unto his brother's wife,
that he spilled it on the ground, lest that he should give seed
to his brother. 10And the thing which he did displeased the
LORD: wherefore he slew him also.

Sandwiched between the story of Joseph's rise to stardom in the land of Egypt, we're endowed with this pleasant account of Judah, Tamar, Er, and Onan. We must remember that as stated in the prior commentary of #37, Jewish tradition upholds the belief that the Torah was entirely dictated by god and transcribed by Moses. There are a variety of approaches as to how and when this all transpired, yet the overall divinity of the Torah, right down to these very stories, is broadly undisputed. In regard to the passage at hand, we can meet in the middle between god done-it and the cave-dwelling myth specialists done-it, and ultimately credit Moses for this emission of lunacy, among other things.

With the underlying theme of our featured story being that of ancient erotica, we can presume the KJV is most accurate in its verse 2 recounting of Judah quickly pouncing on Shuah. The steamy romance continues and they eventually have a brood of three boys. Judah, with his keen eye for women, and particularly for Tamar, cinches an arrangement for his firstborn son, Er. The details run slim here as Moses is eager to get to the good stuff. Verse 7 quickly eradicates Er in basically stating that god didn't like him, so he killed him. Judah's a strong fellow, so only minutes after mourning the murder of Er, he calls on his son Onan, gives him a swift kick in the hiney and says, 'You're gonna go mount Tamar and give your dead brother the boys he would've had whether you like it or not.' Onan doesn't seem to object, yet he decides to 'spill his seed' rather than make some screaming babies. Seems like an easy win-win, but unbeknownst to Onan, there is one other than Judah who has eyes on Tamar and the sexual activities she engages in with Onan; the grand voyeur: god. In the NLT, it appears there wasn't just one instance of sperm spillage, but many. God appears to be taking note, especially paying close attention to the climax, and finally decides he's sick of Onan pulling out, so he simply kills him too. Judah eventually takes care of business when he, conveniently thinking Tamar is a prostitute, gets her pregnant with twins and they live happily ever after.

Moses thought the obvious was on the table for the reader, but he kindly fields some questions:

"You mean, god didn't urge Judah to get the third son, 'Shelah,' to try it out?" asked the reader.

"Uh, obviously not," Moses replied.

"Sorry, I'm so dumb, but if god was watching Onan shoot his sperm on the ground and eventually killed him for it, wouldn't that imply that he also possessed the ability to somehow stop Judah from being 'tricked' and impregnating Tamar?" the reader asked.

"You're right—you really are dumb because you keep asking questions rather than just believing what I wrote and the way I wrote it—*or... the way I heard it from god*," Moses responded.

"Thanks, and just one more. I guess Er was 'wicked' and god killed him for it. Onan wouldn't impregnate Tamar so god killed him too. Hmm, well ok, no problem, both seem perfectly logical. But Judah, other than being the culprit of all of this, solicited a prostitute (Tamar in disguise), and Tamar not only played the prostitute, but tricked Judah. Shouldn't god kill them too?" the reader asked.

"You really are a slow learner. You've read all of my stories and still think I need help or advice with the storyline? If I thought that's how the story should go, I would've written it that way," Moses replied. "Just shut up and believe the story—Ok!? Stop asking questions."

#35

Roiders of the Lost Ark

I-II Samuel; NLT, *pp*

I Sam 4:10 The Philistines defeated the Israelites again 11and they captured the Ark of God.

I Sam 4:18 When the messenger told Eli what had happened to the Ark of God, he fell backward and broke his neck and died.

I Sam 4:19 Eli's daughter-in-law was pregnant. When she heard the Ark had been captured and that Eli and her husband Phinehas had died, she went into labor and 20died in childbirth.

I Sam 5:1 After the Philistines captured the Ark, they took it to Ashdod. 2They carried it into the temple of Dagon and placed it beside an idol of Dagon. 3But the next morning, Dagon had fallen with his face to the ground in front of the Ark! So they put Dagon back in his place. 4But the next morning, Dagon had fallen face down before the Ark again. KJV, *pp*

I Sam 5:6 The hand of the LORD was heavy upon those of Ashdod, and he destroyed them, and smote them with emerods. *5:6 Greek version and Latin Vulgate read tumors; and rats appeared in their land, and death and destruction were throughout the city.*

I Sam 5:8 The lords of the Philistines then said, take the Ark to Gath. 9And after they had carried it about, the hand of the LORD was against Gath with a great destruction; he smote the men of Gath, both small and great, and they had emerods in their secret parts. NLT, *pp*

I Sam 5:10 So they sent the Ark to the town of Ekron, but when the people of Ekron saw it coming they cried out, "They are bringing the Ark of God here to kill us, too!" 11The people begged the Philistines saying, "Please send the Ark of the God of Israel back to its own country, 5:11 Or he will kill us all." For the deadly plague from God had already begun. 12Those who didn't die were afflicted with tumors; and their cries rose to heaven.

I Samuel 6:3 The Philistine priests said, "Send the Ark of God back with a gift. Send a guilt offering so the plague will stop." 4"What sort of offering should we send?" they asked. And they were told, "Make five gold tumors and five gold rats, like those that have ravaged your land. 5Make these things to honor the God of Israel. Perhaps then he will stop afflicting you."

I Samuel 6 KJV, *pp*

6:13 And they of Beth-shemesh were in the valley: and they saw the Ark, and rejoiced to see it. 19And the LORD smote the men of Beth-shemesh, because they had looked into the Ark. He smote 50,070 men and the people lamented, because he smote them with a great slaughter.

II Samuel 6 NLT, *pp*

6:2 Then David led the troops to Baalah to bring back the Ark of God. Uzzah and Ahio were guiding the cart that carried the Ark. 6But the oxen stumbled, and Uzzah reached out his hand and steadied the Ark. 7Then the Lord's anger was aroused against Uzzah, and God struck him dead because of this. Uzzah died right there beside the Ark. 11three months later 12David brought the Ark to the City of David with a great celebration. 13After they carried the Ark six steps, David sacrificed a bull and a calf. 14And David danced before the Lord

with all his might, wearing a priestly garment. 20When David
returned home, Michal, his wife said, "How distinguished the
king of Israel looked today, shamelessly exposing himself to the
servant girls like a vulgar person!" 21David retorted to Michal,
"I was dancing before the Lord, who chose me above your
father and all his family! 22Yes, and I am willing to look even
more foolish than this, but those servant girls you mentioned
will indeed think I am distinguished!" 23So Michal remained
childless throughout her entire life.

Quite imaginative is the celestial punishment of hemorrhoids upon those whom mishandle or wrongly possess this box; or *'Ark.'* Well, to be fair, Uzzah at least was spared from the boilings of the anus, and rather, was divinely zapped and killed for making god angry in trying to keep the box from falling. Now, for the naysayers, and all those who out of undying protection for these texts, remain highly incredulous toward this celestial punishment and dumb it down in order to fortify their narrative, let's address this very tumor in the room; the *'emerod.'*

Deuteronomy 28 begins with a short 14 verse briefing on *"if you obey"* blessings, and as one would expect, it then proceeds with a dominant 54-verse tirade of *"if you do not obey"* curses. We then find our first mention of the emerod in verse 27: The LORD will smite thee with the botch of Egypt, and with the emerods, and with the scab, and with the itch, whereof thou canst not be healed. *[KJV]*

After this mere preview, it's time to get seriously emerodial in the book of Samuel:

- 1 Samuel 5:9: "they had emerods in their secret parts." The "secret parts" are actually the genitals, so the idea here would be hemorrhoids. Strong's Hebrew Dictionary says: "from an unused root meaning to burn; a boil or ulcer (from the inflammation), especially a tumor in the anus or pudenda (the piles):—emerod." The Oxford English Dictionary defines "haemorrhoid" (U.S. "hemorrhoid") as: "a swollen vein or group of veins in the region on the anus. Also (collectively) called piles." Gesenius' Hebrew-Chaldee Lexicon: "tumours of the anus, haemorrhoidal mariscae, protruding from the anus, protruding through tenesmus in voiding." "Tenesmus" is defined as "a continual or recurrent inclination to evacuate the bowels, caused by disorder of the rectum or other illness."
- KJV Dictionary Definition: emerods EM'ERODS, n. With a plural termination. Corrupted from hemorrhoids, Gr. to labor under a flowing of blood. Hemorrhoids; piles; a dilatation of the veins about the rectum, with a discharge of

blood. Definitions from Webster's American Dictionary of the English Language, 1828.

- Most translations say the affliction was "tumors"; the ISV says "tumors of the groin"; and the Darby translation says "hemorrhoids."

Two other fortunate victims that we read of other than Uzzah, were Eli and his daughter-in-law, whose untimely deaths were directly linked to the news of the Ark's capture. Even the poor idol of Dagon was getting brutally vandalized by this box. Otherwise, the preferred infestation of hemorrhoids and rats was sweeping the land of any that wrongfully harbored the Ark. The Philistines, no matter how far they would send the box, couldn't seem to extinguish the flaming lumps, and finally adhered to the great wisdom of their priests. They made a 'guilt offering' of golden mice and hemorrhoids:

I Samuel 6:11and they laid the ark of the LORD upon the cart, and the coffer with the mice of gold and the images of their emerods. *[KJV]*

Brilliant! The problem is, the Bethshemites, who then happily inherited the Ark and these wonderful gifts, lost 50,070 people at the slaughterous hand of god because they had looked inside of it. Or, we might say, a total of 50,073 that god had now *saved* from the boilings of the rectum. Finally, David retrieves his box and gets his wild groove on at the disdain of his wife, Michal. He then makes a couple cocky comments to her and voila, she is then cursed with barrenness.

#34

Familial Cannibalism

Leviticus 26 Compilation; NLT

3"If you follow my decrees and are careful to obey my commands,

6I will rid the land of wild animals and keep your enemies out of your land. 7You will chase down your enemies and slaughter them with your swords. 8Five will chase a hundred, and a hundred of you will chase ten thousand!

14However, if you do not listen to me or obey all these commands, 15and if you break my covenant by rejecting my decrees, treating my regulations with contempt, and refusing to obey my commands, 16I will punish you. I will bring sudden terrors upon you—wasting diseases and burning fevers that will cause your eyes to fail and your life to ebb away. 17I will turn against you, and you will be defeated by your enemies. 18And if, in spite of all this, you still disobey me, I will punish you seven times over for your sins.

21If even then you remain hostile toward me and refuse to obey me, I will inflict disaster on you seven times over for your sins. 22I will send wild animals that will rob you of your children and destroy your livestock. 23And if you fail to learn the lesson and continue your hostility toward me, 24then I myself will be hostile toward you. I will personally strike you with calamity seven times over for your sins.

27If in spite of all this you still refuse to listen and remain hostile toward me, 28then I will give full vent to my hostility. I myself will punish you seven times over for your sins. 29Then you will eat the flesh of your own sons and daughters. I will leave your lifeless corpses piled on top of your lifeless idols and I will despise you. I will take no pleasure in your offerings that should be a pleasing aroma to me.

29And ye shall eat the flesh of your sons, and the flesh of your daughters shall ye eat. [KJV]

33I will scatter you among the nations and bring out my sword against you. 36And for those of you who survive, I will demoralize you in the land of your enemies. You will live in such fear that the sound of a leaf driven by the wind will send you fleeing."

46These are the decrees, regulations, and instructions that the Lord gave through Moses on Mount Sinai as evidence of the relationship between himself and the Israelites.

46These are the statutes and judgments and laws, which the LORD made between him and the children of Israel in mount Sinai by the hand of Moses. [KJV]

After dictating well over 200 mitzvah's (commandments) in the prior chapters of Leviticus, god then brings the fury in chapter 26 with threats of divine brutality and hostility. Violence, disasters, plagues, and familial cannibalism await those who will not listen to him and obey all of his commandments.[31]

Everything seemed fairly kosher at the launch of the chapter. God demands his sabbaths are observed and commences in promising to award the obedient with seasonal rains and favorable harvests. He'll even 'rid the land of wild animals.' Enemies of the obedient will be hunted and slaughtered by the sword. Why heck, five will hunt a hundred and a hundred will hunt ten thousand! This itemizing of perks quickly gets boring for god, and the more preferred onslaught of creative punishments for disobedience dominates the remainder of the chapter, beginning with verse 15. The promises of obliteration escalate right up to a newly devised threat of divine warfare: *the eating of your children.* In fact, this threat gains some traction, earning entries in subsequent books such as Deuteronomy, Jeremiah, Ezekiel, and Zechariah.

> **Deuteronomy 28:45:** If you refuse to listen to the Lord your God and to obey the commands and decrees he has given you, all these curses will pursue and overtake you until you are destroyed. 46These horrors will serve as a sign and warning among you and your descendants forever. 47If you do not serve the Lord your God with joy and enthusiasm for the abundant benefits you have received, 53The siege and terrible distress of the enemy's attack will be so severe that you will eat the flesh of your own sons and daughters, whom the Lord your God has given you. [NLT]

> **Jeremiah 19:9:** I will see to it that your enemies lay siege to the city until all the food is gone. Then those trapped inside

31 *26:14But if ye will not hearken unto me, and will not do all these commandments [KJV]*

will eat their own sons and daughters and friends. They will be driven to utter despair. [NLT]

Ezekiel 5:8: Therefore, I myself, the Sovereign Lord, am now your enemy. I will punish you publicly while all the nations watch. 9Because of your detestable idols, I will punish you like I have never punished anyone before or ever will again. 10Parents will eat their own children, and children will eat their parents. [NLT]

Zechariah 11:9: Then I said, "I will not feed you. Let what is dying die, and what is perishing perish. Let those that are left eat each other's flesh." [NKJV]

This prediction actually came to pass at the siege of Samaria by the Syrians in II Kings 6:26-29, and at the siege of Jerusalem by the Chaldæans, which Jeremiah thus bewails in Lamentations 4:10-11.

Lamentations 4:10: Tenderhearted women have cooked their own children. They have eaten them to survive the siege. 11But now the anger of the Lord is satisfied. His fierce anger has been poured out. [NLT] *11The LORD hath accomplished his fury. [KJV]*

II Kings 6:26: One day as the king of Israel was walking along the wall of the city, a woman called to him, "Please help me, my lord the king!" 27He answered, "If the Lord doesn't help you, what can I do? I have neither food from the threshing floor nor wine from the press to give you." 28But then the king asked, "What is the matter?" She replied, "This woman said to me: 'Come on, let's eat your son today, then we will eat my son tomorrow.' 29So we cooked my son and ate him. Then the next day I said to her, 'Kill your son so we can eat him'" … [NLT]

#33

Ceremonial Purification After Childbirth

Leviticus 12:1-8
NLT

1The Lord said to Moses, 2"Give the following instructions to the people of Israel. If a woman becomes pregnant and gives birth to a son, she will be ceremonially unclean for seven days, just as she is unclean during her menstrual period. 3On the eighth day the boy's foreskin must be circumcised. 4After waiting thirty-three days, she will be purified from the bleeding of childbirth. During this time of purification, she must not touch anything that is set apart as holy. And she must not enter the sanctuary until her time of purification is over. 5If a woman gives birth to a daughter, she will be ceremonially unclean for two weeks, just as she is unclean during her menstrual period. After waiting sixty-six days, she will be purified from the bleeding of childbirth.

6When the time of purification is completed for either a son or a daughter, the woman must bring a one-year-old lamb for a burnt offering and a young pigeon or turtledove for a purification offering. She must bring her offerings to the priest at the entrance of the Tabernacle. 7The priest will then present them to the Lord to purify her.[32] Then she will be ceremonially

32 *12:7 Or to make atonement for her; also in 12:8.*

clean again after her bleeding at childbirth. These are the instructions for a woman after the birth of a son or a daughter.

8If a woman cannot afford to bring a lamb, she must bring two turtledoves or two young pigeons. One will be for the burnt offering and the other for the purification offering. The priest will sacrifice them to purify her, and she will be ceremonially clean."

KJV

6And when the days of her purifying are fulfilled, for a son, or for a daughter, she shall bring a lamb of the first year for a burnt offering, and a young pigeon, or a turtledove, for a sin offering, unto the door of the tabernacle of the congregation, unto the priest: 7who shall offer it before the LORD, and make an atonement for her; and she shall be cleansed from the issue of her blood. This is the law for her that hath born a male or a female. 8And if she be not able to bring a lamb, then she shall bring two turtles, or two young pigeons; the one for the burnt offering, and the other for a sin offering: and the priest shall make an atonement for her, and she shall be clean.

The laughably ludicrous book of Leviticus is renown for its fatiguing and shameless addressing of nearly every freaky facet and juicy crevice that god could think of to spin laws out of. When god and Moses were high on Mount Sinai in every sense of the phrase, they deemed it fit to adorn this bloody issue with its very own chapter.

Although it's the shortest chapter of the Torah, it overdelivers with a sucker punch to the gut of every woman. Favoritism, unworthiness, uncleanness, and animal sacrifices abound, yet leading this pack of atrocities is the inference of 'sin' in verse 6. The NLT stands alone among all of the major translations including the Tanakh, the Septuagint, and the Vulgate, in conveniently attenuating verse six (and eight) by replacing 'sin' with 'purification.' Let's see how these eminent theologians treat this concept of the woman's sin in childbirth:

Ellicott's Commentary:

> '...whilst the sin offering was to atone for sinful and violent expressions which she may have heedlessly uttered in the hours of labour and agony.'

Benson Commentary:

> '...Because of her ceremonial uncleanness, which required a ceremonial expiation.'

Matthew Henry's Concise Commentary:

> 'Increase and multiply, Gen. 1:28, is become to the fallen race a direful curse; communicates sin and misery.'

Jamieson-Fausset-Brown Commentary:

> '...but a burnt offering and sin offering, in order to impress the mind of the parent with recollections of the origin of sin, and that the child inherited a fallen and sinful nature.'

Matthew Poole's Commentary:

> 'For a sin-offering; either because of her ceremonial uncleanness,

which required a ceremonial expiation; or for those particular sins relating to the time and state of child-bearing, of which she is justly presumed to be guilty, which might be many ways.'

Gill's Exposition of the Entire Bible:

'The Jews commonly refer this to some sin or another, that the childbearing woman has been guilty of in relation to childbirth, or while in her labour; and it is not unlikely that she may sometimes be guilty of sin in some way or other, either through an immoderate desire after children, or through impatience and breaking out into rash expressions in the midst of her pains; so Aben Ezra suggests, perhaps some thought rose up in her mind during childbirth because of pain, or perhaps spoke with her mouth; meaning what was unbecoming, rash, and sinful.'

Keil and Delitzsch:

'For her restoration to the Lord and His sanctuary, she was to come and be cleansed with a sin-offering and a burnt-offering, on account of the uncleanness in which the sin of nature had manifested itself; because she had been obliged to absent herself in consequence for a whole week from the sanctuary and fellowship of the Lord.'

Rabbi Shlomo Ephraim Luntschitz:

'There, the penalty for eating of the Tree of Knowledge is, for man, the hardship of labor in the field and, for woman, the hardship of labor in childbirth. Since the birthing mother's suffering derives from Eve's sin, she thereafter is required to bring an offering in atonement of that sin. In the process of labor the childbearing woman cries out in pain against God, committing her own sin that implicates her in Eve's.'

Implicates her?

#32

Doggone Dogs

Matthew 15:21-28
NLT

21Then Jesus left Galilee and went north to the region of Tyre and Sidon. 22A Gentile woman who lived there came to him, pleading,

"Have mercy on me, O Lord, Son of David! For my daughter is possessed by a demon that torments her severely."

23But Jesus gave her no reply, not even a word. Then his disciples urged him to send her away.

"Tell her to go away," they said. "She is bothering us with all her begging."

24Then Jesus said to the woman,

"I was sent only to help God's lost sheep—the people of Israel."
25But she came and worshiped him, pleading again,

"Lord, help me!"

26Jesus responded,

"It isn't right to take food from the children and throw it to the dogs."

27She replied, "That's true, Lord, but even dogs are allowed to eat the scraps that fall beneath their masters' table."

28 "Dear woman," Jesus said to her, "your faith is great. Your
request is granted." And her daughter was instantly healed.

Well, be of good cheer my dear fellow dogs, our friendly Saint Paul at least tries to dilute this a tad with his 'neither Jew nor Gentile' bit in Galatians 3. Regardless of this exciting news, we still must confront this peculiar monstrosity of a story that we find in both Matthew and Mark. In every which way one may attempt to slice, dice, cut, and water down the ingredients of these mere 7 verses, there is no escaping its literal emphasis of exclusivity.

In a verse by verse breakdown through the modern lens of the JST version, we can further investigate its contents:

> 22: A non-Jewish woman in whom no discrimination or prejudices were found, begged Jesus for the healing of her demon possessed daughter.
>
> 23: Jesus ignored her and his chosen followers told him to send her away as she was bothering them with her request. "Jesus Christ she's annoying!" they cried.
>
> 24: Jesus then decided to reply to her and said,
>
> "No. I'm only here for *my* chosen people—*my* children."
>
> 25: In her inferiority, the woman persisted in continuing to beg Jesus for help.
>
> 26: Jesus responded, "No. My healing powers are not for you, for your children, or for anyone that you love. In fact, anything I share with my children, is not right for me to share with you. It's like taking candy from a baby and tossing it to maggots—to put it mildly. Ya get me?"
>
> 27: The non-Jewish, inferior, and battered woman replied, "You're so right, and though I'm just a maggot, I would happily eat the scraps of your children."
>
> 28: Jesus replied, "Haha, good answer lady. Ok, changed my mind. Forget what I said. You seem to know your place. It's actually right for me to do this now. She's healed."

Now of course this couldn't have gone another way such as:

> 23: Jesus turned and said, "Woman, I am here for all mankind. That whole separatist, isolationist, and elitist game of favoritism and nepotism that my partners and I within the trinity put together in choosing a 'special people'—is out of style now. We changed our mind. So…ya…..we love everyone equally now! So…great news! She's healed now!"

Well dogs…oh well. Can't get everything. Let's lick our wounds and move on.

#31

Ass Redemption Rules

Exodus 13:11-16; 22:30
NLT

11"This is what you must do when the Lord fulfills the promise he swore to you and to your ancestors. When he gives you the land where the Canaanites now live, 12you must present all firstborn sons and firstborn male animals to the Lord, for they belong to him. 13A firstborn donkey may be bought back from the Lord by presenting a lamb or young goat in its place. But if you do not buy it back, you must break its neck. However, you must buy back every firstborn son. 14And in the future, your children will ask you, 'What does all this mean?' Then you will tell them, 'With the power of his mighty hand, the Lord brought us out of Egypt, the place of our slavery. 15Pharaoh stubbornly refused to let us go, so the Lord killed all the firstborn males throughout the land of Egypt, both people and animals. That is why I now sacrifice all the firstborn males to the Lord—except that the firstborn sons are always bought back.' 16This ceremony will be like a mark branded on your hand or your forehead. It is a reminder that the power of the Lord's mighty hand brought us out of Egypt."

22:30"You must also give me the firstborn of your cattle, sheep, and goats. But leave the newborn animal with its mother for seven days; then give it to me on the eighth day."

KJV 13:13-16; 22:30

13And every firstling of an ass thou shalt redeem with a lamb; and if thou wilt not redeem it, then thou shalt break his neck: and all the firstborn of man among thy children shalt thou
redeem. 14And it shall be when thy son asketh thee in time to come, saying, What is this? that thou shalt say unto him, By strength of hand the LORD brought us out from Egypt, from
the house of bondage: 15and it came to pass, when Pharaoh would hardly let us go, that the LORD slew all the firstborn in the land of Egypt, both the firstborn of man, and the firstborn of beast: therefore I sacrifice to the LORD all that openeth the matrix, being males; but all the firstborn of my children I
redeem. 16And it shall be for a token upon thine hand, and for frontlets between thine eyes: for by strength of hand the LORD brought us forth out of Egypt.

22:30Likewise shalt thou do with thine oxen, and with thy sheep: seven days it shall be with his dam; on the eighth day thou shalt give it me.

Dear brethren, before we begin today's devotional with the words of two encouraging commentaries on this passage, we must understand a couple things about the donkey, otherwise nothing beautiful can come of this.

1. God's creation, the donkey; was unclean. It did not have a cloven (split) hoof, and it did not chew the cud (the act of regurgitating partly digested food in order to chew on it again before it gets sent back through the digestive tract.)
2. Because the first-born of all beasts were appropriated to god by his command; and because many of them were unclean and unfit to be sacrificed to him, there was no other way of offering them to god, but by redemption. In the case of the donkey, if it were not redeemed, its neck was to be broken.

Let's see how this cleverly applies to us today with a commentary from Shawn Bumpers of Calvary Chapel, Birmingham:

There were many different types of unclean animals but God is very specific here in these verses … talking about a donkey. In scripture, the donkey – an unclean animal – is a picture of man … perhaps you can think of a few reasons … what's the old saying, "Stubborn as a mule?" I think God is telling us something here … According to God, donkeys were unclean animals and because it was unclean, the firstborn of a donkey could not be sacrificed to God, so it was redeemed by a lamb. If the donkey could not be redeemed through the sacrifice of a lamb, then it had to be killed. God chose to sacrifice The Lamb. Jesus went to the cross because He loves you. He didn't go to the cross because you were good enough or you had worked hard enough … you were a stubborn donkey. But God loves you and so He chose to "provide Himself a lamb" (Genesis 22).

Let's continue with a commentary from Reverend George van Popta:

The Israelite had a choice. If he wanted to keep the donkey (after

> *all, donkeys were important as beasts of burden) – he could redeem it with a lamb. He then would have to bring a lamb to the tabernacle for sacrifice. The lamb would have to die for the donkey. If he did not want to sacrifice a lamb, then he had no choice but to break the donkey's neck. He had to kill it. God had adopted Israel as His own – to be, as it were, His firstborn son. As a sign of that adoption, God said every firstborn son in Israel is Mine. As a memorial of that evening when God saved Israel and destroyed Egypt, the Israelites were to devote their eldest sons to God, and to sacrifice the firstborn of their clean livestock. It was a sign, a symbol, a commemoration of how the Lord had brought them out of Egypt. Every firstborn creature – man or domestic animal – must be given to the Lord. But since the donkey was unclean, it could not be presented in sacrifice. What then? Should it be allowed to go free from the universal law? No, it could not. God allows no exceptions. The donkey is rightfully his, and yet it cannot be offered to him. That unclean animal, that donkey (let the reader not be too greatly offended) is us. Like it or not, we are the donkey. We are rightly the property of the Lord – the Lord who made us. But the problem is that we, because of our sins, are unacceptable to God. Our sins make us unclean. There is only one thing to do with the unclean – break their necks. Destroy them. Get them away from the presence of God. Or ... redeem them. Redeem them with a lamb, the clean, pure, spotless Lamb of God, Christ Jesus. The Lamb of God must stand in our stead. If not, we must die eternally in the land of the broken necks.*

'God is telling us something here.' Shawn is right and urges us to apply some introspection: Are you an unclean, unacceptable ass? According to Rev. Popta, you certainly are. In connecting the dots, beginning with commemorating the murder of all the firstborn of Egypt, we can clearly see how this applies to our lives. Are you the dog from the prior passage, or the ass? Blessings.

#30

Forbidden Incense

Leviticus 10:1-3; 6-7
NLT

1Aaron's sons Nadab and Abihu put coals of fire in their
incense burners and sprinkled incense over them. In this way,
they disobeyed the Lord by burning before him the wrong
kind of fire, different than he had commanded. 2So fire blazed
forth from the Lord's presence and burned them up, and
they died there before the Lord. 3Then Moses said to Aaron,
"This is what the Lord meant when he said, 'I will display my
holiness through those who come near me. I will display my
glory before all the people.'" And Aaron was silent.

6Then Moses said to Aaron and his sons Eleazar and Ithamar,
"Do not show grief by leaving your hair uncombed or by
tearing your clothes. If you do, you will die, and the Lord's
anger will strike the whole community of Israel. However, the
rest of the Israelites, your relatives, may mourn because of the
Lord's fiery destruction of Nadab and Abihu. 7But you must
not leave the entrance of the Tabernacle or you will die, for
you have been anointed with the Lord's anointing oil." So they
did as Moses commanded.

KJV

1And Nadab and Abihu, the sons of Aaron, took either of them his censer, and put fire therein, and put incense thereon, and offered strange fire before the LORD, which he commanded them not. 2And there went out fire from the LORD, and devoured them, and they died before the LORD. 3Then Moses said unto Aaron, This is it that the LORD spake, saying, I will be sanctified in them that come nigh me, and before all the people I will be glorified. And Aaron held his peace.

6And Moses said unto Aaron, and unto Eleazar and unto Ithamar, his sons, Uncover not your heads, neither rend your clothes; lest ye die, and lest wrath come upon all the people: but let your brethren, the whole house of Israel, bewail the burning which the LORD hath kindled. 7And ye shall not go out from the door of the tabernacle of the congregation, lest ye die: for the anointing oil of the LORD is upon you. And they did according to the word of Moses.

We had another mishap at camp. Boys will be boys, and sure enough, they just had to go play games in the administrative tent. Now these weren't just any games, and these weren't just any boys. These two were the sons of Aaron; the nephews of Moses, and they were playing with fire—literally. Not only that, this was the wrong kind of fire. Well god will be god and will not be outclassed, so he responded by striking them dead with his own set of fire beams. These two boys were well deserving of divine execution by means of incineration as they were well aware of the camp rules laid out in Exodus 30:

The Lord's words to Moses regarding the Altar of Incense:

30:7"Every morning when Aaron maintains the lamps, he must burn fragrant incense on the altar. 8And each evening when he lights the lamps, he must again burn incense in the Lord's presence. This must be done from generation to generation. 9Do not offer any unholy incense on this altar, or any burnt offerings, grain offerings, or liquid offerings."

Exodus 30:34Then the Lord said to Moses, "Gather fragrant spices—resin droplets, mollusk shell, and galbanum—and mix these fragrant spices with pure frankincense, weighed out in equal amounts. 35Using the usual techniques of the incense maker, blend the spices together and sprinkle them with salt to produce a pure and holy incense. 36Grind some of the mixture into a very fine powder and put it in front of the Ark of the Covenant, where I will meet with you in the Tabernacle. You must treat this incense as most holy. 37Never use this formula to make this incense for yourselves. It is reserved for the Lord, and you must treat it as holy. 38Anyone who makes incense like this for personal use will be cut off from the community."

(Though much conjecture abounds as to just what this 'wrong kind of fire' was that Nadab and Abihu conjured up, we can surmise it was likely a product of the wrong *['unauthorized'; 'forbidden']* incense formula.)

Soon after the pyrodrama, Moses turns to Aaron and says "Seeee! Told ya, brother. God means business." Aaron is a good, subservient older brother, and though his sons have just been burned to death, he doesn't say anything. Though Moses, being the good brother and uncle that he is, consoles Aaron and his other two nephews by telling them not to grieve for their loss. He follows with a stern warning: 'If you do, god will kill you and his anger will strike everyone.' Thankfully, the extra empathy of Moses kicks in, and he then says, 'but ya know, it's cool if your other relatives and fellow campers wanna mourn a bit.' Moses then adds one more warning: 'And don't you walk out that door just yet, or you're dead.'

We conclude with the realization that in this story, among many, god, being the all-loving god, was working really hard to get his chosen people to love him one way or the other. In fact, this story holds such significance, that twice in the book of Numbers, we're reminded of the vile disobedience of Nadab and Abihu:

Numbers 3:4 But Nadab and Abihu died in the Lord's presence in the wilderness of Sinai when they burned before the Lord the wrong kind of fire, different than he had commanded.

Numbers 26:61 But Nadab and Abihu died when they burned before the Lord the wrong kind of fire, different than he had commanded.

#29

Gate of the Gods

Leviticus 8
NLT, *pp*

4The whole community of Israel assembled at the Tabernacle.
5Moses announced: "This is what the Lord has commanded
us to do." 6Then he presented Aaron and his sons and washed
them. 7He put the official tunic, holy garments, and turban
with the badge of holiness on Aaron. 10Then Moses anointed
the Tabernacle with anointing oil, making it holy. 11He sprinkled the oil on the altar seven times, making it holy. 12Then
he poured anointing oil on Aaron's head, making him holy.
13Next Moses put the tunics, holy garments and special head
coverings on Aaron's sons. 14Then Moses presented the bull
for the sin offering. Aaron and his sons laid their hands on the
bull's head, 15and Moses slaughtered it. Moses took some of
the blood, and with his finger he put it on the four horns of
the altar and he poured out the rest of the blood at the base
of the altar, making it holy by purifying it. 16Then Moses
took the fat of the internal organs, the liver, and the kidneys
and burned it on the altar. 18Then Moses presented the ram
for the burnt offering. Aaron and his sons laid their hands
on the ram's head, 19and Moses slaughtered it. Then Moses
took the ram's blood and splattered it on all sides of the altar.
20He cut the ram into pieces, and he burned the head, some
of its pieces, and the fat on the altar. 21Moses then burned

the entire ram on the altar as an offering. It was a pleasing aroma, a special gift for the Lord, as the Lord had commanded him. 22Then Moses presented the ram of ordination. Aaron and his sons laid their hands on the ram's head, 23and Moses slaughtered it. Then Moses took some of its blood and put it on the lobe of Aaron's right ear, his right thumb, and his right big toe. 24Next Moses presented Aaron's sons and put some of the blood on the lobes of their right ears, their right thumbs, and their right big toes. He then splattered the rest of the blood on all sides of the altar. 25Next Moses took the fat of the internal organs, the liver, and the kidneys. 26On top of the fat he placed a cake of unleavened bread, a cake made with olive oil, and a wafer spread with olive oil. 28Moses then burnt these offerings on the altar. It was a pleasing aroma, a special gift for the Lord. 29Then Moses lifted up the breast as an offering to the Lord. 30Next Moses took anointing oil and some blood from the altar, and he sprinkled them on Aaron and his sons making them and their garments holy. 31Then Moses said to Aaron and his sons, "Eat the remaining meat and bread. 34All we have done today was commanded by the Lord. 35Stay at the entrance of the Tabernacle for seven days, and do everything the Lord requires. If you fail to do this, you will die, for this is what the Lord has commanded."

The veracity of 'god's word' becomes highly suspect when passages such as this undergo some quick name changes. In playing letter jumble with Moses, Aaron, and Israel, and exchanging 'the Lord' to 'the god,' or 'the gods,' we suddenly have the people of Sariel attending the grand exhibition of animal slaughterings, sacrifices, and blood ritual ceremonies performed by their high priests, Semos and Ranao, in that they may communally appease the gods. Taking it one blasphemous step further, we can cut this slightly edited passage and paste it in a leather bound book like that of the Bible; title it something like 'Gate of the Gods,' and presto, we have an occultic Mesopotamian book, detailing the mystical rituals of a wandering blood cult. We could then fill the pages with all sorts of instructions on how to please the gods and offer them special aromas, such as exercising unique methods with birds. Maybe Ranao could rip the head off of a bird, pour its blood around an altar, and then grasp it by the wings and tear it open. Then, he could burn it on the altar and offer a sweet savor to the gods. In fact, this altar would have a perpetually burning fire; never to be quenched, day or night. Ceaseless smoke from the burning heads, fat, flesh, liver, and kidneys from the animals offered as oblations from the community, would forever fill the nostrils of the gods and sustain their favor.

Finally, and most enjoyably, hand this book to anybody, preferably the biblically devout, and relish the barrage of responses. It's highly likely that most will not recognize the plagiarism, including the bird sequence from Leviticus 1:14-17, and the law of the perpetual fire on the altar of burnt offering from Leviticus 6:12-13. This simple little exercise can be applied to countless stories within the Bible and inevitably garner responses such as: "demonic," "wicked," "satanic," "amoral," and "idolatrous." More informal and certainly more likely responses, among many, may include: "that's insane," "sounds like an occult gathering," "that's what those crazy ancient barbarians used to do," and to top it off, "good thing we don't serve a god like that."

The proposition that an infinite entity of boundless and inexplicable composition; of towering omnipotence and omniscience; of immeasurable benevolence and of incalculable superiority to humans—met with a man atop a mountain and commanded such things, is the absolute and unequivocal zenith of the unfathomable.

#28

Kill Everyone

Exodus 32:25-35
NLT

25Moses saw that Aaron had let the people get completely out of control, much to the amusement of their enemies. 26So he stood at the entrance to the camp and shouted, "All of you who are on the Lord's side, come here and join me." And all the Levites gathered around him. 27Moses told them, "This is what the Lord, the God of Israel, says: Each of you, take your swords and go back and forth from one end of the camp to the other. Kill everyone—even your brothers, friends, and neighbors." 28The Levites obeyed Moses' command, and about 3,000 people died that day. 29Then Moses told the Levites, "Today you have ordained yourselves for the service of the Lord, for you obeyed him even though it meant killing your own sons and brothers. Today you have earned a blessing." 30The next day Moses said to the people, "You have committed a terrible sin, but I will go back up to the Lord on the mountain. Perhaps I will be able to obtain forgiveness for your sin." 31So Moses returned to the Lord and said, "Oh, what a terrible sin these people have committed. They have made gods of gold for themselves. 32But now, if you will only forgive their sin—but if not, erase my name from the record you have written!" 33But the Lord replied to Moses, "No, I will erase the name of everyone who has sinned against me.

34Now go, lead the people to the place I told you about. Look! My angel will lead the way before you. And when I come to call the people to account, I will certainly hold them responsible for their sins."
35Then the Lord sent a great plague upon the people because they had worshiped the calf Aaron had made.

32:26-29, :35
KJV, *pp*

26Moses stood in the gate of the camp, and said, Who is on the LORD's side? And all the sons of Levi gathered themselves
around Moses. 27And he said unto them, Thus saith the LORD God of Israel, Put every man his sword by his side, and go throughout the camp, and slay every man his brother, and every man his companion, and every man his neighbour.
28And the children of Levi obeyed the word of Moses: and
there fell that day about three thousand men. 29For Moses had said, Consecrate yourselves today to the LORD, even every man upon his son, and upon his brother; that he may bestow
upon you a blessing this day. 35And the LORD plagued the people, because they made the calf, which Aaron made.

Welcome back to the epic saga of Exodus 32. In #54, we covered the first half of the chapter; celebrating Moses as the master crisis negotiator, having successfully dissuaded god from destroying everyone. (The KJV provides a more decorative outcome with Moses ultimately getting *the LORD to repent of the evil which he thought to do unto his people.*[33]) The chapter then proceeds to derail into further derangement.

Let's review the order of events starting at the beginning of the chapter:

1. Moses and god were hanging out too long so the Israelites fell into boredom.
2. The Israelites make a golden calf to worship and they get their party on.
3. God flies into a rage and tells Moses he's going to destroy them.
4. Moses tells god to relax and so god changes his mind.
5. Moses and god adjourn their meeting and Moses descends the mountain.
6. Moses then sees the calf and finds the people dancing, and he flies into a rage.
7. Moses then tells the Levites that god is now saying to kill everyone.
8. The Levites proceed to slay 3,000 people.
9. Moses and god reconvene, and Moses asks god to forgive the people.
10. God says no and then sends a plague upon the people.

As undeniably preposterous as this brilliant order of events may be, I'm absolutely convinced it's exactly how the author intended. Fortunately for his sake, most aren't reading these 'fulfilled' portions of the Bible, and for those that do, they simply 'choose to believe,' rather than apply some critical thinking and rationale to its contents.

33 Exodus 32:14 [KJV]

Maybe, at the very minimum, we can find a morsel of a lesson here in noting the humility of Moses. All within one chapter, he pens his own fall from hero to zero. His remarkable swaying of the mind of god quickly turns futile as the plot twist features the double whammy raging of both he and god. Only one of great humility would proceed in sharing the utterly embarrassing psychopathic inanity of delivering a blessing to those who killed their own sons, brothers, and neighbors. Well, such is the illustrious prose of Moses, and he continues to pen his downward spiral of bassackwardsry as he runs back up the hill to ask god to forgive the people. (Yes, a tad late, and yes, after he's granted a blessing upon the Levite murderers.) Although, this time around, god shall not be negotiated with, and he strikes the people with a plague.

Nice goin Mosiebaby. Your original negotiation in successfully getting god to change his mind, bought everybody about a nanosecond until he decided to change it back.

#27

David the Mighty Foreskinner

I Samuel 18:22-27
NLT

22Then Saul told his men to say to David, "The king really
likes you, and so do we. Why don't you accept the king's offer
and become his son-in-law?" 23When Saul's men said these
things to David, he replied, "How can a poor man from a
humble family afford the bride price for the daughter of a
king?" 24When Saul's men reported this back to the king,
25he told them, "Tell David that all I want for the bride price
is 100 Philistine foreskins! Vengeance on my enemies is all I
really want." But what Saul had in mind was that David would
be killed in the fight. 26David was delighted to accept the
offer. Before the time limit expired, 27he and his men went
out and killed 200 Philistines. Then David fulfilled the king's
requirement by presenting all their foreskins to him. So Saul
gave his daughter Michal to David to be his wife.

KJV

22And Saul commanded his servants, saying, Commune
with David secretly, and say, Behold, the king hath delight
in thee, and all his servants love thee: now therefore be the
king's son in law. 23And Saul's servants spake those words in
the ears of David. And David said, seemeth it to you a light
thing to be a king's son in law, seeing that I am a poor man,

and lightly esteemed? 24And the servants of Saul told him, saying, On this manner spake David. 25And Saul said, Thus shall ye say to David, The king desireth not any dowry, but an hundred foreskins of the Philistines, to be avenged of the king's enemies. But Saul thought to make David fall by the hand of the Philistines. 26And when his servants told David these words, it pleased David well to be the king's son in law: and the days were not expired. 27Wherefore David arose and went, he and his men, and slew of the Philistines two hundred men; and David brought their foreskins, and they gave them in full tale to the king, that he might be the king's son in law. And Saul gave him Michal his daughter to wife.

Well golly gee David, you little snipping whippersnapper of a foreskinner, we are all so proud of you. Of course it goes without saying that your direct descendant, Jesus, was also certainly proud of you, and it's only a few verses earlier in this same chapter that we read of god being with you in all of your successes.[34] Well I'll be doggone David! Jumping genitals! You legendary shearman—the whole world is proud of you!

You know dear brethren, *including all the children that are present for today's sermon,* this is a story of romance & love, obedience, faith, and valor. You see, the penis and genitalia altogether are of grave concern throughout much of god's word. It is unabashedly enveloped in numerous stories and steeped in traditions and laws by the command of god. When Saul puts David to the test, we realize his love for Michal is deep; his obedience to his master—unwavering; his faith in god to assist in all tasks—unrivaled; and his valor—limitless, as he returns with a double portion of fresh penis skin. It's a defining moment in both the Bible and David's life as it's the first and only mention of a man of god committing a slew of murders in order to retrieve and deliver the prized peels. Well, in all fairness, we don't really know if the cutting or the killing came first, though we're at will to imagine the worst when considering the overall nature of the story.

Dear brethren, in closing, let us not only remember the heroism of David,[35] but let us also be mindful of those who made this story possible.

Let us honor David's men in their assistance in capturing the bounty.

Let us honor those in both camps of Saul and David whom assisted in counting the bounty.

Let us honor the fallen Philistines, whom gave all plus a bonus.

---

34 I Samuel 18:14

35 I Samuel 18:14

Let us honor Michal whom must have been overwhelmed with flattery and great joy by the bounty laid before her and her father.

Lastly, let us honor god, whom knows all, sees all, and directs the paths of the righteous. In the case of David, and again, as we're reminded of earlier in the chapter, god was with him through all, and we can be absolutely sure, dear brethren, he was with him (or at least did not halt him) in his capturing of this bounty.

Blessings.

And children, if you have any further questions about today's sermon or the story itself, I'm sure your parents will be happy to discuss it with you in further detail.

#26

A Fishy Tale

Matthew 17:24-27
NLT

24On their arrival in Capernaum, the collectors of the temple tax came to Peter and asked him, "Doesn't your teacher pay the Temple tax?"

25"Yes, he does," Peter replied. Then he went into the house.

But before he had a chance to speak, Jesus asked him, "What do you think, Peter? Do kings tax their own people or the people they have conquered?" 26"They tax the people they have conquered," Peter replied.

"Well, then," Jesus said, "the citizens are free! 27However, we don't want to offend them, so go down to the lake and throw in a line. Open the mouth of the first fish you catch, and you will find a large silver coin. Take it and pay the tax for both of us."

KJV

24And when they were come to Capernaum, they that received tribute money came to Peter, and said, Doth not your master pay tribute? 25He saith, Yes. And when he was come into the house, Jesus prevented him, saying, What thinkest thou, Simon? of whom do the kings of the earth take custom or tribute? of their own children, or of strangers? 26Peter saith unto him, Of strangers. Jesus saith unto him, Then are the children free. 27Notwithstanding, lest we should offend them, go thou to the sea, and cast an hook, and take up the fish that first cometh up; and when thou hast opened his mouth, thou shalt find a piece of money: that take, and give unto them for me and thee.

Things are getting a little fishy here. Either this tilapian tale is entirely allegorical, or it's ripped from the 5th century BC historian and geographer— Herodotus and his legend of the Ring of Polycrates, or, in accordance with mainstream Bible believers, it's entirely literal and a tallied miracle of Jesus.

Let's visit the allegorical route. You know, the common route one is forced to take when the subject at hand is too outrageously absurd to bear a literal interpretation. Here is a common allegorical view of this passage:

'Jesus was using an analogy between the kingdom of God and the kingdoms of this world. In the kingdom of God, God is the king and the disciples are his sons. They have the privilege of intimacy with God, and this intimacy supersedes the physical temple and its need for physical maintenance. Jesus himself is the way to God (John 14:6) and the true temple (John 2:21). His name, Immanuel, means "God with us" (Matt. 1:23). The disciples have intimacy with God through him. So, concluded Jesus, his disciples, as sons of the kingdom, are "free." But if, to avoid offense, the sons wish to pay anyway, God the king has plenty of resources that he gives to his sons. The miracle has a double symbolic significance. First, it confirms Jesus's claim that he has a unique status as Son of God. It implies also that his followers through their relationship to him inherit an analogous status. They too are sons, because of their relationship to him. Second, the miracle shows that God can supply directly whatever resources are appropriate.'

Heading back to ancient Greece and approximately 450 years before Jesus, we have this fable from the pen of Herodotus:

'Polycrates, ruler of the island of Samos, worried that he was tempting fate with his great prosperity. He tried to introduce some counterbalancing misfortune into his life by throwing a precious signet ring into the sea, but it was swallowed by a large fish and returned to the king by a fisherman.'

'This is a story that people in the first century CE would have been familiar with, especially in Capernaum - a fishing village. The author, Herodotus, is commonly referred to as "The Father of History" and was a primary source for historical accounts. Because of this, there is a strong possibility that Jesus and his disciples had heard or even read the story of Polycrates and the account of getting inexplicable treasure from a fish would have struck a chord — good joke material, in other words.'

Now, let's dive into the hugely populated ocean of those who believe this literally happened word for word. After all, Jesus leaves us no real reason to believe it's wholly symbolic or parabolic. The instantaneous channeling of a fish; the magical automating of its coordinates to find the specific hook of Peter's line; and above all, the mysterious origin and reveal of a valid coin upon it being caught, is easily believable if one is to believe in the many other miracles and improbabilities of the Bible. Why Jesus needed to create a whole fishing expedition out of this, versus magic-wanding a coin into the hand or mouth of Peter to quickpay the taxes—is beyond me. Maybe this commentary from Dr. Gerald M. Bilkes will help:

This miracle proved the Lord's omniscience, for He knew of this fish in the sea with a coin in his mouth. Moreover, it proved the Lord's omnipotence, for He made it come to Peter's hook. Christ speaks to Peter with such calm confidence. If the Lord could discern the money of the fish in the sea, could He not discern your need, child of God? And if the Lord could provide in this need, would He not know how to provide in your need?

Yes, he would certainly know.

Please wire magic funds to *****04801 for payment of my taxes.

#25

The 10 Plagues of Egypt

Exodus 7-11; NLT, *pp*

7:3 I will make Pharaoh's heart stubborn so I can multiply my miraculous signs and wonders in the land of Egypt. 4then Pharaoh will refuse to listen to you so I will bring down my fist on Egypt and I will rescue my people. 5By my power, the Egyptians will know I am the Lord.

River turned to Blood *(the Lord told Moses)* 7:16"Tell Pharaoh the Lord says: 'Let my people go, so they can worship me. 17I will strike the water of the Nile with my staff, and the river will turn to blood. 18The fish will die, and you will not be able to drink of it.'"20Aaron struck the Nile with his staff and the river turned to blood!

Frogs 8:1The Lord told Moses, "Tell Pharaoh the Lord says: 'Let my people go, so they can worship me. 2If you refuse, I will send a plague of frogs across your entire land.'" 6Aaron raised his hand over the waters of Egypt, and frogs came up and covered the whole land!

Gnats 8:16The Lord told Moses, "Tell Aaron, 'Raise your staff and strike the ground. The dust will turn to swarms of gnats throughout Egypt.'"17...Aaron struck the ground and gnats infested the land, covering the Egyptians and their animals. All the dust turned into gnats.

Flies 8:20The Lord told Moses, "Tell Pharaoh the Lord says: 'Let my people go, so they can worship me. 21If you refuse, I will send swarms of flies 22and will spare only my people. Then you will know I am the Lord.'" 24…and all of Egypt was thrown into chaos by the flies.

Livestock 9:1The Lord told Moses, "Tell Pharaoh the Lord says: 'Let my people go, so they can worship me. 2If you refuse, 3the Lord will strike all your livestock with a deadly plague.'" 6The next day all the livestock of the Egyptians died, but the Israelites didn't lose one animal.

Boils 9:8The Lord said to Moses and Aaron, "Have Moses toss ashes from a kiln into the air while Pharaoh watches." 10…As Pharaoh watched, Moses threw the ashes into the air, and boils broke out on people and animals. 12But the Lord hardened Pharaoh's heart.

Hail 9:13The Lord told Moses, "Tell Pharaoh the Lord says: 'Let my people go, so they can worship me. 14If you don't, I will send more plagues and you will know that there is none like me in all the earth. 16I have spared you to show you my power and to spread my fame throughout the earth.'" 22The Lord told Moses, "Lift your hand to the sky so hail may fall throughout all of Egypt." 23Moses lifted his staff and the Lord sent a hailstorm against Egypt. 25It left Egypt in ruins. Hail struck everywhere except where the people of Israel lived.

Locusts 10:1The Lord told Moses, "Return to Pharaoh. I have made him stubborn so I can display my miraculous signs. 2and so you can tell your children and grandchildren of how I made a mockery of the Egyptians so you will know I am the Lord." 12The Lord told Moses, "Raise your hand over the land to bring the locusts. Let them devour every plant." 13Moses raised his staff 14And locusts swarmed over the land of Egypt.

Darkness 10:20But the Lord hardened Pharaoh's heart again, so he refused to let the people go. 21Then the Lord said to Moses, "Lift your hand toward heaven, and the land of Egypt will be covered with a darkness so thick you can feel it." 22Moses lifted his hand and a darkness covered the entire land of Egypt for three days. 23During that time the people could not see each other, and no one moved. But there was light as usual where the people of Israel lived.

Angel of Death 10:27But the Lord hardened Pharaoh's heart once more, and he would not let them go. 11:4Moses told Pharaoh, "This is what the Lord says: At midnight tonight 5All the firstborn sons will die in every family in Egypt. Even the firstborn of all the livestock will die. 6A loud wail will rise throughout the land of Egypt, a wail like no one has heard before or will ever hear again. 7But among the Israelites it will be so peaceful that not even a dog will bark."

First and foremost, let us not forget the staffshifting sorcery from passage #38 that kicked off this series of unfortunate events. In the case that one can adopt such a flight of fancy as a literal and historic account, then the subsequent plagues of doom from our passage come as easily credible. Highlights such as Aaron's staff turning the Nile River to blood, the attack of the frogs, targeted hailstorms, and the lord's mass murder of every firstborn boy and animal are but extra sprinkles from the cabinet of god's literal arsenal of weapons.

If we apply the remove-and-rebrand exercise to this block of chapters and name it something like, '*The Titan of Antraepides*,' it immediately becomes a standard dust-collecting volume of mythology. In spite of that, this historically undocumented, yet foundational event of the Israelites and their 430 years of enslavement in Egypt, along with their exodus of approximately 2 million people, is constantly emphasized and brought to our attention throughout the Bible. Though quite shocking and almost embarrassing for those who uphold the entire saga as a historical event, are the obvious mammoth-size holes scattered throughout.

We begin with the cheat-move and arrogance of god in 7:3. God makes it clear that the main objective of this campaign is to largely display his miraculous signs and wonders. (The more impressive and sanitary disappearing acts, like those of Enoch and Elijah, are off the table.) It's only been 430 years of enslavement for god's chosen people, and now, it's finally time to implement the hardening-of-Pharaoh's-heart trick. Now, this trick will ensure that Pharaoh cannot possibly glitch and grant freedom to the Israelites at each request of Moses. Every time Pharaoh's assumably softer, more pragmatic heart is in need of some godly hardening, it then results in another imaginative catastrophe. Though the laws of nature stand in magical suspense in order to execute these supernatural acts of devastation, it is clearly overburdening, or not the will of this omnipotent god of love to accomplish the entire mission without blood, torture, and murder. It is then he, in the most exhausting and repetitious manner throughout many instances in the

Bible, who reminds the Israelites that 'I am the Lord your God who brought you out from the land of Egypt.'

Maybe the joke was actually on Moses all along. After all, god wants to be worshipped and repeatedly tells Moses to ask Pharaoh to free his people. Each time he does, god pulls the genius trick-move and hardens Pharaoh's heart so he'll say 'no,' giving god yet another excuse to drop some more heavenbombs. Brilliant!

The biggest tease of all has to be the ninth plague; the plague of darkness. In this creative plague, the Egyptians are smothered by a 'darkness so thick you can feel it,' however, the Israelites are unaffected and still have light. Seems like the perfect getaway plan, though absolutely not before all the firstborn sons and livestock are killed. Thankfully, that midnight mayhem is still celebrated today.

#24

They Will Eat Their Children & Friends

Jeremiah 19:1-12
NLT

1This is what the Lord said to me: "Go and buy a clay jar. Then ask some of the leaders of the people and of the priests to follow you. 2Go out through the Gate of Broken Pots to the garbage dump in the valley of Ben-Hinnom, and give them this message. 3Say to them, 'Listen to this message from the Lord, you kings of Judah and citizens of Jerusalem! This is what the Lord of Heaven's Armies, the God of Israel, says: I will bring a terrible disaster on this place, and the ears of those who hear about it will ring!

4For Israel has forsaken me and turned this valley into a place of wickedness. The people burn incense to foreign gods—idols never before acknowledged by this generation, by their ancestors, or by the kings of Judah. And they have filled this place with the blood of innocent children. 5They have built pagan shrines to Baal, and there they burn their sons as sacrifices to Baal. I have never commanded such a horrible deed; it never even crossed my mind to command such a thing! 6So beware, for the time is coming, says the Lord, when this garbage dump will no longer be called Topheth or the valley of Ben-Hinnom, but the Valley of Slaughter.

7For I will upset the careful plans of Judah and Jerusalem. I will allow the people to be slaughtered by invading armies, and I will leave their dead bodies as food for the vultures and wild animals. 8I will reduce Jerusalem to ruins, making it a monument to their stupidity. All who pass by will be astonished and will gasp at the destruction they see there. 9I will see to it that your enemies lay siege to the city until all the food is gone. Then those trapped inside will eat their own sons and daughters and friends. They will be driven to utter despair.'"

10"As these men watch you, Jeremiah, smash the jar you brought. 11Then say to them, 'This is what the Lord of Heaven's Armies says: As this jar lies shattered, so I will shatter the people of Judah and Jerusalem beyond all hope of repair. They will bury the bodies here in Topheth, the garbage dump, until there is no more room for them. 12This is what I will do to this place and its people, says the Lord. I will cause this city to become defiled like Topheth.'"

We could've done without the melodramatic jar skit, Jerry. Then again, I guess we can expect anything after reading your enlightening rotten underwear story found in passage #39. Well, there I am again in my unbelief. I have to remind myself that you are yet another who hears directly from the god of the universe and that I must take your word for it. With that said, let's see what god told you here:

- *The people burn incense to foreign gods that don't exist.* Ouch.
- *They fill their temple with the blood of innocent children.* Sick.
- *They have built shrines to Baal who doesn't exist.* Yikes.
- *They have sacrificed their sons to Baal.* Nasty.

Unforgivable is the act of shedding *any* blood of *any* child, but equally bruising to the self esteem of the infinitely supreme god is the offering of incense and the building of shrines to Baal. God commences with Jeremiah:

- *I have never commanded child sacrifice—it has never crossed my mind!*

Ah, the climactic juncture. I wonder what will happen next. God couldn't possibly attempt to one-up child sacrifice could he? God returns with the verdict:

- *'So I'll tell ya what...I will upset their plans.'*
  Hmm...Good so far.
- *'I will allow the people to be slaughtered.'*
  Hmm...Sounds about right. Ok.
- *'Their dead bodies will be food for vultures and wild animals.'*
  Uh-oh...Here we go.
- *'I will see to it that all the food in the city is gone.'*
  Oh I see where this is going...
- *'Now get ready for the kicker Jerrybaby...Those trapped in the city will eat their own sons and daughters and even their friends! I shall not be one-upped! They thought their child sacrifice was something!? How about some familial cannibalism?'*

Great.

- *'Oh and see that jar I had you bring along and shatter? Check this out...THAT is the people. Ohhh SNAP! I will shatter these people so bad that they will be irreparable. How about that for an analogy?'*
  Wow. Yeah you got me. So creative & poetic.
- *'Thanks bud. And check this out...There will be so many bodies piled up in the valley that there will be no more room! Speaking of poetry and that valley, I want to rename it something more fitting. This slaughtering will be so bad that I want it named "The Valley of Slaughter." Like it?'*
  Yeah...Perfect. Genius even.
- *'Thank you not to sneer.'*
  You're welcome.

#23

She Will Secretly Eat Her Newborn

Deuteronomy 28:45-49; 53-63
NLT

45"If you refuse to listen to the Lord your God and obey
his commandments, all these curses will overtake you until
you are destroyed. 46These horrors will serve as a sign and
warning among you and your descendants forever. 47If you
do not serve the Lord your God with joy and enthusiasm for
the abundant benefits you have received, 48you will serve your
enemies whom the Lord will send against you. You will be left
hungry, thirsty, naked, and lacking in everything. The Lord
will put an iron yoke on your neck, oppressing you harshly
until he has destroyed you. 49The Lord will bring a distant
nation against you from the end of the earth, and it will swoop
down on you like a vulture. 53The siege and terrible distress of
the enemy's attack will be so severe that you will eat the flesh
of your own sons and daughters, whom the Lord your God
has given you. 54The most tenderhearted man among you will
have no compassion for his own brother, his beloved wife, and
his surviving children. 55He will refuse to share with them the
flesh he is devouring—the flesh of one of his own children—
because he has nothing else to eat during the siege and terrible
distress that your enemy will inflict on all your towns. 56The
most tender and delicate woman among you—so delicate she
would not so much as touch the ground with her foot—will

be selfish toward the husband she loves and toward her own son or daughter. 57She will hide from them the afterbirth and the new baby she has borne, so that she herself can secretly eat them. She will have nothing else to eat during the siege and terrible distress that your enemy will inflict on all your towns. 58If you refuse to obey all the words of instruction that are written in this book, and if you do not fear the glorious and awesome name of the Lord your God, 59then the Lord will overwhelm you and your children with indescribable plagues. These plagues will be intense and without relief, making you miserable and unbearably sick. 60He will afflict you with all the diseases of Egypt that you feared so much, and you will have no relief. 61The Lord will afflict you with every sickness and plague there is, even those not mentioned in this Book of Instruction, until you are destroyed. 62Though you become as numerous as the stars in the sky, few of you will be left because you would not listen to the Lord your God. 63Just as the Lord has found great pleasure in causing you to prosper and multiply, the Lord will find pleasure in destroying you."

As the entire Torah is nearing the finish line in this fifth and final book of Deuteronomy, the author (assumedly Moses), laboriously sets the seal on every jot and tittle of its contents and places limitless importance on each and every god-given commandment within. As mentioned in passage #34, the litany of extreme threats of domination, destruction, and despair for disobeying any of these commandments begins in verse 15 of this chapter. Somehow, among the unhinged barrage of damnation, Moses manages to make it a whole 53 verses until he can no longer resist revealing one of god's favorite threats...

Let's hear it for the grand of gore...The signet of sinister...

The hellaciously horrifying...Drum roll please. . . . .

Coming to you from God and Moses....

THE EATING OF YOUR CHILDREN!

Be it known, that Moses, as the conduit and voice of god, leaves absolutely no ambiguity as to what laws these divine threats of violence apply to. On four occasions within this one chapter, Moses hammers home the all-encompassing applicability of these threats. Earliest in the chapter is verse 15: "But if you refuse to listen to the Lord your God and do not obey all the commands and decrees I am giving you today, all these curses will come and overwhelm you."

Dr. WA Liebenberg elaborates on the Torah and its laws:

> "The Torah is an extension of YHWH's grace because it links to salvation. Deut 6:24 states, 'YHWH commanded us to do all these statutes, to fear YHWH our God, for our good always, that he might preserve us alive, as it is at this day.' Therefore, living a Torah lifestyle is for our physical welfare. Observing YHWH's Commandments protects us from the problems of the world. Deut 28:45 states, 'Moreover all these curses shall come on you, and shall pursue you, and overtake you, till you are destroyed; because you listened not to the voice of YHWH your God, to keep his commandments and

> his statutes which he commanded thee.' Torah observance gave Israel the promise that they would be secure from the plagues and the curses that the ungodly nations experienced. Besides the physical benefit of Torah observance, Y'shua linked Torah observance with eternal reward. Matt 5:18-19 states, 'Verily I say unto you, Till heaven and earth pass, one jot or one tittle shall in no wise pass from the law, till all be fulfilled. Whoever therefore shall break one of these least commandments, and shall teach men so, he shall be called the least in the kingdom of heaven: but whoever shall do and teach them, the same shall be called great in the kingdom of heaven.' The Torah is an extension of grace because it gives us salvation and provides us with the hope that obedience brings eternal reward."

Here's an enjoyable 20 (just 3.26%) of the 613 laws god delivered to Moses, each of which are most certainly bound by the rules and threats of our chapter:

> **A Woman Must:** offer animal sacrifices after her period (Lev. 15:28-30) and after giving birth (Lev. 12:6-8). Drink a magic potion if suspected of adultery (Num. 5:30). **You Must Not:** Eat shellfish (Lev. 11:10). Intermarry with gentiles (Deut. 7:3). Have sex with a woman during her period (Lev. 18:19). Work on the sabbath (Exod. 35:2). Eat bread with yeast during passover (Exod. 12:15). Wear clothing mixed with linen and wool (Deut. 22:11). Use the formula for the incense offering for yourselves (Exod. 30:37). Offer up yeast or honey (Lev. 2:11). Be defiled by sitting where a menstruating woman has sat (Lev. 15:20). Put olive oil or frankincense in the meal-offering of a woman suspected of adultery (Num. 5:15). **You Must:** Put tassels on the corners of clothing (Num. 15:38). Break the neck of the firstborn donkey if it is not redeemed (Exod. 13:13). Destroy all Canaanites (Deut. 7:1-6; 16). Circumcise (Lev. 12:3). Cut off the hand of the woman who grabs the genitals of the man who is attacking her husband (Deut. 25:11-12) **Regulations:** Beating slaves (Exod. 21:20-21). One with a physical blemish shall not serve beyond the altar (Lev.

21:23). No uncircumcised male may eat the passover meal (Exod. 12:48). An animal with damaged testicles may not be offered as a sacrifice (Lev. 22:24).

#22

Deviled Ham

Gen 9:18-27
NLT

18The sons of Noah who came out of the boat with their
father were Shem, Ham, and Japheth. 19From these three
sons of Noah came all the people who now populate the earth.
20After the flood, Noah began to cultivate the ground, and
he planted a vineyard. 21One day he drank some wine he had
made, and he became drunk and lay naked inside his tent.
22Ham, the father of Canaan, saw that his father was naked
and went outside and told his brothers. 23Then Shem and
Japheth took a robe, held it over their shoulders, and backed
into the tent to cover their father. As they did this, they looked
the other way so they would not see him naked. 24When
Noah woke up from his stupor, he learned what Ham, his
youngest son, had done. 25Then he cursed Canaan, the son
of Ham: "May Canaan be cursed! May he be the lowest of
servants to his relatives." 26Then Noah said, "May the Lord,
the God of Shem, be blessed, and may Canaan be his servant!
27May God expand the territory of Japheth! May Japheth
share the prosperity of Shem, and may Canaan be his servant."

KJV

18And the sons of Noah, that went forth of the ark, were
Shem, and Ham, and Japheth: and Ham is the father of

Canaan. 19These are the three sons of Noah: and of them
was the whole earth overspread. 20And Noah began to be an
husbandman, and he planted a vineyard: 21and he drank of
the wine, and was drunken; and he was uncovered within his
tent. 22And Ham, the father of Canaan, saw the nakedness
of his father, and told his two brethren without. 23And Shem
and Japheth took a garment, and laid it upon both their
shoulders, and went backward, and covered the nakedness of
their father; and their faces were backward, and they saw not
their father's nakedness. 24And Noah awoke from his wine,
and knew what his younger son had done unto him. 25And
he said, Cursed be Canaan; A servant of servants shall he be
unto his brethren. 26And he said, Blessed be the LORD God
of Shem; And Canaan shall be his servant. 27God shall enlarge
Japheth, And he shall dwell in the tents of Shem; And Canaan
shall be his servant.

In this Epic of Gilgamesh, I mean Epic of Atrahasis, I mean the Legend of Ra and Hathor, I mean Noah's Flood *(the more modern of the four and just one in a huge variety of flood myths)*, we must first accept these infallible words of god: 'from these three sons of Noah came all the people who now populate the earth.' Now that we have established the exact origin of all civilization, we may proceed with the next historical account of our distant ancestors.

Noah was enjoying his retirement at the ripe age of 600. His days at sea had driven him to the grape, earning himself the honorary title of the Bible's first drunk. Each afternoon, Noah would close the doors of Ararat Winery and resign himself to his tent. Oftentimes, he would turn to his three boys and issue a perplexing warning, 'Stay outta me tent laddies, for fear ye may never grow to feel like real men.' They never quite understood what that meant, or why Noah would always follow it with a snicker & a squeal just before turning in.

One day, curiosity got the better of Noah's son, Ham. Upon entering the prohibited tent, he was immediately met with an overwhelmingly putrid stench, of which rivaled the spice of the zoo from the year-long ark expedition. Hearing a strange monotonous drivel and amidst the haze of odors, he stood in utter shock; enraptured at the sight of this domain of neglect and infestation. Through his squint and beyond the excrements, he could see what looked like legs peering out from behind a pile of animal slop and bottles. The drivel became increasingly agitated as Ham slowly tiptoed his way to the body. There, upon his final step, he nearly collapsed out of sheer astonishment. His wide eyes couldn't help but take in the rotund and fully nude wine-soaked body of his dad as he lay there on his back, violently muttering and foaming at the mouth. Ham furiously darted out of the tent—hysterically screaming for his brothers; "Guys! GUYS!! You gotta go in there! It's just weird…I, I….can't even explain it. Dad's passed out—his junk is all out…Just…I don't know—bring a blanket and cover him up! But try not to look at him too much!!" The brothers did just as they were told and scolded Ham thereafter: "You dummy

Ham," said Shem. Don't you realize Dad's gonna hate you for what you did!? You just doomed thousands of your own people!" "Huh? I did??" said Ham. "Uhh…Duh…Obviously." Japheth retorted. Just then, they heard a maniacal shrieking from the tent followed by curses, obscenities, and profanities; "You nosy little pervert I oughta slap you silly!" yelled Noah. Suddenly, Noah fell head-first out of the tent and pulled himself up by the robe of Shem. "You deviled Ham you!" screamed Noah. "Didn't I tell you NOT to come in my tent!!?? So I'll tell you what! I CURSE YOUR SON—MY GRANDSON!! IN FACT, HE AND HIS PEOPLE WILL FOREVER BE THE SLAVES OF THE LINE OF SHEM AND JAPHETH!!!"

True story folks. As Prof. Osvaldo D. Vena, ThD. states, 'it is meant to justify Israel's conquest of Canaan later in the book of Joshua.'

Got it. Sounds justified.

#21

Kosher Deli

Leviticus 11
NLT, *pp*

1The Lord said to Moses and Aaron, 2"Give these instructions
to the people of Israel. Of all land animals, these are those you
can eat. 3Any with split hooves and chews the cud. 4Do not
eat those that do not both chew the cud and have split hooves.
The camel chews the cud but does not have split hooves 7The
pig has split hooves but does not chew the cud; both are ceremonially unclean for you. 8Do not eat their meat or touch
their carcasses. 9Of sea animals, you may eat anything if it has
both fins and scales. 10Never eat those that do not have both
fins and scales. 11Never touch their dead bodies. 13Never eat
the eagle, the vulture, 14the kite, falcons, 15ravens, 16the owl,
the seagull, hawks, 17the cormorant, 19the stork, herons, the
hoopoe, and the bat. 21You may eat winged insects that walk
along the ground and can jump. 23All other winged insects
that walk along the ground are detestable to you. 27Animals
that walk on all fours and have paws are unclean. If you touch
their carcass, you will be defiled until evening. 28If you pick
up its carcass, you must wash your clothes, and you will
remain defiled until evening. 29Of small animals that scurry
along the ground, these are unclean for you: the rat and the
lizard. 31Those of this kind are unclean for you. If you touch
their carcass, you will be defiled until evening. 32If such dies

and falls on something, such as wood or fabric, that object will be unclean. You must dip it in water, and it will remain defiled until evening. After, it will be ceremonially clean. 33If such an animal falls into a pot, the pot will be defiled and must be smashed. 34If the water from the pot spills on any food, the food will be defiled. Anything in the pot will be defiled. 35Any object on which the carcass of such an animal falls will be defiled. If it is an oven or hearth, it must be destroyed; it is defiled. 36though if the carcass falls into a spring or a cistern, the water is still clean. 37If the carcass falls on seed grain to be planted, the seed will still be clean. 38But if the seed is wet when the carcass falls on it, the seed will be defiled. 39If an animal you are permitted to eat dies and you touch it, you will be defiled until evening. 40If you eat any of its meat or carry its carcass, you must wash your clothes, and you will remain defiled until evening. 41All small animals that scurry along the ground are detestable; you must never eat them 42such as those that slither on their bellies, as well as those with four legs and those with many feet. 43Do not defile yourselves by touching them. 44I am the Lord your God. You must consecrate yourselves and be holy, as I am holy. 45For I, the Lord, am the one who brought you up from the land of Egypt, that I might be your God. 47By these instructions you will know what is unclean and clean, and which animals may be eaten and which may not be eaten."

Following the divine incineration of Nadab and Abihu, chapter 11 heats things up with the oppressively tedious categorizing of permitted and prohibited foods. Moses, being the meticulous mental giant that he is, demonstrates his unparalleled ability to retain and transcribe every finicky nuance that god can throw at him. He finds himself so engrossed in the new and finely tuned dietary laws, that it never crosses his mind to ask why grandpa Noah and company had it so easy when they got off the boat:

Genesis 9:1-3:

> *1And God blessed Noah and his sons, and said unto them, Be fruitful, and multiply, and replenish the earth. 2And the fear of you and the dread of you shall be upon every beast of the earth, and upon every fowl of the air, upon all that moveth upon the earth, and upon all the fishes of the sea; into your hand are they delivered. 3Every moving thing that liveth shall be meat for you; even as the green herb have I given you all things.*

God, in his unspeakable vastness of all things infinite, is keenly interested in ratcheting up his kosher menu, even to the point of deeming much of his own creation as unclean. For instance, he places towering importance on his design of an animal's hoof and seems to highly favor the process of chewing the cud, which is a portion of food that is regurgitated from the rumen compartment of the stomach and chewed on for a second time before returning to the digestive system. He then breaks the hearts of seafood fans, banning delicacies such as crab, shrimp, mussels, oysters, scallops, and lobster because they lack the equipment of both fins and scales. The list continues, and great defilement, along with ceremonial uncleanness, follows anyone who may touch the carcass of any of these cataloged animals. This defilement even applies to inanimate objects such as an oven, which must be destroyed if grazed by the carcass. Additionally, the carcass cannot touch wet seeds or they'll be defiled. (If they're dry seeds, that's okay.) But hey, if one of these carcasses falls into a water reservoir, no problem—the water is still good. Snakes, lizards, etc.; don't even touch them or you'll be defiled. By adhering to these laws, the people will be set apart and holy as god is holy. God then reminds them that he brought them out of Egypt.

The two commentaries below speak on behalf of scholars in the field and the overall general consensus in regard to the grounds by which these regulations serve. It must be noted, god is not simply giving a lesson in sanitation here, but rather demanding the separation and holiness of his people by the mere obedience of his decrees. After all, the people had somehow managed to make it this far without this comprehensive breakdown of restrictions.

Pulpit Commentary:

> These concluding verses (44-47) give a religious sanction to the previous regulations, and make them matters of sacred, not merely sanitary or political obligation. They were to sanctify themselves, that is, to avoid uncleanness, because God is holy, and they were God's. They were thus taught that ceremonial cleanness of the body was a symbol of holiness of heart, and a means of attaining to the latter.

Matthew Henry's Commentary:

> These laws seem to have been intended as a test of the people's obedience, as Adam was forbidden to eat of the tree of knowledge; and to teach them self-denial, and the government of their appetites.

#20

The First Sacrifice

Genesis 4:1-5
KJV

1And Adam knew Eve his wife; and she conceived, and bare Cain, and said, I have gotten a man from the LORD. 2And she again bare his brother Abel. And Abel was a keeper of sheep, but Cain was a tiller of the ground. 3And in process of time it came to pass, that Cain brought of the fruit of the ground an offering unto the LORD. 4And Abel, he also brought of the firstlings of his flock and of the fat thereof. And the LORD had respect unto Abel and to his offering: 5but unto Cain and to his offering he had not respect. And Cain was very wroth, and his countenance fell.

NLT

1Now Adam had sexual relations with his wife, Eve, and she became pregnant. When she gave birth to Cain, she said, "With the Lord's help, I have produced a man!" 2Later she gave birth to his brother and named him Abel.

When they grew up, Abel became a shepherd, while Cain cultivated the ground. 3When it was time for the harvest, Cain presented some of his crops as a gift to the Lord. 4Abel also brought a gift—the best portions of the firstborn lambs from his flock. The Lord accepted Abel and his gift, 5but he did not accept Cain and his gift. This made Cain very angry, and he looked dejected.

Welcome to the top 20. In honor of this milestone, we will commemorate the Bible's first mention of propitiatory offerings which come in the form of crops and animal sacrifices. These gifts, offered to god as appeasements for reasons such as adoration and expiation, play an essential role throughout much of the narrative of the Bible. In a book that places an almost indescribable importance on blood and especially that of animals, it is of little shock that Cain's dismal offering of crops was met with disdain when compared to the fruit of Abel's slaughterhouse.

The Cambridge Bible for Schools and Colleges states:

> *'This is the first mention of sacrifice in Scripture. Its origin is not explained, nor is an altar mentioned. Man is assumed to be by nature endowed with religious instincts, and capable of holding converse with God. Worship was man's mode of approach to the Deity; and sacrifice was its outward expression. The purpose of the offering was (1) propitiatory, to win favour, or to avert displeasure; and (2) eucharistic, in expression of gratitude for blessings on home or industry. It was deemed wrong to approach God with empty hands, that is, without an offering or gift, Exodus 23:15[36]; Exodus 25:30[37].'*

This excerpt from the Cambridge commentary sheds a perfect light on all that is perfectly bad. Indeed it is correct in that the biblical origin of sacrifice is unexplained and appears out of nowhere. Though historically speaking, there is absolutely nothing unique or original about the practice of animal sacrifices and blood rituals—especially for those attempting to appease their gods. Various sects and cultures from around the world had long been accustomed to this form of *'worship as a mode of approaching a deity,'* with the purely barbaric concept of animal sacrifice being their means of *'outward expression.'* Regarding the assumption that *'man is by nature endowed with religious instincts, and capable of holding converse with God,'* and thus equates

36 …No one may appear before me without an offering.

37 Place the Bread of the Presence on the table to remain before me at all times.

to the murdering and mutilation of animals in order that their blood and meat be offered to gain favor and atonement with the divine, is catastrophically absurd. Cambridge continues by reminding us that *'it was deemed wrong to approach god with empty hands; without an offering or gift'*—and yes, we can very much expect this sort of ideology from a primitive and deeply depraved society. Sadly, our ancestors who delved in such wretched practices were too mentally stymied and blind to see the recurring flatline response from all things above within the grandiosity of the infinite universe, to all things below—right down to the smallest particles of dust.

Cambridge may have mistakenly revealed the ironclad case against the silly notion of animal sacrifices and blood rituals being that of divine origin as the Bible eventually purports. As we clearly find in the commentary, the root of these practices come strictly from the mind of man. Oddly enough, the Bible is one of the only examples where we find the deity directly commanding this form of propitiation. Somehow, a bizarre game of connect-the-sacrifice-dots leads us to the master plan of the human sacrifice of Jesus; thus allowing a convenient, yet highly unjustified disregard for the utter inanity of propitiation.

#19

Sexecutions

Leviticus 20
NLT, *pp*

1The Lord said to Moses, 2"Give the people of Israel these
instructions. If anyone offer their children as a sacrifice to
Molech, the people of the community must stone them to
death. 6I will also turn against those who put their trust in
mediums or in those who consult the spirits of the dead. I
will cut them off from the community. 7Set yourselves apart
to be holy, for I am the Lord your God. 8Keep all my decrees
by putting them into practice, for I am the Lord who makes
you holy. 9Anyone who dishonors[38] father or mother must be
put to death. Such a person is guilty of a capital offense. 10If a
man commits adultery with his neighbor's wife, both the man
and the woman must be put to death. 11If a man violates his
father by having sex with one of his father's wives, both must
be put to death. 12If a man has sex with his daughter-in-law,
both must be put to death. 13If a man practices homosexuality, having sex with another man as with a woman, both
men have committed a detestable act. They must both be put
to death, for they are guilty of a capital offense. 14If a man
marries both a woman and her mother, the man and both
women must be burned to death. 15If a man has sex with

38 *[Greek version reads anyone who speaks disrespectfully of. Compare Matt 15:4; Mark 7:10.]*

an animal, he must be put to death, and the animal must be killed. 16If a woman presents herself to an animal to have intercourse with it, she and the animal must be put to death. 17If a man marries his sister, the daughter of either his father or his mother, and they have sexual relations, it is a shameful disgrace. They must be publicly cut off from the community. Since the man has violated his sister, he will be punished for his sin. 18If a man has sexual relations with a woman during her menstrual period, both of them must be cut off from the community, for together they have exposed the source of her blood flow. 19Do not have sexual relations with your aunt. 20If a man has sex with his uncle's wife, he has violated his uncle. Both will be punished and they will die childless. 21If a man marries his brother's wife, it is an act of impurity. He has violated his brother, and the guilty couple will remain childless. 22You must keep all my decrees and regulations by putting them into practice; otherwise the land I am giving to you will vomit you out. 24…I am the Lord your God, who has set you apart from all other people. 25You must make a distinction between ceremonially clean and unclean animals, and between clean and unclean birds. 26You must be holy because I, the Lord, am holy. I have set you apart from all other people to be my very own. 27Men and women among you who act as mediums or who consult the spirits of the dead must be put to death by stoning."

It is of crucial importance that we remember the celebrated provenance of these very words and of course those of the entire Torah. It is unanimously accepted within Jewish tradition and among the limitless denominations of Bible believers that indeed, these words, also referred to as the Mosaic Law, are the very words of god. After all, with regard to the question of the authorship of the Bible, the remaining three options listed below present direct defeaters for the very pillars the Bible hangs on:

1. God and Moses camped out on Mount Sinai and made all this up together.
2. God delivered it to Moses as 'divine revelation.'
3. Moses made all of it up.

Concerning option #1, we can be fairly certain that an omniscient and omnipotent deity would lack nothing, would need nothing, and especially wouldn't need any help—especially that of early man. Option #2 introduces a sort of divine download theory; one in which god beamed this mountain of glorious information into the brain of Moses—and additionally granted him the most extraordinary retention known to man so that he may transcribe the verbatim words of god from memory. Option #3...ya...the most likely. Although, if we obediently place our trust in the words of Moses, or whomever may have written the Torah, we can then confidently embrace the hundreds of instances where the scriptures state '*the Lord said to Moses.*' We can also rely on the veracity of Exodus 24:4 as any deviation creates a domino effect of defeaters:

'Then Moses carefully wrote down all the Lord's instructions.' [NLT]

'And Moses wrote down all the words of the LORD.' [NASB]

Regardless of which flavor of authorship one prefers, they all come with outrageous implications. As stated, the most popular of all is the belief that these are the very words of god. Therefore, putting it as bluntly as the Bible does, god commands the execution of homosexuals;

dishonorable or disrespectful children; *(children who curse their parents, KJV, pp)* adulterers; necromancers; anyone who has engaged in bestiality—including the animal; and for participants in other sexual activities such as various forms of incest. It's quite convenient for Moses and Aaron that god *now* enacts these laws regarding incest as they both came directly from the incestual relationship of their Father Amram and their Great Aunt, (Amram's Aunt) Jochabed. Let's of course not mention the incestual relationship of the grand patriarch; the father of the 3 major religions, and to whom all was promised; Abraham—and his sister, Sarah. (Half-sister to be fair.) Sadly, the more sensible and practical source of authorship, is the mind of man.

Finally, we make it to the trendy and hilarious fallback of the modern hipster Christian; the safe haven of *'Well Jesus never said anything about THAT!'*—i.e., homosexuality, bestiality, incest, etc. Jesus spoke very clearly about 'sexual immorality' and the union of marriage between a man and a woman, though he didn't have to. His assertions of his divine nature and equality with god as the 'I AM' before Abraham, and that he and the Father are one, reveal all.

#18

Broken Stones and Other Disqualifications

Leviticus 22
NLT, *pp*

1The Lord said to Moses, 2"Tell Aaron and his sons to be very
careful with the sacred gifts that the Israelites set apart for
me, so they do not bring shame on my holy name. I am the
Lord. 3In all future generations, if any of your descendants is
ceremonially unclean when he approaches the sacred offerings
consecrated to the Lord, he must be cut off from my presence.
4If any of Aaron's kin have a skin disease or any kind of discharge that makes him ceremonially unclean, he may not eat
from the sacred offerings until he has been pronounced clean.
He also becomes unclean by touching a corpse, or by having an
emission of semen, 5or by touching a small animal or someone
who is ceremonially unclean. 6Any who is defiled will remain
unclean until evening. He may not eat of the offerings until he
has bathed in water. 8He may not eat an animal that has died
a natural death or has been torn apart by wild animals; this
would defile him. I am the Lord. 9The priests must follow my
instructions or they will be punished for their sin and will die
for violating my instructions. I am the Lord who makes them
holy. 10No one outside a priest's family may eat the sacred
offerings including guests and hired workers of a priest's home.
11If the priest buys a slave, the slave may eat from the sacred
offerings. If his slaves have children, they may share his food.

12If a priest's daughter marries outside the priestly family, she may no longer eat the sacred offerings. 14Any such person who eats the offerings without realizing it must pay the priest for the amount eaten, plus 20 percent. 18...If you present a burnt offering to the Lord, 19it will be accepted if it is a male animal with no defects. 20Animals with defects will not be accepted by the Lord. 21If you bring a peace offering to the Lord, you must offer a perfect animal. 22Do not offer an animal that is blind, crippled, injured, or that has a wart, a skin sore, or scabs. 24If an animal has damaged testicles or is castrated, you may not offer it to the Lord. 25...Such animals will not be accepted, for they are mutilated or defective. 27When a calf or lamb or goat is born, it must be left with its mother for seven days. After the eighth day, it will be acceptable as a gift to the Lord. 28Do not kill a mother animal and her offspring on the same day. 29When you bring a thanksgiving offering to the Lord, sacrifice it properly so you will be accepted. 30Eat the entire sacrificial animal on the day it is offered. 31You must keep all my commands, for I am the Lord. 32Do not bring shame on my holy name, for I will display my holiness among the people of Israel. I am the Lord who makes you holy. 33It was I who rescued you from the land of Egypt, that I might be your God. I am the Lord."

Let us commence with this holy book of the Torah, and let us not be led into temptation in heretically hypothesizing its origin as was presented in the prior passage of #19. Let us remove all doubt and any lack of faith; that we may positively uphold the many instances of 'The Lord said to Moses' as an absolute declaration of truth. Any substitution, such as the blasphemous 'Nobody said to Moses,' will certainly lead to a myriad of colossal cracks in the overall narrative. Thus we must again lay our trust, our hope and our faith in these very words of Moses; upholding them as the ultimately true, infallible, and divine words of god. Therefore, we are blessed to be endowed with such a book as that of Leviticus. A book that explicitly reveals the nature of god and comes brimful with his direct commands regarding sex, blood, semen, testicles, menstruation, deformities, disabilities, animal sacrifice, burning at the stake, yeast, odors, bestiality, mold, skin diseases, secretions, split hoofs, stoning, the killing of dishonorable children and homosexuals, shellfish, tattoos, haircuts, and the mixing of fabrics—to name a small handful. In matters of disobedience, we're granted the equally important threats[39] of tumultuous tyrannical terror from above, such as the eating of your own children—if they haven't already been abducted by wild animals.

'An emission of semen.' Rather, for the sake of censoring the Bible; *'A man whose seed goeth from him.'* [KJV] One can only wonder just what the necessary steps may have been in revealing such damnable news. The spentman likely felt the pressure of the ever watchful eyes of god, knowing that on each depletion, he must fess up for fear of being publicly exposed by the divine voyeur. God then continues to voice his disdain for the flaws in his creation (including additional rules regarding genitalia), by applying the same set of rules to animals as those laid out for Aaron and his descendants in Leviticus 21:

> 21:16Then the Lord said to Moses, 17"Give the following instructions to Aaron: In all future generations, none of your descendants who has any defect will qualify to offer food to

39 Leviticus 26

his God. 18No one who has a defect qualifies, whether he is blind, lame, disfigured, deformed, 19or has a broken foot or arm, 20or is hunchbacked or dwarfed, or has a defective eye, or skin sores or scabs, or damaged testicles. ('or hath his stones broken.' KJV) 21No descendant of Aaron who has a defect may approach the altar to present special gifts to the Lord. Since he has a defect, he may not offer food to his God."

Well, now there we are again…One just has to wonder what entailed a broken-stones reveal. Maybe it was something easy and rudimentary such as:

'Hi priest, I'd like to sacrifice animals to god.'

'Sure. Drop your drawers.'

Forging beyond the nutsy, we're met with plenty of other divine delicacies, including the enforcement of great protection over the sacrificial meat of the carcass. Thankfully, the priest's daughter is forbidden to eat it if she has married outside the family. Phew…we wouldn't want the dead animal to be consumed by just anybody.

#17

Burn Her to Death and Other Instructions

Leviticus 21
NLT, *pp*

1The Lord said to Moses, "Give the following instructions to
the priests, the descendants of Aaron. A priest must not make
himself ceremonially unclean by touching the dead body of
a relative. 2The only exceptions are his closest relatives—his
mother or father, son or daughter, brother, 3or his virgin sister.
5The priests must not shave their heads or trim their beards or
cut their bodies. 6They must be set apart as holy to their God,
for they are the ones who present the gifts to the Lord, gifts of
food for their God. 7Priests may not marry a woman defiled
by prostitution, or a woman who is divorced, for the priests are
set apart as holy to their God. 8You must treat them as holy
because they offer up food to your God. You must consider
them holy because I, the Lord, am holy, and I make you holy.
9If a priest's daughter defiles herself by becoming a prostitute,
she also defiles her father's holiness, and she must be burned
to death. 10The high priest has the highest rank of all. The
anointing oil has been poured on his head, and he is ordained
to wear the priestly garments. He must never leave his hair
uncombed, (uncovered) or tear his clothing. 11He must not
defile himself by going near a dead body. He may not make
himself ceremonially unclean even for his father or mother.
12He must not defile the sanctuary by leaving it to attend to

a dead person, for he has been made holy by the anointing oil of his God. 13The high priest may marry only a virgin. 14He may not marry a widow, a woman who is divorced, or a woman who has defiled herself by prostitution. She must be from his own clan 15so that he will not dishonor his descendants. 17... In all future generations, none of your descendants who has any defect will qualify to offer food to his God. 18...whether he is blind, lame, disfigured, deformed, 19or has a broken foot or arm, 20is hunchbacked or dwarfed; has a defective eye, skin sores, scabs, or damaged testicles. 21No descendant of Aaron with a defect may approach the altar to offer gifts and food to his God. 23He may not enter the room behind the inner curtain or approach the altar, this would defile my holy places. I am the Lord who makes them holy."

The limelight of Leviticus continues and rightfully so, as one can never get enough of the very words of god. Call me a little too nosy in my constant trespassing into prohibited territory of this '*Old* Testament' and especially that of the hallowed Torah, though I for one have a keen interest in what the purported unchanging god of the universe and creator of all has to say. If of grave concern to god, then of grave concern to me. These, being the likes of what has already been covered, such as testicular trivialities, semen stipulations, menstruation memos, blood briefings, slaughters and sacrifices, execution of evil-doers, and the list goes on—a LOT. Though, for this one, I thought we might head on out to the Theology Acrobatics and Maneuvering Aces Club and enjoy one of their trendy concoctions. It's one of many containing an extremely strong dilution of water, giving it a smooth, easy-to-swallow watered-down finish. It's called the 'Divinely Inspired Cocktail.' We can largely credit this drink to one of Paul's best epiphanies in II Timothy 3:16:

> '*All scripture is given by inspiration of God, and is profitable for doctrine, for reproof, for correction, for instruction in righteousness.*'

Paul was certainly well studied in the writings of what later became the 'Old Testament;' (the '*scripture*' he refers to here in II Timothy) and though obvious, the Don Stewart Commentary states:

> 'At the time Paul wrote to Timothy, the New Testament had not yet been completed. Therefore, it is argued, that it is probably better to limit his statement to the Old Testament writings.'

It could've been a reference to both testaments, (what may have existed of the New Testament) but it doesn't matter. It's not only a direct statement from Paul, but also a reinforcement for the many instances, implications, and inferences of the foundational principle we read of throughout the entire Bible and what the majority has always accepted prior to and after its canonization, in that it is indeed, the divine word of god. It just so happens that Paul's version, somehow allows for an easier swallow—as mystifying as that may be. There's something in the modern believer that promotes a natural gravitation to the 'Divinely Inspired' designation, versus 'Direct from god,' which should understandably be deemed as the interchangeable or equivalent option. *(i.e., It's not of man.)* Dare we assume otherwise? Dare we cross into forbidden territory in assuming it was completely inspired by man and man alone? (Thus purely defeating any 'divine' status of authorship.)

Well, let's drink up anyway. Cheers my friends! Swallow the divinely inspired cocktail with peace and joy in relying on the divinity of these commands, such as burning the priest's daughter to death for her sin; the law of the beard, and that of the testicles!

"Oh, hey—by the way—-you dumb, disfigured, reprobate roaches of the Earth down there, when I told Moses, 'In all future generations,' I meant it!" -God

#16

Rest or Die

Exodus 31:12-17
NLT

12The Lord then gave these instructions to Moses: 13"Tell the people of Israel: 'Be careful to keep my Sabbath day, for the Sabbath is a sign of the covenant between me and you from generation to generation. It is given so you may know that I am the Lord, who makes you holy. 14You must keep the Sabbath day, for it is a holy day for you. Anyone who desecrates it must be put to death; anyone who works on that day will be cut off from the community. 15You have six days each week for your ordinary work, but the seventh day must be a Sabbath day of complete rest, a holy day dedicated to the Lord. Anyone who works on the Sabbath must be put to death. 16The people of Israel must keep the Sabbath day by observing it from generation to generation. This is a covenant obligation for all time. 17It is a permanent sign of my covenant with the people of Israel. For in six days the Lord made heaven and earth, but on the seventh day he stopped working and was refreshed.'"

Exodus 35:1-3
NLT

1Then Moses called together the whole community of Israel and told them, "These are the instructions the Lord has commanded you to follow. 2You have six days each week for your ordinary work, but the seventh day must be a Sabbath day of complete rest, a holy day dedicated to the Lord. Anyone who works on that day must be put to death. 3You must not even light a fire in any of your homes on the Sabbath."

Numbers 15:32-36
NLT

32One day while the people of Israel were in the wilderness, they discovered a man gathering wood on the Sabbath day. 33The people who found him doing this took him before Moses, Aaron, and the rest of the community. 34They held him in custody because they did not know what to do with him. 35Then the Lord said to Moses, "The man must be put to death! The whole community must stone him outside the camp." 36So the whole community took the man outside the camp and stoned him to death, just as the Lord had commanded Moses.

If there's one commandment that modern christians (and much of modern man) have conveniently sponged away from the stone tablets, it's the fourth; that ye shall honor and keep the sabbath. Of course this absolving has nothing to do with the inevitable and very necessary growth of mankind in exiting the sand and shedding the robe. It's even worse. The accommodation of one enjoying their weekend is of divine revelation; one that bears witness with ones spirit, and most of all, is part of the 'fulfillment' of Jesus Christ. In other words, the original words of god (words of Jesus) are quite beneficially negated... again...and again....and again. *'Ya...that whole DIE if you violate this commandment thing...I changed my mind on that one too.'*

Be that as it may, we cannot forget the countless millions who uphold this observance with great reverence, and we can't exactly blame them. Those of the various religions and Christian denominations who adhere to the sabbatarian way of life in masochistically sabotaging their Saturdays (and Sundays for those who see it as such), find they are merely upholding the very words and commands of god; that this law be kept and observed in perpetuity from generation to generation as a permanent sign of the covenant with Israel.

Matthew Henry's Concise Commentary:

> Ex. 31:12-17 'Shabath' signifies rest, or ceasing from labour. The thing signified by the sabbath is that rest in glory which remains for the people of God; therefore the moral obligation of the sabbath must continue, till time is swallowed up in eternity.

Forgive my curiosity, but what happened to the death sentence for violators, such as that wretched scoundrel in Numbers 15 who dared to gather wood on such a day? It's interesting to note that the unforgivable trespass of this sorely mischievous man was first met with the crushing punishment of: Nothing. Up to this point, we have a god who takes great pride in the personal delivery of divine domination, destruction, demolition, and disaster, yet somehow, this trespasser managed to escape immediate execution from above; falling into the hands of dumbfounded men who (supposedly) had no idea how to sentence him. It's only then that we find god steps in and helps them out a little; commanding they carry out an old pastime in stoning him to death.

Keil and Delitzsch Biblical Commentary on the Old Testament:

> This was "a sign between Jehovah and Israel for all generations, to know (i.e., by which Israel might learn) that it was Jehovah who sanctified them," viz., by the sabbatical rest (see at Exodus 20:11). It was therefore a holy thing for Israel (Exodus 31:14), the desecration of which would be followed by the punishment of death, as a breach of the covenant.

This idea that a gargantuan force was (*and for many, still is*) reduced to an unquantifiably small finicky freakazoid on the weekends—is rather odd, wouldn't you say? This god, who bears down on the human race from beyond the clouds with a frantic all seeing eye; wildly jittering behind an immeasurably huge magnifying glass for 24-48 hours in hopes of the perfect roll call—is unspeakably absurd. It was then… And it is now.

Have a good & busy weekend!

#15

The Return of the Shapeshifting Wand of Doom

Exodus 17:3-6
NLT, *pp*

3Tormented by thirst, the people of Israel continued to argue
with Moses. "Why did you bring us out of Egypt? Are you
trying to kill us with thirst?" 4Then Moses cried out to the
Lord, "What should I do with these people? They are ready to
stone me!" 5The Lord said to Moses, "Walk out in front of the
people. Take your staff and call some of the elders of Israel to
join you. 6I will stand before you on the rock at Mount Sinai.
Strike the rock, and water will come out. Then the people will
be able to drink." So Moses struck the rock and water gushed
out as the elders looked on.

Numbers 20:2-12, 24
NLT, *pp*

2There was no water for the people to drink at that place, so
they rebelled against Moses and Aaron. 3The people said, "If
only we had died in the Lord's presence with our brothers!
4Why have you brought the Lord's people into this wilderness
to die? 5Why did you make us leave Egypt and bring us here?
This land has no grain, no figs, no grapes, no pomegranates,
and no water to drink!" 6Moses and Aaron turned away and
went to the entrance of the Tabernacle, where they fell face
down on the ground. Then the glorious presence of the Lord

appeared to them, 7and the Lord said to Moses, 8"You and Aaron must take the staff and assemble the entire community. As the people watch, speak to the rock over there, and it will pour out its water. You will provide enough water from the rock to satisfy the whole community and their livestock."
9So Moses took the staff from the place where it was kept before the Lord.
10Then he and Aaron summoned the people. "Listen!" he shouted. "Must we bring you water from this rock?"
11Then Moses struck the rock twice with the staff, and water gushed out. The entire community and their livestock drank.
12But the Lord said to Moses and Aaron, "Because you did not trust me enough to demonstrate my holiness to the people of Israel, you will not lead them into the land I am giving them!"
24"The time has come for Aaron to join his ancestors in death. He will not enter the land I am giving the people of Israel, because the two of you rebelled against my instructions concerning the water at Meribah."

Numbers 27:12-14
NLT, *pp*

12One day the Lord said to Moses, "Climb one of the mountains of Abarim and look out over the land I have given the people of Israel.
13After you have seen it, you will die like your brother, Aaron,
14for you both rebelled against my instructions in the wilderness of Zin. When the people of Israel rebelled, you failed to demonstrate my holiness to them at the waters of Meribah."

The almighty shapeshifting wand of Moses returns. The accolades of this divinely possessed magic stick are many, including transmutating into a snake, bringing forth the plagues of hail, locusts, darkness, and the parting and closing of the Red Sea. Of course this staff mustn't be confused with the supercharged staff of Aaron; another instrument of superior sorcery, known for its skills in transmutating into a predatory snake, turning the Nile river into blood, and sprouting flowers and almonds.

This latest episode of wonders and wizardry begins with the continuation of the Israelites arduous exodus from Egypt as they find themselves dying of thirst. Of all feats of nature the creator of the universe is most proud of, and one we are endlessly reminded of, is the rescuing of his people from Egyptian slavery. Though it's yet another instance where the god of the punishing plagues and miraculous mayhem has neglected to provide basic necessities for his people as they journey the desert. The people even wish to return to Egyptian slavery; bemoaning the unbearable living conditions. We do find a couple last minute lifelines in the prior two chapters; one where god tells Moses to toss a tree into the water, thus purifying it and making it drinkable; and the raining down of the legendary manna; the *angel food*,[40] freshly baked in the ovens of heaven; like that of wafers, made with coriander seed and honey. Although Moses and god have been on speaking terms for quite some time now, Moses manages to wait until the last second to talk with god about this latest affair of thirst. God tells Moses to equip himself with his staff to which he responds,

"Is there some peculiar power which emanates from this staff?"

"Oh yes…there is," replies god with a sprinkle of delight.

Directly thereafter, we find one of the Bible's greatest impossibilities and one that is flippantly accepted by many as objectively true. The waterdown community finds great difficulty in massaging this tale into one of poetry or fanciful figurative fluff, so the ensuing opening act of spellbinding sorcery, and the following rock show, whereupon

40 Psalm 78:25

water gushes forth for all, remains as true as steel. Moses and Aaron, the rock star brothers of the desert, get another crack at it after they manage to lead the tribe into yet another quandary of thirst.

This time around, they both have a meeting with god:

"Hey," said Moses, "We're all dying of thirst down here again and everyone wants to go back to slavery in Egypt because this desert sucks."

"Alright, alright," said god. "Check this out. For this act…Take the staff as a kind of decoy, BUT…Only speak to the rock this time."

Moses and Aaron proceed and successfully pull off the stunt by striking the rock. The community drinks of the water, though someone is quite mad…

"You two dummies—I TOLD you to SPEAK to the rock! Now…I have to kill both of you!" god exclaimed.

"But, ummm…We got the water! The thirst of your people is quenched now!" yelled Moses.

"I DON'T CARE!" retorted god.

And thus…the fate of these two patriarchs.

#14

The Cozbi Show

Numbers 25
NLT

1While the Israelites were camped at Acacia Grove, some of
the men defiled themselves by having sexual relations with
local Moabite women. 2These women invited them to attend
sacrifices to their gods, so the Israelites feasted with them and
worshiped the gods of Moab. 3In this way, Israel joined in
the worship of Baal of Peor, causing the Lord's anger to blaze
against his people. 4The Lord issued the following command
to Moses: "Seize all the ringleaders and execute them before
the Lord in broad daylight, so his fierce anger will turn away
from the people of Israel." 5So Moses ordered Israel's judges,
"Each of you must put to death the men under your authority
who have joined in worshiping Baal of Peor." 6Just then one
of the Israelite men brought a Midianite woman into his tent,
right before the eyes of Moses and all the people, as everyone was weeping at the entrance of the Tabernacle. 7When
Phinehas son of Eleazar and grandson of Aaron the priest saw
this, he jumped up and left the assembly. He took a spear
8and rushed after the man into his tent. Phinehas thrust the
spear all the way through the man's body and into the woman's
stomach. So the plague against the Israelites was stopped, 9but
not before 24,000 people had died. 10Then the Lord said to
Moses, 11"Phinehas son of Eleazar and grandson of Aaron the

priest has turned my anger away from the Israelites by being as zealous among them as I was. So I stopped destroying all Israel as I had intended to do in my zealous anger. 12Now tell him that I am making my special covenant of peace with him. 13In this covenant, I give him and his descendants a permanent right to the priesthood, for in his zeal for me, his God, he purified the people of Israel, making them right with me." 14The Israelite man killed with the Midianite woman was named Zimri son of Salu, the leader of a family from the tribe of Simeon. 15The woman's name was Cozbi; she was the daughter of Zur, the leader of a Midianite clan. 16Then the Lord said to Moses, 17"Attack the Midianites and destroy them, 18because they assaulted you with deceit and tricked you into worshiping Baal of Peor, and because of Cozbi, the daughter of a Midianite leader, who was killed at the time of the plague because of what happened at Peor."

Welcome to the original Cozbi Show. In this prequel to passage #40 (where we explored the bloody aftermath of this tale), we get our first introduction to 'Baal of Peor,' or 'Lord of the Opening.' What a scene it must've been that day; one filled to the brim with openings, sacrifices, crying, executions, blood, and a decimating plague. Moses takes the cake after adding the final icing by gifting the young virgins to his captains, just after demanding the execution of the remaining men, women, and boys.

Though we turn our attention to a true warrior of god. One who knew how to take matters into his own hands, thereby achieving great commendation from god himself. He even stayed the fury of the heavens in this mass murder of Moabites, minimizing the casualties to an even 24,000. His keen observation for those attempting to play opening games, coupled with his proficiency with the spear, proved his worth as a deadly assassin for god. Let's hear it for the one and only, the soldier of purification, the instrument of impalement, the agent of atonement, thee who is awarded the crown of god's special covenant of peace; it is he, Phinehas the Zealous. Quite zealous indeed…What exactly was happening in the tent? The story reads as though Phinehas is one that is very quick on his feet, leaving no time for bodily engagement by any means. Hmmm…Well, I guess we must assume the worst. We know Moses is frequently unabashed in his writings, so it's odd that he would leave out such details.

Maybe the JST version can assist the script and help us understand as to why this act of sheer heroism was so monumental; even earning Phinehas an honorable mention in the Psalms:

'There at the tent, they wailed, wept, and moaned at the sight. Upon the horizon, a great many heaps of human flesh were scattered about; many of orgies and many of slain. Thousands by the minute were both emitting, and conversely, dying, having been stricken by a divine plague. It was then when it happened…Time stood still and the heavens froze…Phinehas had seen Zimri and Cozbi dive into a tent. Overwhelmed with utter shock, yet intent on making his mark, he grabbed a hold of his freshly sharpened spear and sprinted toward the tent. Suddenly, Moses began to hear voices again. It was the heavens begging for immediate intervention: "Don't let him stick it inside of her! Don't let him do it Phinehas!! Hurry!!!" Moses then fell to the ground and began violently convulsing at the very thought of what may happen inside the tent. And just before Zimri could pierce Cozbi, Phinehas pierced them both with his spear; killing them before the congregation and the heavens; thus, saving our planet and the entire universe. Soon after the cataclysmic shockwave of turmoil and suspense had subsided, Moses began to hear voices again. This time, it was god himself…again…"Ya know Mose, I don't know if ya know, but you got yourself a good lil boy there in Phin. Sheesh—he stopped me from killing y'all! What a kick in the pants. Anyway, I'm gonna go ahead and chalk up this whole mess as one of assault by trickery and deceit, and give you, my favorite folks, the victim card. It's not like boys, especially *my* boys, to willingly go out and have sex with women. Oh and by the way, this Cozbi character is an additional culprit. What a weird lady. How dare she jump into that tent with my Israelite boy. Like—what was she going to do to him? Sexually assault him?? It's too bad, if it weren't for her, poor Zimri may have lived. Ya so anyway…Eradicate them. Completely and utterly destroy them."'

Friends, guard your openings. Amen.

#13

God's Guide on Hebrew Slaves: *A Special Loophole*

Exodus 21:1-8
NLT

1These are the regulations you must present to Israel.

{Concerning Hebrew slaves} 4If his master gave him a wife while he was a slave and they had sons or daughters, then only the man will be free in the seventh year, but his wife and children will still belong to his master. 5But the slave may declare, 'I love my master, my wife, and my children. I don't want to go free.' 6If he does this, his master must present him before God. Then his master must take him to the door or doorpost and publicly pierce his ear with an awl. After that, the slave will serve his master for life. 7When a man sells his daughter as a slave, she will not be freed at the end of six years as the men are. 8If she does not satisfy her owner, he must allow her to be bought back again. But he is not allowed to sell her to foreigners, since he is the one who broke the contract with her.

KJV

1Now these are the judgments which thou shalt set before them.

{Concerning Hebrew slaves} 4If his master have given him a wife, and she have born him sons or daughters; the wife and her children shall be her master's, and he shall go out by

himself. 5And if the servant shall plainly say, I love my master,
my wife, and my children; I will not go out free: 6then his
master shall bring him unto the judges; he shall also bring
him to the door, or unto the door post; and his master shall
bore his ear through with an aul; and he shall serve him for
ever. 7And if a man sell his daughter to be a maidservant, she
shall not go out as the menservants do. 8If she please not her
master, who hath betrothed her to himself, then shall he let her
be redeemed: to sell her unto a strange nation he shall have no
power, seeing he hath dealt deceitfully with her.

...Moses had returned to the dark cloud.

"Welcome back bud," said god. "I've whipped up some additional laws I wanna share with you."

Moses was merrier than Moloch at sundown.

"Great! What are they god!?"

"Well young man, it's time I award you with my laws & regulations on slavery."

Moses nearly came undone. He floated in ecstasy; anesthetized by the radiating words of god propelling forth as dazzling bolts of lightning. His robe shone brightly; his body surged with happiness; his beard bore a fresh singe and his tingler was a'tinglin'. "Do tell me more!" Moses excitedly exclaimed.

"Well, now let's just calm down a little Mosie-baby. You'll have more to add on this in the future, so let's just focus on a couple details for now."

"Sounds sensationally slavish my scintillating slavedriver. But can I ask a question ol' pal?"

"How there could be a single question when I'm about to institute my rules and advocation of slavery is beyond me, but...sure...Shoot."

"Well...I'm certain this would *never* happen, but what if one day...ya know... People label slavery as *'wrong,'* going so far as to say that you actually *didn't* advocate for it, or hand down and administer these laws and regulations...?"

"Ha ha ha ha Haaaaaa. Foolish boy. Why would anyone ever cast doubt on our meetings and what I have to say? Why heck, you're already making it abundantly clear with your exemplary word for word transcriptions; to the extent of incessantly reminding the readers of every time I say something (hence your many "And the Lord said unto Moses"). So...Why would they doubt that? What—you think they'll pick & choose which one's I really said to you and which one's you may have just made up? Come on. They won't be that dumb in the future will they? Nah. Plus, my words resonate. I am god; the creator of the universe and of all things. My words and actions bear witness to my divinity. For instance, let me enlighten you on a tricky sanction I've come up with to keep a slave for life (one that only a deity extraordinaire could invent): As you'll eventually write in Leviticus[41], *'You may treat slaves as your property, passing them on to your children as a permanent inheritance. You may treat them as slaves, but never treat your fellow Israelites this way.'* Concerning the fellow Israelite slave, he is to be freed in the seventh year. If it so happens that his master grant him a wife and they have children during his term of slavery, these perks shall remain as property of the master and they are not to be freed with the slave. Now here's the caveat, champ. If the slave just happens to love his wife and children and doesn't want to abandon them, he can take a vow of lifelong slavery and forever remain the property of his master. Then of course…he can keep his wife and kids. By the way, Israelite daughters belong to their slaveowners for life…just as long as these daughters continue to…'*please them.*'"

"Sound good?" god asked.

"No," Moses replied…

"It sounds absolutely amazingly fantastic!!"

41 25:44-46

#12

Zipporah the Zenith Zapper

Exodus 4:24-26
NLT

24On the way to Egypt, at a place where Moses and his family
had stopped for the night, the Lord confronted him and was
about to kill him. 25But Moses' wife, Zipporah, took a flint
knife and circumcised her son. She touched his feet with the
foreskin and said, "Now you are a bridegroom of blood to me."
26(When she said "a bridegroom of blood," she was referring
to the circumcision.) After that, the Lord left him alone.

KJV

24And it came to pass by the way in the inn, that the LORD
met him, and sought to kill him. 25Then Zipporah took a
sharp stone, and cut off the foreskin of her son, and cast it at
his feet, and said, Surely a bloody husband art thou to me.
26So he let him go: then she said, A bloody husband thou art,
because of the circumcision.

Señora Zipporah
Snipporah of Torah
The Tipsnipping Maiden
La Crotcha Transforma

Let's unzip this wanger of a story shall we? Moses, our dearest, most illustrious autobiographer, must have had some serious PTSD while penning this lovely account. Nonetheless, we must applaud his brevity in packing such a hugely cockeyed plonker of a story into a tiny winky dinky three scriptures.

The host of heaven frenetically swarmed 'round the clock; counting down the seconds before Gershom, the firstborn son of Moses and Zipporah, turned 9 days old. Millions upon millions of celestial eyes were affixed to the trousers of Gershom; terrified at the impending violation of the code of the covenant set forth in Genesis 17:9-14:

> 9Then God said to Abraham, "Your responsibility is to obey the terms of the covenant. You and all your descendants have this continual responsibility.
>
> 10This is the covenant that you and your descendants must keep: Each male among you must be circumcised.
>
> 11You must cut off the flesh of your foreskin as a sign of the covenant between me and you.
>
> 12From generation to generation, every male child must be circumcised on the eighth day after his birth. This applies not only to members of your family but also to the servants born in your household and the foreign-born servants whom you have purchased.
>
> 13All must be circumcised. Your bodies will bear the mark of my everlasting covenant.
>
> 14Any male who fails to be circumcised will be cut off from the covenant family for breaking the covenant." [NLT]

Moses was about to get himself murdered by god, when Zipporah the Zenith Zapper saved the day by slicing off the offending hood of skin. The Hacker of Hephzibah then proceeded to touch Gershom's feet (genitals) with the peel. *(Zipporah touched the foreskin of Gershom to Gershom's genitals from which it had been removed. "Feet" is one of the Hebrew euphemisms for genitals. She thus had physically circumcised Gershom, then immediately she symbolically used the removed foreskin to touch his genitals.)* God and the heavenly host let out a sigh of relief and...The End.

I must now yield to the greater wisdom of greater minds:

"The arrangement was made with Abraham when God claimed for Himself all of his being, and put the seal of His promise upon the most personal member of his anatomy. It was a seal that dedicated his descendants to God with their very own blood in a painful operation that would cause a mother to squirm...Such a mother was Zipporah... Only now did Zipporah understand how important it was, the seal of the promise, the familial brand. Only then would she be convinced to cut, to mutilate the manhood of her son in order to redeem his father, her husband. For this she would call him her 'bridegroom of blood.'" —*Pastor Bror Erickson, MDiv*

Barnes Commentary, pp:

> Literally, "a husband of blood." The marriage was now sealed by blood. By this rite, Zipporah had recovered Moses; purchasing his life by the blood of her child.

Pulpit Commentary, pp: ... *"a bridegroom of blood."*

> The words are clearly a reproach; and the gist of the reproach seems to be that Moses was a husband who cost her dear, causing the blood of her sons to be shed in order to keep up a national usage which she regarded as barbarous.

#11

Stone the Rebellious Child

Exodus 21:17
NLT

17Anyone who dishonors[42] father or mother must be put to death.

KJV

17And he that curseth his father, or his mother, shall surely be put to death.

Leviticus 20:9
NLT

9Anyone who dishonors father or mother must be put to death. Such a person is guilty of a capital offense.

KJV

9For every one that curseth his father or his mother shall be surely put to death: he hath cursed his father or his mother; his blood shall be upon him.

Deuteronomy 21:18-21
KJV

18If a man have a stubborn and rebellious son, which will not obey the voice of his father, or the voice of his mother, and

42 Greek version reads '*anyone who speaks disrespectfully of.*'

that, when they have chastened him, will not hearken unto them: 19then shall his father and his mother lay hold on him, and bring him out unto the elders of his city, and unto the gate of his place; 20and they shall say unto the elders of his city, This our son is stubborn and rebellious, he will not obey our voice; he is a glutton, and a drunkard. 21And all the men of his city shall stone him with stones, that he die: so shalt thou put evil away from among you; and all Israel shall hear, and fear.

Within Exodus and Leviticus, we find god and Moses hard at work in grinding out all offenses that are punishable by banishment or death. These include the likes of breaking the sabbath (such as the evil wood-gatherer found in passage #16), remaining uncircumcised, engaging in sex during menstruation, committing holy oil or incense ingredient infringement, eating bread with yeast during the exciting commemoration of the murder of all the Egyptian firstborn (Passover), and eating god's food (food offered to god), to name just a handful. I'm sure both of these old pals look back on their 40 day adventure of being really high on Mount Sinai and regret leaving plenty of twisted combinations on the table. Though in giving it their best shot, they made sure to thrice address the rebellious child, leaving no ambiguity as to the sentencing.

Gill's Exposition of the Entire Bible *[pp]* lends a lovely illumination:

'He that curseth his father, or his mother,.... Though he does not smite them with his hand, or with any instrument, yet smites them with his tongue, reviles and reproaches them, speaks evil of them, wishes dreadful imprecations upon them, curses them by the name explained, as the Targum of Jonathan calls it, by the name Jehovah, wishing the Lord would curse them, or that his curse might light upon them, see Proverbs 20:20, shall surely be put to death; or be killed with casting stones on him, as the Targum of Jonathan, or with stoning; so Jarchi, who observes, that wherever it is said, "his blood be upon him", it is meant of stoning, as it is of the man that curses his father or his mother, Leviticus 20:9 which was after this manner, the place of stoning was two cubits high, to which the malefactor with his hands bound was brought; from whence one of the witnesses against him cast him down headlong, and if he did not die, then they took up stones and cast on him, and if he died not, then all present of Israel came and stoned him.'

Oh how symphonic it is to hear the sputtering, splattering, spittery of sludgery come oozing out of the mouths of scriptural acrobatic aces when trying to "explain" (water-down and justify) these phenomenally funked up passages. At least ol' Gilligan sticks with the script in the above commentary, and as a bonus, provides some nice visuals regarding stoning.

Let me remind you that these scriptures, commanding the execution of your child, are the alleged words of god. Can one censor god? Can one actually reshape the words, wishes, and commands of the almighty perfect creator of the universe and yet retain the integrity of the book by which this creator is extolled as the absolute source? Those who wish to endorse the Bible as a whole, and especially its unmistakable bedrock—being that of the Torah, which purportedly contain the direct words of god, simply cannot without unraveling most, if not all of what the Bible presents. Though I would very much like to censor god and his psychopathic agent; Moses, by presenting a simple, yet far superior message, and one that comes from a far superior degree of morality, which unsurprisingly comes naturally for most of humankind: Nothing under the sun would move me to kill my child. Nothing.

In light of these scriptural passages of Exodus, Leviticus, and Deuteronomy, those who cling to either the 'god of the era' claim; or the more popular 'that was the old testament,' you are utterly disgraceful, shameful, and sick.

#10

Lotsa Love

Genesis 19:30-38
NLT

30Afterward Lot left Zoar because he was afraid of the people
there, and he went to live in a cave in the mountains with
his two daughters. 31One day the older daughter said to her
sister, "There are no men left anywhere in this entire area, so
we can't get married like everyone else. And our father will
soon be too old to have children. 32Come, let's get him drunk
with wine, and then we will have sex with him. That way we
will preserve our family line through our father." 33So that
night they got him drunk with wine, and the older daughter
went in and had intercourse with her father. He was unaware
of her lying down or getting up again. 34The next morning
the older daughter said to her younger sister, "I had sex with
our father last night. Let's get him drunk with wine again
tonight, and you go in and have sex with him. That way we
will preserve our family line through our father." 35So that
night they got him drunk with wine again, and the younger
daughter went in and had intercourse with him. As before, he
was unaware of her lying down or getting up again. 36As a
result, both of Lot's daughters became pregnant by their own
father. 37When the older daughter gave birth to a son, she
named him Moab. He became the ancestor of the nation now
known as the Moabites. 38When the younger daughter gave

birth to a son, she named him Ben-ammi. He became the ancestor of the nation now known as the Ammonites.

We now enter the dangerously fun territory of the top 10, and there's no better way to commemorate this landmark than by honoring two unsung heroes of our past:

The Fair... The Fertile... The Potent...

The Trade-Off Twins of Tricks & Traps...

The Lotsa Love - Daughters of Lot.

These girls were having quite the week. It all started when Dad had offered them up for a round of gang rape but he was denied. Next, they were swiftly displaced and fleeing to Zoar as god was about to rain down some serious fireballs on their homeland of Sodom. To rub salt into the wound, they then witness their Mommy crystallize into a saltsicle. Soon after their arrival in Zoar, they found the inhabitants to be scary people, and that did it. Dad and the girls agreed to set out for the mountains in hopes of finding some much needed peace and tranquility. After settling in a swanky cave, Lot excused himself for a nap and it was girl-time for the girls. They sat on the cliffside of their new abode and overlooked the breathtaking aftermath of divine decimation. Across the plains, they could see faint plumes of smoke from the charred ruins of their city.

"Hey there's Mom," said big sis.

"Haha...Salty in life, salty in death," replied little sis.

"Ha...you're right..."

Little sister lay her head on her big sister's shoulder and let out a big sigh...

"What a weird week this has been. I have so much tension."

"Ha...yeah...me too...and this week's about to get even weirder."

"What do you mean?"

"Oh gosh little sis...What do you think I mean? Let's have sex with dad."

"Hmm…Ok…I think you're right…Like—I ain't losing my virginity to any of those Zoarian clowns down there."

"Yep. Neither am I. We're keeping things in the family. Plus, Dad is a righteous man. I bet he'll be immortalized and written about by men of renown[43] in generations to come!"

"Ooo that's kinda hot actually…Alright…haha…I'm in. Let's do him! I mean, let's do it! But you go first big sis."

"Pshh…No problem…Me tonight, you tomorrow night. I wonder what our babies will be like!"

Little did they know, the fate of humankind would rest on their ~~shoulders~~ loins. From their offspring would come great nations, kingdoms, empires, and a lineage that would lead directly to none other than the savior of the world; Jesus Christ.[44] (Jesus would even reference Lot and his wife in Luke 17:32.)

Night had fallen, and the potent petunias were ready for a juicy game of tag.

"Deeeeamn that was an all-nighter. Dad may be old, but he ain't too old! Alright. Your turn."

The little sister moved in.

"Holy sons of Sodom, what have we been missing! Wow. Youch… but like…Wow."

As the story goes, the girls had planned a little drunk fest, having somehow spared their wine amidst losing everything else. Or…Lot wasn't drunk at all. I'll let you decide. Nevertheless, the righteous man, Lot, had shot twice (or a lot more) and hit twice, and the new and improved Ladies of Lot bore his children.

---

43 II Peter 2:7-8

44 Matt. 1:1-17, Luke 1:32; 3:23-38, Ruth 4:22, Acts 13:22-23, Romans 1:3, II Tim. 2:8, Heb. 7:14, Rev. 5:5; 22:16

#9

Bloody Sheets

Deuteronomy 22:13-17; 20-21
NLT

13Suppose a man marries a woman, but after sleeping with her, he turns against her 14and publicly accuses her of shameful conduct, saying, 'When I married this woman, I discovered she was not a virgin.' 15Then the woman's father and mother must bring the proof of her virginity to the elders as they hold court at the town gate. 16Her father must say to them, 'I gave my daughter to this man to be his wife, and now he has turned against her. 17He has accused her of shameful conduct, saying, "I discovered that your daughter was not a virgin." But here is the proof of my daughter's virginity.' Then they must spread her bed sheet before the elders.

20But suppose the man's accusations are true, and he can show that she was not a virgin. 21The woman must be taken to the door of her father's home, and there the men of the town must stone her to death, for she has committed a disgraceful crime in Israel by being promiscuous while living in her parents home. In this way, you will purge this evil from among you.

KJV

13If any man take a wife, and go in unto her, and hate her, 14and give occasions of speech against her, and bring up an

evil name upon her, and say, I took this woman, and when I
came to her, I found her not a maid: 15then shall the father of
the damsel, and her mother, take and bring forth the tokens
of the damsel's virginity unto the elders of the city in the gate:
16and the damsel's father shall say unto the elders, I gave my
daughter unto this man to wife, and he hateth her; 17and, lo,
he hath given occasions of speech against her, saying, I found
not thy daughter a maid; and yet these are the tokens of my
daughter's virginity. And they shall spread the cloth before the
elders of the city.

20But if this thing be true, and the tokens of virginity be not
found for the damsel: 21then they shall bring out the damsel
to the door of her father's house, and the men of her city shall
stone her with stones that she die: because she hath wrought
folly in Israel, to play the whore in her father's house: so shalt
thou put evil away from among you.

Deuteronomy *('second law' or 'repetition of the law')* is a second iteration of a great many laws, decrees, and regulations given to Moses by god. In fact, Moses reminds us of their divine origin a painstaking 53 times in Deuteronomy alone. This must be distinctly understood, or nothing wonderful can come of the passage I am going to relate. Thus we commence and further investigate what god himself had delivered to Moses, or simply that which Moses was too embarrassed to take credit for.

One of the best wedding gifts the father and mother of the bride could receive, was the bloody sheets from the wedding night; proving a successfully broken hymen, and evidence ('tokens') of their daughter's virginity. On the contrary, clean sheets after consummation, was a newlywed husband's worst nightmare. Blood or no blood, it would certainly make for a peculiar meeting with the elders and any other perverted parasites that cared to attend the examination at the town gate. The thought of old, crusty, original rabbis—giddy with excitement as their beady eyes, draped in unkempt eyebrows—strenuously inspect the sheets; oohing, aahing, smelling, and giggling, while hoping for any speck, spot, or splash of blood, is unthinkably grotesque—no matter the era, no matter the culture, and no matter the tradition. Fortunately for these appointed men of god; shrouded in vestments and other costumes, it's a win-win as their sadistic desires will be fulfilled one way or the other. It's quite possible that as much as they wished to find even a morsel of red juice from that cute little Jewish girl, they'll find even more gratification in her execution.

Following the final verdict of untainted sheets, immediate hysteria sweeps the council. Deafening moans and groans burst forth, robes are torn, and the pre-owned non-bleeder is marched to the door of her father's home.

"You didn't bleed on those sheets? Well how about this. For the shame you've brought upon your husband, your Father and Mother, *and* the entire community, your blood will now splatter the home of your family as tokens of your impurity."

And off they go, *purging the evil from among themselves* by way of communal stoning—right there on the porch of the bride's father and mother.

What an inexpressible travesty for the father; giving his daughter's hand in marriage just a day before he is faced with cleaning her mutilated corpse off of his porch. Though considering all we have come to know regarding this clan of the morally and mentally destitute, it wouldn't be a surprise if he had as little empathy and regard for human life as the the merciless savage that manufactured this utter trash.

Yet again, as stated earlier, it's imperative that we remember just where these decrees, laws, regulations, and framework for these rituals came from. They did not come from Moses. According to Moses, they came from god.

#8

Baldy & the Bears

II Kings 2:23-24
NLT

23Elisha left Jericho and went up to Bethel. As he was walking along the road, a group of boys from the town began mocking and making fun of him. "Go away, baldy!" they chanted. "Go away, baldy!" 24Elisha turned around and looked at them, and he cursed them in the name of the Lord. Then two bears came out of the woods and mauled forty-two of them.

KJV

23And he went up from thence unto Beth-el: and as he was going up by the way, there came forth little children out of the city, and mocked him, and said unto him, Go up, thou bald head; go up, thou bald head. 24And he turned back, and looked on them, and cursed them in the name of the LORD. And there came forth two she bears out of the wood, and tare forty and two children of them.

The chapter of the passage at hand leads us on a fantastical flight of fancy, filled with magic, mystery, and murder. It begins with Elijah being chased by Elisha, his apprentice. On three different occasions, Elijah tells Elisha to stay put, but he refuses. On the final instance, they reach an impasse at the Jordan River. Elijah is purely unfazed. As a seasoned magician who has quite the lengthy list of accolades, such as the power to summon lethal fire-beams, terminate rain on demand for years at a time, revive the dead, command automatic refills of flour and oil, and one whom even the ravens swear allegiance to, such an impasse is no match. He simply took his cloak, struck the water with it and the river divided. *"Come on slick,"* said Elijah. Once they had crossed to the other side, Elijah decided to level with Elisha:

"Listen up cueball, I'm about to ditch this planet. What is it that you really want from me??"

"Oh Elijah, I want to be just like you! In fact, I want double the powers that you have!"

"Pfft…Riiiight. Well…whatever - I'll be gone anyway. Tell ya what…Here's the game—if you see me when I'm taken from you, then fine - wish granted. If not, then…eh, answer's no."

Suddenly, a chariot of fire, drawn by horses of fire, crashed the meeting and took Elijah up to heaven. Elisha quickly seized Elijah's cloak, which had fallen when he was taken up. *"My precious,"* Elisha said in a throaty rasp. Intent on testing the word of Elijah, he returned to the bank of the river and said, *"Where are you and god now, Elijah!? A deal is a deal!"* He then struck the water and it divided as it had for Elijah. The eyes of Elisha glinted as he stared at the cloak. As he made his way to the other side, he incessantly whispered, *"It's mine."*

One day, some of the men of the city approached Elisha about the widespread water problem. Elisha then requested a bowl with salt in it. He went to the spring that supplied the water and threw the salt in it, purifying it entirely and indefinitely.

A short time had passed and Elisha had grown exceedingly insecure about his bald head. He wasn't getting any chicks and he couldn't shake his idol calling him names just before taking off in his chariot. As the keeper of the magical cloak, he vowed severe retribution for anyone who might hurl the next insult.

We now reach the story behind the two verses that stand in contention for '*The Most Psychotic Back to Back Verses of the Bible Award.*'

Elisha was on a scenic stroll to Bethel when suddenly, he came to a dead stop, horrified and paralyzed by shock, as forty-two unruly children began to chant the unimaginable: "Go away baldy! Go away bald head! Haha!" Elijah mustered up the courage to turn around as a man must face his assailants, and that's when it happened. Like a fiery spear between the eyes, so it came; the defiling defamator of doom, clear as day and thunderous as a crowd: "EGGHEAD!!!" Elisha clenched firmly to his cloak and cursed them in the name of the lord with a loud shriek. Immediately, two bears, sent from god himself, came rushing out of the woods and ripped the children to shreds. Moments later, it was all quiet on the Bethel front.

Elisha snickered, turned back around, and calmly said, *'See ya.'*

#7

Covenantal Addicktion

Genesis 17:9-14; 23-27
NLT

9Then God said to Abraham, "Your responsibility is to obey the terms of the covenant. You and all your descendants have this continual responsibility. 10This is the covenant that you and your descendants must keep: Each male among you must be circumcised. 11You must cut off the flesh of your foreskin as a sign of the covenant between me and you. 12From generation to generation, every male child must be circumcised on the eighth day after his birth. This applies not only to members of your family but also to the servants born in your household and the foreign-born servants whom you have purchased. 13All must be circumcised. Your bodies will bear the mark of my everlasting covenant. 14Any male who fails to be circumcised will be cut off from the covenant family for breaking the covenant."

23On that very day Abraham took his son, Ishmael, and every male in his household, including those born there and those he had bought. Then he circumcised them, cutting off their foreskins, just as God had told him. 24Abraham was ninety-nine years old when he was circumcised, 25and Ishmael, his son, was thirteen. 26Both Abraham and his son, Ishmael, were circumcised on that same day, 27along with all the other men and boys of the household, whether they were born there or bought as servants. All were circumcised with him.

On any given evening, stare into the void of eternity in absolute resignation, and behold the wondrous insignificance of our infinitesimally small existence. In the grand scheme of the universe, our Milky Way, being just one of an estimated 100-200 billion observable galaxies, is an inconsequential speck of dust, while Earth; one of an estimated 100 billion planets within the Milky Way alone, is a mere fraction of an incalculably smaller speck of dust. In all reality, it's nearly impossible to understand just how small we really are, especially when considering the incomprehensible rate of expansion of the universe that occurs every second. Once you've reached this state of awareness; one that is truly cognizant of the impossibility of grasping just how terrifyingly microscopic and dreadfully lonely our place in the universe really is, only then, can the sheer magnitude of the madness within our passage be understood.

Let's first appreciate the spirited buildup to the scriptures in focus. In Genesis 12, we read of the call of Abram. God promises to make a great nation out of Abram; to make his name great; to bless his descendants; and that through him, the whole earth would be blessed. In Genesis 15, god then promises Abram that his descendants will be innumerable, like that of the stars, and that they will inherit the land of Canaan as part of this covenant. Genesis 17 then begins with god appearing to Abram, and he continues in promising him countless descendants; great wealth; kingdoms, and kings within his lineage. Abram then earns a name change to Abraham as god promises to make him the father of many nations.

Abraham is delightfully delirious having just won the world. God then steps a foot closer and says, *"Um, yaa.... There's just one thing I need from ya to seal the deal. This...uh, may come as a bit of a surprise, especially at your ripe ol' age of 99, but it's imperative that you obey what I'm gonna need ya to do. Oh and not only you... Ya know all those descendants I promised you? Ya, well... I'm gonna need them to also follow suit."* Abraham was ready for anything...(so he thought.) *"Sit down bud,"* said god. It felt like an eternity for Abraham as he sat in great anticipation; anxiously awaiting this obligatory duty. God then turned to Abraham and politely said, *"I'm gonna need you to cut off that skin on the tip of your penis."*

God wanted to establish this covenantal addicktion to the appendage (known as 'Brit Milah'; '*covenant of circumcision*'), very early on to emphasize its extraordinary importance. Of the 31,102 total verses in the Bible (23,145 in the Old Testament), circumcision makes its mark at #408.

On any given day, stare into the void of eternity and imagine a god who is (or even *was*—makes no difference) concerned with the tip of the penis. Imagine this god, this uncreated source; this zenith of perfection, omnipotence, and omniscience and the creator of all things, stooping down from the vast corridors of his domain and demanding the foreskin of men as a covenantal seal. However repulsively absurd the concept, it still managed to go viral.

#6

Jephthah's Vow

Judges 11:29-39
NLT

29At that time the Spirit of the Lord came upon Jephthah, and he went throughout the land of Gilead and Manasseh, including Mizpah in Gilead, and from there he led an army against the Ammonites. 30And Jephthah made a vow to the Lord. He said, "If you give me victory over the Ammonites, 31I will give to the Lord whatever comes out of my house to meet me when I return in triumph. I will sacrifice it as a burnt offering." 32So Jephthah led his army against the Ammonites, and the Lord gave him victory. 33He crushed the Ammonites, devastating about twenty towns from Aroer to an area near Minnith and as far away as Abel-keramim. In this way Israel defeated the Ammonites.

34When Jephthah returned home to Mizpah, his daughter came out to meet him, playing on a tambourine and dancing for joy. She was his one and only child; he had no other sons or daughters. 35When he saw her, he tore his clothes in anguish. "Oh, my daughter!" he cried out. "You have completely destroyed me! You've brought disaster on me! For I have made a vow to the Lord, and I cannot take it back." 36And she said, "Father, if you have made a vow to the Lord, you must do to me what you have vowed, for the Lord has given you a great victory over your enemies, the Ammonites. 37But first let me do this one thing: Let me go up and roam in the hills and weep with my friends for two months, because I will die a virgin." 38"You may go," Jephthah said. And he sent her away for two months. She and her friends went into the hills and wept because she would never have children. 39When she returned home, her father kept the vow he had made, and she died a virgin.

Jephthah's fifteen minutes of fame lasts a whole 2 chapters in the Bible. He gets a couple extra minutes when he would later go on to be venerated and celebrated as a mighty man of god and a hero of the ages by Samuel and the author of Hebrews (presumably our friend Paul).

Our engagement spans a quick 10 verses, beginning with a statement that demands the attention of any inquisitive mind: 'The Spirit of the Lord came upon Jephthah.' Surely there is no greater foundation. All subsequent affairs must indeed be that of a divine nature.

Now operating under the agency of the spirit of the lord, Jephthah the genius makes a wildly creative vow to burn and kill whatever first comes out of his house as a sacrifice to the lord if he may grant him victory over the Ammonites.

Jephthah then leads a successful killing spree *('a very great slaughter'; KJV)* in his annihilation of 20 towns. (Par for the course when god is the golfer.) He cleans up and makes his way home. Upon entering the front yard, he's joyously greeted by his one and only child—his daughter.

"Hi daddy!"

"Ah dangit."

"What is it daddy!?"

"Well I made a vow to the lord and figured our cat or maybe our dog Phinehas would come out first—but you did, and so ya, I need to kill you. Well actually…I vowed to burn you to death."

"Oh ok daddy! Well hey. Listen. A deal's a deal and whatever you vowed you must complete! I think my friends and I will go on a camping trip though…Just to mourn that I'll die a virgin."

After a couple months passed, she returned home, feeling refreshed and ready.

"Hi daddy! I'm back! I'm ready for you to burn me now!"

"Welcome back sweetheart. Thanks, let's get a move on."

In a similar sick and twisted story, we're told that an angel of the lord intervened and thus saved that child from being murdered. Unfortunately for Jephthah and his daughter, they wouldn't be so lucky. They were now bound by the newly-created laws within Deuteronomy and Numbers, in that a vow to god must be fulfilled, and if unfulfilled, it is counted as a sin.

Keil and Delitzsch Biblical Commentary on the Old Testament:

> Jephthah no doubt intended to impose a very difficult vow upon himself. And that would not have been the case if he had merely been thinking of a sacrificial animal. Even without any vow, he would have offered, not one, but many sacrifices after obtaining a victory…(Note: "What kind of vow would it be if some great prince or general should say, 'O God, if Thou wilt give me this victory, the first calf that meets me shall be Thine!'" -Pfeiffer, dubia vex. p. 356.)…In his eagerness to smite the foe, and to thank God for it, Jephthah could not think of any particular object to name, which he could regard as great enough to dedicate to God; he therefore left it to accident, i.e., to the guidance of God, to determine the sacrifice. He shrank from measuring what was dearest to God, and left this to God himself" (P. Cassel in Herzog's Real-encycl.). Whomsoever God should bring to meet him, he would dedicate to Jehovah, and indeed, as is added afterwards by way of defining it more precisely, he would offer him to the Lord as a burnt-offering.

Jamieson-Fausset-Brown Bible Commentary:

> 31. whatsoever cometh forth of the doors of my house to meet me—This evidently points not to an animal, for that might have been a dog; which, being unclean, was unfit to be offered; but to a person, and it looks extremely as if he, from the first, contemplated a human sacrifice.

#5

Sex & Suspicion ~ *A Magic Potion Game by God*

Numbers 5:11-31
NLT, *pp*

11And the Lord said to Moses, 12"Give the following instructions to the people of Israel. Suppose a man's wife is unfaithful to her husband 13and has sex with another man, but neither her husband nor anyone else knows about it. She has defiled herself, even though there was no witness. 14If her husband becomes jealous and is suspicious of his wife and needs to know whether or not she has defiled herself, 15the husband must bring his wife to the priest. He must also bring an offering of barley flour to be presented as a jealousy offering to prove whether or not she is guilty. 16The priest will then present her to stand trial before the Lord. 17He must take holy water in a clay jar and pour into it dust he has taken from the Tabernacle floor. 18When the priest has presented the woman before the Lord, he must loose her hair and place in her hands the jealousy offering of proof to determine whether her husband's suspicions are justified. The priest will stand before her, holding the jar of bitter water that brings a curse to those who are guilty. 19The priest will then put the woman under oath and say to her, 'If no other man has had sex with you, and you have not defiled yourself while under your husband's authority, may you be immune from the effects of this bitter water that brings on the curse. 20But if you have been unfaithful to your husband, 21may the people know that the Lord's curse is upon you when he makes you infertile, causing your womb to shrivel and your abdomen to swell. 22Now may this water that brings the curse enter your body and cause your abdomen to swell and your womb to shrivel.' And the woman will be required to say, 'Yes, let it be so.' 23And the priest will write these curses on a piece of leather and wash them off into the bitter water. 24He will make the woman drink the bitter water that brings on the curse. When the water enters her body, it will cause bitter suffering if she is guilty. 25The priest will take the jealousy offering from the woman's hand, lift it up before the Lord, and carry it to the altar. 26He will take a handful of the flour and burn it on the altar, and he will require the woman to drink the water. 27If she has defiled herself by being unfaithful to her husband, the water that brings on the curse will cause bitter suffering. Her abdomen will swell and her womb will shrink and her name will become a curse among her people. 28But if she has not defiled herself and is pure, then she will be unharmed and will still be able to have children. 29This is the ritual law for dealing with suspicion. If a woman goes astray and defiles herself while under her husband's authority, 30or if a man becomes jealous and is suspicious that his wife has been unfaithful, the husband must present his wife before the Lord, and the priest will apply this entire ritual law to her. 31The husband will be innocent of any guilt in this matter, but his wife will be held accountable for her sin."

Once again, our vignette opens with the crowning jewel of calamity: *'And the Lord said to Moses.'* In other words, whatever may follow, be it that of rites and rituals of ceremonial sorcery and magic; entailing the accompaniment of a priest and his chalice of bewitchery—rest assured, comes directly from god. We can then put our minds at ease and bask in the serenity of what god, Jesus, and the holy spirit *(as one triune being)* have to say.

Peering down from his cockpit, the grand voyeur debuts the magic potion game; an advanced support system for the husband who may be suspicious of his wife's faithfulness. Included is a test developed by heaven's best wizards and warlocks; one administered by the priest, which eliminates the necessity of evidence, and one the husband is expected to impose based on mere paranoia. To make things interesting, god has even disengaged multiple force fields and god-modes; suspending insta-peril via omniscient status—allowing for a level playing field, at least until it's god's turn to activate the potion with poison.

Sex & Suspicion

A MAGIC POTION GAME by GOD

OBJECT: To reach a verdict on the husband's suspicions of infidelity.

PLAYERS: 1. Husband 2. Wife 3. Priest 4. God

SETUP:

1. The husband brings his wife and barley flour to the priest at the tabernacle.
2. The priest will put dust from the tabernacle floor into a clay jar filled with holy water.
3. The priest will supply a leather scroll.

GAMEPLAY:

1. The priest will present the woman before the lord to stand trial.
2. The priest will then loose the woman's hair and place the elixir of bitter water in her hands.
3. The priest will put the woman under oath and begin to utter incantations and curses of the elixir:

- May god cause your womb to shrivel and discharge and cause your belly to swell upon consumption if guilty.
- May god grant you immunity upon consumption if innocent.

4. She must agree to the terms by saying 'Amen, Amen.'
5. The priest will write the curses on the leather scroll and wash them off into the elixir.
6. The priest will then make the woman drink the elixir.
7. The priest will take the clay jar with the elixir from the woman and will lift it up to the lord.
8. He will then take the clay jar to the altar and will burn a handful of the barley flour on the altar.
9. The priest will again make the woman drink the elixir.

Somewhere in steps 6 through 9, the chalice of agony or exoneration is activated by god. Of course, the only way for the woman to fail this test is for the cursed elixir to cause a miscarriage, which in this case, would be known as an abortion.

After some success, Moses added a flyer to the tabernacle bulletin that read:

Are you getting suspicious of your wife? Are you thinking she may be growing someone else's baby? Act Now. Call 1-800-NUM-BERS. (Opt. #5) (For males only.)

#4

Evil Twin, Evil Mother ~ *A Hallmark Tale*

Genesis 27
NLT, *pp*

1One day when Isaac was old and turning blind, he called for Esau, his firstborn son, and said, 2"I am old now and I don't know when I may die. 3Go and hunt some venison for me. 4Prepare my favorite dish, and I will pronounce the blessing that belongs to you before I die." 5But Rebekah overheard what had been said. 6So she said to her son Jacob, "I overheard your father say to Esau 'prepare me a meal then I will bless you in the Lord's presence before I die.' 8Now, do as I tell you. 9Bring me two young goats and I'll prepare your father's favorite dish. 10Then take the food to your father so he can eat it and bless you before he dies." 11"But Esau is a hairy man, and my skin is smooth. 12What if my father touches me? He'll see that I'm trying to trick him, and then he'll curse me instead of blessing me," Jacob replied. 13But his mother replied, "Then let the curse fall on me! Just do what I tell you." 14So Jacob went out and got the young goats and Rebekah prepared the meal. 15Then she took Esau's clothes and 16covered his arms and his neck with the skin of the young goats. 18Then Jacob took the meal to his father. "My father?" he said. "Yes, my son," Isaac answered. "Who are you—Esau or Jacob?" 19Jacob replied, "It's Esau. I've done as you asked. Here is the venison. Now sit up and eat it so you can give me your blessing." 20Isaac asked, "How did you find it so quickly, my son?" "The Lord your God put it in my path!" Jacob replied. 21Then Isaac said to Jacob, "Come closer so I can touch you and know that you really are Esau." 22Jacob went closer, and Isaac touched him. "The voice is Jacob's, but the hands are Esau's," Isaac said. 23But he did not recognize Jacob, because his hands felt hairy just like Esau's. 24"Are you really my son Esau?" he asked. "I am," Jacob replied. 25Then Isaac said, "Now, bring me the venison." So Jacob took the food to his father, and Isaac ate it. 26Then Isaac said, "Come closer and kiss me, my son." 27So Jacob went over and kissed him. And when Isaac caught the smell of his clothes, he was convinced, and he blessed his son. He said, "Ah! The smell of my son is like the smell of the outdoors, which the Lord has blessed! 28From the dew of heaven and the richness of the earth, may God always give you abundant harvests and bountiful wine. 29May many nations become your servants, and bow to you. May you be the master over your brothers, and may your mother's sons bow down to you. All who curse you will be cursed, and all who bless you will be blessed." 30As soon as Isaac had finished blessing Jacob, Esau returned from his hunt. 31Esau prepared the meal and brought it to his father. Then he said, "Sit up, my father, and eat my venison so you can give me your blessing." 32But Isaac asked him, "Who are you?" Esau replied, "It's your firstborn son, Esau." 33Isaac began to tremble uncontrollably and said, "Then who just served me venison? I have already eaten it, and I blessed him just before you came. And that blessing must stand!" 34When Esau heard his father's words, he let out a loud cry. "Oh father, what about me? Bless me, too!" he begged. 35But Isaac said, "Your brother was here, and he tricked me. He has taken your blessing." 36Esau exclaimed, "No wonder his name is Jacob, for now he has cheated me twice. First he took my rights as the firstborn, and now has stolen my blessing. Haven't you one blessing for me?" 37Isaac said to Esau, "I have made Jacob your master and have declared that his brothers will be his servants—what

is left for me to give you?" 38Esau pleaded, "But do you have
only one blessing? Oh father, bless me, too!" Then Esau broke
down and wept. 39Finally, Isaac, said to him, "You will live
away from the richness of the earth, and away from the dew
of the heaven above. 40You will live by your sword, and you
will serve your brother."

For some, it may come as a bit of a surprise that such a low-grade Hallmark tale about an evil twin and venison would directly lead to the origin of the "Israelites." For others, it's just one more fragment of commonplace cheese within the Bible's casserole of chaos, and this fragment begins in Genesis 25.

Isaac was keeping the incestual family tradition alive when he married his grossly underaged cousin, Rebekah. She became pregnant with twins and the two struggled with each other in her womb. When she asked god why this was happening, he told her the two sons in her womb would be rivals, and the older would serve the younger. When delivery day came, Rebekah first popped out a furry redheaded critter and they named him Esau. She then popped out a devious prankster of a critter and they named him Jacob.

As the years passed, Esau won the heart of Isaac as he could cook some mean venison. Jacob, on the other hand, was favored by Rebekah (and god).

One day, Esau was on the brink of starvation and begged Jacob for some of his stew. Jacob said, "Sure, just trade me your birthright as the firstborn son." They shook on it and Esau ate up.

Some time later, when Isaac was old and blind, he called for Esau.

"Yes, Dad?" said Esau.

Isaac burst with excitement, "Well there's my lil gingerman! Listen bud, I'm an old man and I don't know when I may die. I'd like to order me up some nice venison and then seal the deal in giving you all you are owed as the firstborn before I expire. I don't care about your dumb little stew thing between you and your trickster brother. I'm old and not in the mood. I've dealt with enough in my life—heck, your gramps and god nearly murdered me; mom's been acting weird, and who knows, her and Jacob may plot against me in my blindness. I'd just like to go in peace."

"Ok Dad! Sounds good! I'll be back in a wee bit with the venison!"

Once Esau was on his way, Rebekah seized the moment and called for Jacob.

"Yes, Mother?" said Jacob.

"Well there's my lil deviant!" said Rebekah. "Listen bud. God assured me this day would come and now it's time to act. Your invalid father is about to give everything to that freckle-faced twerp. So I'm gonna dress you in an Esau costume and send you in with your father's favorite dish. That ol' fart is blind as a bat; tell him that you're Esau and get the blessing before he dies!"

"Ok Mother! Sounds good! I'll go trick Dad and steal the blessing!"

Meanwhile, Esau returned with the meal, though much to his dismay, it was too late. The evil mother and the evil twin had prevailed. Even Isaac, whose ailments had clearly infiltrated his brain, remarked with a sneer when pressed by Esau: "Too late carrot! In fact, you will not reap of the blessings bestowed upon your brother and you will live by the sword. Oh, and you will serve Jacob now."

Esau never had a chance. Our dear Paul and Malachi solidify this by quoting the words of god: 'Jacob have I loved, but Esau have I hated.' From the onset, god was dead set on this wicked cheat becoming the progenitor of the Israelites. The account of this pivotal moment in history is found in Genesis 32 when Jacob and an angel get into an all-night wrestling match. The angel dislocates Jacob's hip and proceeds to change Jacob's name to Israel, and thus, we have the eponymous patriarch of the Israelites. Cool story, Moses.

#3

Passover

Exodus 12
NLT, *pp*

1While the Israelites were still in the land of Egypt, the Lord spake unto Moses and Aaron and said, 3"Announce to the community of Israel that each family must choose a lamb for a sacrifice, one animal for each household. 6…Then the community of Israel must slaughter their lamb at twilight. 7They are to take some of the blood and smear it on the sides and top of the doorframes of their houses. 12On that night I will pass through the land of Egypt and strike down every firstborn son and firstborn male animal in the land of Egypt. I will execute judgment against all the gods of Egypt, for I am the Lord! 13But the blood on your doorposts will serve as a sign, marking the houses where you are staying. When I see the blood, I will pass over you. This plague of death will not touch you when I strike the land of Egypt. 14This is a day to remember. Each year, from generation to generation, you must celebrate it as a special festival to the Lord. This is a law for all time. 15For seven days the bread you eat must be made without yeast. Anyone who eats bread made with yeast during the seven days of the festival will be cut off from the community of Israel. 17Celebrate this Festival of Unleavened Bread as a permanent law, for it will remind you that I brought you out of the land of Egypt. 18The bread must be made without yeast from the evening of the fourteenth day of the first month until the evening of the twenty-first day of that month. 19During those seven days, there must be no trace of yeast in your homes. Anyone who eats anything made with yeast during this week will be cut off from the community of Israel. 20During those days you must not eat anything made with yeast." 21Then Moses said to them, "Go, pick out a lamb for each of your families, and slaughter the Passover animal. 22Drain the blood into a basin. Then take a bundle of hyssop branches and dip it into the blood. Brush the hyssop across the top and sides of the doorframes of your houses. And no one may go out through the door until morning. 23For the Lord will pass through the land to strike down the Egyptians. But when he sees the blood on the top and sides of the doorframe, the Lord will pass over your home. He will not permit his death angel *('the destroyer'; KJV)* to enter your house and strike you down. 24These instructions are a permanent law that you and your descendants must observe forever. 26When your children ask, 'What does this ceremony mean?' 27You will reply, 'It is the Passover sacrifice to the Lord, for he passed over the houses of the Israelites in Egypt. And though he struck the Egyptians, he spared our families.'" 28So the people of Israel did as the Lord had commanded. 29That night at midnight, the Lord struck down all the firstborn sons in the land of Egypt, from the firstborn son of Pharaoh, who sat on his throne, to the firstborn son of the prisoner in the dungeon. Even the firstborn of their livestock were killed. 30…Loud wailing was heard throughout the land of Egypt. There was not a single house where someone had not died. 31Pharaoh sent for Moses and Aaron during the night. "Get out!" he ordered. "Leave my people—and take the rest of the Israelites with you!" 36The Lord caused the Egyptians to look favorably on the Israelites, and they gave the Israelites whatever they asked for. So they stripped the Egyptians of their wealth!

42On this night the Lord kept his promise. So it must be commemorated every year by all the Israelites, from generation to generation. 43Then the Lord said to Moses and Aaron, "These are the instructions for the festival of Passover. No outsiders are allowed to eat the Passover meal. 48No uncircumcised male may ever eat the Passover meal. If there are foreigners among you who want to celebrate the Lord's Passover, let all their males be circumcised."

I, along with most of the world, stand in solidarity in memorializing the millions of Jews from the Holocaust and the countless millions of all who lost their lives at the hand of a genocidal warlord, less than only a century ago. The unspeakably horrific massacring of innocent men, women, and children will forever remain etched on the core of earth's crust as one of the greatest atrocities known to mankind.

Oddly enough, one of the most important Jewish holidays celebrates a Holocaust that far pre-dates that of World War II. Every year, both religious and cultural Jews from around the world unite for a week of lavish meals and rituals in shameless observance of *'Passover'*; *the midnight murder of every Egyptian firstborn son—compliments of* 'the destroyer', *or the* 'angel of death'; *better known as* 'god.' This short body of facts alone should be enough for anyone to stamp this 'holiday' as astronomically absurd, categorically obscene, and completely reprehensible—yet somehow, it remains a sacred observance. For the Jews, I suppose it's easier to celebrate when god 'passed-over' the house of their people and murdered someone else's child rather than their own, though comparably, I don't think they, nor the world would find it kosher if the Germans declared an annual week-long celebration honoring the slaughter of countless Jewish children in World War II. On that note, we of the world have failed the Egyptians. In the very face of such an audacious Jewish holiday, we have yet to institute the Annual Feast of Overkill; a time when we solemnly remember this holocaust of the Egyptian firstborn. For Egypt, it must be a strange time of year to find a nearby nation and its kin around the world, reverently celebrating the execution of your ancestors firstborn sons. Though exceedingly brazen, the Egyptians likely *(and accurately)* chalk it up as another wildly ridiculous myth.

Let's review some key points regarding this holiday like none other. After all, what other large-scale annual celebration honors the mass murder of children?

- God's 'Harden-Pharaoh's-Heart trick' leads us to this 10th and final plague of Egypt.
- God commands that each family slaughter an animal and smear their doorframes with its blood.
- God then kills every firstborn son in Egypt and *passes-over* the homes with the smeared blood.
- God's efficiency is unrivaled; *Verse 30: There was not a single house where someone had not died.*
- God declares the perpetual celebration of this event as a law for all time. *[Verses 14-17; 24-27]*
- God declares that if anyone wants to celebrate the Passover, they must be circumcised.

God's severely stymied omniscience is concerning. Apparently he wouldn't know what houses his chosen people were in, so he needed the blood of their slaughtered animals as a 'sign'; that he may '*pass over*' their home. God's severely stymied omnipotence is alarming, yet unsurprising as the insatiably bloodthirsty nature of god prefers the more unsanitary hands-on approach, versus a more pragmatic purging. Therefore, we can rest assured, the ensuing midnight raid in the murdering of not only the firstborn sons, but also the firstborn animals, was one of an extreme bloodbath.

But fret not! Rejoice! In verse 36, his omnipotence has been restored as he's 'caused the Egyptians to look favorably on the Israelites!' Cool! Great timing.

#2

A Test of Faith: *Burn Your Son*

Genesis 22:1-18
NLT, *pp*

1Some time later, God tested Abraham's faith. "Abraham!"
God called.

"Yes," he replied. "Here I am." 2"Take your son, your only
son—yes, Isaac, whom you love so much—and go to the land
of Moriah. Go and sacrifice him as a burnt offering on one of
the mountains, which I will show you." 3The next morning
Abraham got up early. He saddled his donkey and took two
of his servants with him, along with his son, Isaac. Then he
chopped wood for a fire for a burnt offering and set out for
the place God had told him about. 4On the third day of their
journey, Abraham looked up and saw the place in the distance.
5"Stay here with the donkey," Abraham told the servants. "The
boy and I will travel a little farther. We will worship there, and
then we will come right back." 6So Abraham placed the wood
for the burnt offering on Isaac's shoulders, while he himself
carried the fire and the knife. As the two of them walked on
together,

7Isaac turned to Abraham and said, "Father?"

"Yes, my son?" Abraham replied.

“We have the fire and the wood, “but where is the sheep for the burnt offering?”

8“God will provide a sheep for the burnt offering, my son,” Abraham answered. 9When they arrived at the place where God had told him to go, Abraham built an altar and arranged the wood on it. Then he tied his son, Isaac, and laid him on the altar on top of the wood. 10And Abraham picked up the knife to kill his son as a sacrifice. 11At that moment the angel of the Lord called to him from heaven, “Abraham! Abraham!”

“Yes,” Abraham replied. “Here I am!”

12“Don’t lay a hand on the boy!” the angel said. “Do not hurt him in any way, for now I know that you truly fear God. You have not withheld from me even your son, your only son.” 13Then Abraham looked up and saw a ram caught by its horns in a thicket. So he took the ram and sacrificed it as a burnt offering in place of his son. 14Abraham named the place Yahweh-Yireh; as it is said to this day, “On the mountain of the Lord it will be provided.” 15Then the angel of the Lord called again to Abraham from heaven. 16and said, “Because you have obeyed me and have not withheld your only son, I swear by my own name that 17I will certainly bless you. I will multiply your descendants beyond number, like the stars in the sky and the sand on the seashore. Your descendants will conquer the cities of their enemies. 18And through your descendants all the nations of the earth will be blessed—all because you have obeyed me.”

Abraham…The grand patriarch…The father of three faiths…The man, the myth, the legend…A man set in motion by the activation of a unique set of traits; those that would find their way through the crippled helix of moral depravity and colonize the molecular fabric of his third great grandson, Moses. Both would be equally encoded with an attuned ear for hearing voices (especially those of the divine), and a readiness to execute their wishes on command. Today we call this schizophrenia. Additionally, those who wish to burn their children are imprisoned. Nevertheless, we are much obliged for the many clinical mental disorders that plagued this family lineage of fictional characters; those of which inspired countless stories such as this within our passage. Stories that give us invaluable insight into the true moral nature of the god of the Bible.

Building up to this massively iconic story, there's a key feature in Abraham's meteoric rise to superstardom that conveniently remains unmentioned among those who uphold and teach the sacrality of this 'test of Abraham's faith' found in Genesis 22. Beginning with Genesis 12 and through chapter 17, we find a staggering 18 instances where god himself promises Abraham fame, glory, land, and descendants like that of the stars. God's fatiguing redundancy overemphasizes the fact that the deal is sealed. Heck, Abraham even whacked the top wing of his wanger to secure the agreement at the command of god.

We arrive at chapter 22 and the voices in Abraham's head return with an additional stipulation: *"Hey man, it's me again, god. You're doin good bud, but, um, yaa…. There's just one more thing I need from ya to seal the deal. Soo…I'm gonna need you to go ahead and burn your son. You know—to me…as a sacrifice."* Abraham obeys, and this *obedience*, exegetically speaking, is one of the defining moments that has created a fathomless chasm in dividing the faithful from the infidel (or any thinking agent).

It's simply incomprehensible in finding these faithful adherents, many even being family and friends, deriving lessons out of this disastrous debris of delusion, concocted from a clinically twisted mind. I question every ounce of their very nature and especially their morality; the supposed morality that comes from god. Like little mentally debilitated minions, they rush to their safe haven at the end of the story where Abraham is relieved of this duty in an attempt to intellectualize their sad and obvious miniature stature of a human being. Of course what follows as the gotcha hammer-fall is the cliche parallel of *"and seeeee, god went all the way in killing his son!"* Though quite embarrassingly, in revering just this one story, their mental framework is overtly displayed as one that is stripped of the beauty of true love and empathy, and warped into believing an infinitely flawed logical fallacy: *'It's in the Bible, so it's ok.' (Or, 'The Bible says so.')*

Simply put, the Bible, and any 'holy book,' especially those containing the purported words of god, should contain nothing that we as humans would be unwilling to do and should make no requests that would violate our moral nature. Yes, the very moral nature that naturally defies the moral nature of god.

#1

The Worst of the Lot

Genesis 19:1-8; NLT

> 1That evening the two angels came to the entrance of the city of Sodom. Lot was sitting there, and when he saw them, he stood up to meet them. Then he welcomed them and bowed with his face to the ground. 2"My lords," he said, "come to my home to wash your feet, and be my guests for the night. You may then get up early in the morning and be on your way again." "Oh no," they replied. "We'll just spend the night out here in the city square." 3But Lot insisted, so at last they went home with him. Lot prepared a feast for them, complete with fresh bread made without yeast, and they ate. 4But before they retired for the night, all the men of Sodom, young and old, came from all over the city and surrounded the house. 5They shouted to Lot, "Where are the men who came to spend the night with you? Bring them out to us so we can have sex with them!" 6So Lot stepped outside to talk to them, shutting the door behind him. 7"Please, my brothers," he begged, "don't do such a wicked thing. 8Look, I have two virgin daughters. Let me bring them out to you, and you can do with them as you wish. But please, leave these men alone, for they are my guests and are under my protection."

Judges 19:1-29; NLT, *pp*

> 1There was a Levite who brought home a woman to be his

concubine. 2But she became angry with him; *(she was unfaithful [KJV, pp])* and returned to her father's home. After four months, 3her husband set out to persuade her to come back. When he arrived, her father welcomed him. 4Her father urged him to stay awhile. 10On the fifth day, he took his concubine and headed toward Jerusalem. 14...When they came to Gibeah, 15they stopped to spend the night. 16That evening an old man came home from his work in the fields. 17When he saw the travelers sitting in the town square, he asked them where they were from and where they were going. 18..."We are on our way to the hill country of Ephraim, which is my home. I traveled to Bethlehem, and now I'm returning home. But no one has taken us in for the night," the man replied. 20"You can stay with me, but whatever you do, don't spend the night in the square," the old man said. 21So he took them home with him and they ate and drank together. 22While they were enjoying themselves, a crowd of troublemakers from the town surrounded the house. They began beating at the door and shouting to the old man, "Bring out the man who is staying with you so we can have sex with him." 23The old man stepped outside to talk to them. "No, my brothers, don't do such an evil thing. This man is a guest in my house, and such a thing would be shameful. 24Here, take my virgin daughter and this man's concubine. I will bring them out to you, and you can abuse them and do whatever you like. But don't do such a shameful thing to this man." 25But they wouldn't listen to him. So the Levite took hold of his concubine and pushed her out the door. The men of the town abused her all night, taking turns raping her until morning. Finally, at dawn they let her go. 26At daybreak the woman returned to the house where her husband was staying. She collapsed at the door of the house and lay there until it was light. 27When her husband opened the door to leave, there lay his concubine with her hands on the threshold. 28He said, "Get up! Let's go!" But there was no answer. So he put her body on his donkey and took her home. 29When he got home, he took a knife and cut his concubine's body into twelve pieces. Then he sent one piece to each tribe throughout all the territory of Israel.

Genesis sits high atop the throne as the nucleus of this immortal thorn. Impervious to the annals of time, it remains an indomitable nerve center, permeating much of mankind as a clutching force. It would be unbecoming to deny the profound and even psychological effects that such foundational stories and elements found in Genesis have on society today. We find the story of god creating all things, the garden of Eden, the serpent and the fall of man, the first murder, Noah's Ark, the Tower of Babel, Abraham the patriarch, and shortly thereafter, we find ourselves engrossed in the opening passage of Genesis 19; the crowning jewel of our countdown.

Beginning in signature prose, Moses pens a spicy and utterly gratuitous story as a prelude to the destruction of Sodom and Gomorrah. (Of course we must bear in mind, this story is just one in the ocean of the Torah that god himself dictated to Moses.)

Lot was the nephew of Abraham and one who was favored by god. One particular evening, he welcomed a couple angels into his home. After a nice supper with unleavened bread it was time to retire and snuggle up in bed. With salty mamma in her 'kerchief and Lot in his cap, they settled their brains for a long evening's nap. When out on the lawn there arose such a clatter, Lot sprang from his bed to see what was the matter.

"Hey you in there!" they shouted. "We want us some sex with your guests! Send 'em on out bud!" Lot stepped out onto his porch and kindly appealed to the crowd.

"Ah, come on guys—I know you're looking for a new orifice or two, but these guys just got in and they're my guests. I'll make a deal with ya—you leave my guests alone, and I'll give you my two daughters to do whatever you wish! Oh and they're both virgins! Sound good?"

Aww, Lotty baby. Your compassion as an innkeeper brings tears to my eyes. Even Peter gives you a shoutout in his book—pronouncing you a 'righteous man' and one who was 'sick of the shameful immorality of those around him.'

Such an enrapturing soap, sizzling with sodomites, angels, and a father offering up his daughters as sex slaves, was enough of a hit to get a near replication from the pen of Samuel in the book of Judges. Though like any good fish-story, embellishments will follow—and those usually being the fantasies of the storyteller. Samuel's need for a little more climax entails a twist in the script at the porch scene. This time, the innkeeper offers his virgin daughter and one of his new guests (the lady who came with the Levite man; *his concubine*) as sex slaves to a rowdy group of Benjamites in lieu of their demand for the Levite. Upon their rejection, the Levite heroically saves himself and the innkeeper's daughter by forcing his concubine out the door as a final offer. After a dusk till dawn gang-rape, the woman returns to the porch as a lifeless corpse. Upon opening the door, the Levite says, *"Alrighty—up & at 'em!"* but there was no response.

He saddles her up and when he gets home, he cuts her body into twelve pieces and sends one piece to each tribe of Israel. This gesture unites the armies of Israel and god directs a bloody avenging in the overthrow of the the tribe of Benjamin.

REFERENCES

Commentary #73/The Rich Man and Lazarus

Martin, Ernest L., Ph.D, "The Real Meaning of Lazarus and the Rich Man" (2019, Oct. 29) https://www.mercyonall.org/posts/the-real-meaning-of-lazarus-and-the-rich-man

Commentary #59/The Scapeman

Guzik, David "Leviticus Chapter 24" Enduring Word Bible Commentary . (2022, Aug. 31) https://enduringword.com/bible-commentary/leviticus-24

Commentary #58/The Story of Samson The Myth of Hercules

Manning, Joseph "Making Sense of Samson" (2012, Jul. 20) https://ancientwordtour.wordpress.com/2012/07/20/making-sense-of-samson

Meshel, Dr. Naphtali "Samson the Demigod?" TheTorah.com. (2019, Jun. 14) https://www.thetorah.com/article/samson-the-demigod

Terry, Eso "Samson, the Sun God" (2018, June) https://www.esotericdaily.com/2018/06/samson-sun-god.html

Corollary, Mathisen "Samson and the Seven Locks of His Head" Star Myths of the World (2015, Jan 16) https://www.starmythworld.com/mathisencorollary/2015/01/samson-and-seven-locks-of-his-head.html

Commentary #57Divine Retribution: ***Lashing with Leprosy***

Yitzhaq Feder, "Tzaraat in Light of Its Mesopotamian Parallels"

TheTorah.com (2017)
https://www.thetorah.com/article/tzaraat-in-light-of-its-mesopotamian-parallels

Rabbi Rosenfeld, Dovid "Tzara'at versus Leprosy" aish.com. (2021) https://aish.com/tzaraat-versus-leprosy/

Rabbi Shurpin, Yehuda "Is Tzaraat Leprosy?" (2020) https://www.chabad.org/library/article_cdo/aid/4714280/jewish/Is-Tzaraat-Leprosy.htm

Fox, Tamar "Tzaraat--A Biblical Affliction" My Jewish Learning. (2018, Jul. 23)
https://www.myjewishlearning.com/article/tzaraat-a-biblical-affliction

Gillen, Dr. A. L. "Biblical Leprosy: Shedding Light on the Disease that Shuns." Answers in Genesis (2015)
https://answersingenesis.org/biology/disease/biblical-leprosy-shedding-light-on-the-disease-that-shuns

Deffinbaugh, Robert L. "The Sin Offering" (Leviticus 4:1-5:13; 6:24-30) | Bible.org. (2004, May 18)
https://bible.org/seriespage/5-sin-offering-leviticus-41-513-624-30

Schamberg, Dr. Jay F. The Biblical World, 1899 13:3, 162-169 The Nature of the Leprosy of the Bible. From a Medical and Biblical Point of View

Rabbi Blank, Glenn "The Hidden Meaning of Tzara'at." (2000, Apr. 08)
https://www.lehigh.edu/~gdb0/simcha/tzaraat.htm

Torah Insights - Chabad Lubavitch of Greenwich. "The Gift of Pleasure" (2019, Apr. 05)
https://www.chabadgreenwich.org/templates/blog/post_cdo/aid/2197590/PostID/90127

Milgrom, Jacob, (1991). "Leviticus 1–16: A New Translation with Introduction and Commentary."

Commentary #56/Generational Hexes

Bradley, M. "The 6 Steps To Breaking a Generational Curse." Bible Knowledge. (2021) https://www.bible-knowledge.com/six-steps-to-breaking-a-generational-curse

Klok, Duane V. "Breaking Generational Curses" | Walking By Faith. (2020) https://walkingbyfaith.tv/breaking-generational-curses

Commentary #55/*Deuteronomy Compilation:* Highlights of the 10 613 Commandments

Hecht, Mendy "The 613 Commandments (Mitzvot)" (2009, Mar.) https://www.chabad.org/library/article_cdo/aid/756399/jewish/The-613-Commandments-Mitzvot.htm

Rich, Tracey "A List of the 613 Mitzvot (Commandments)" - Judaism 101 (JewFAQ). (2022) https://www.jewfaq.org/613_commandments

Rabbi Ullman, Yirmiyahu "Origin of the Torah" www.rabbiullman.com. (2004, Jan. 31) https://ohr.edu/1438

Rabbi Amaru, Joshua "Torah min Ha-shamayim" | Yeshivat Har Etzion. (2015, Apr. 3) https://www.etzion.org.il/en/philosophy/issues-jewish-thought/issues-mussar-and-faith/torah-min-ha-shamayim

Commentary #54/Mosaissism

Kaiser, W. C. (1991). Toward Old Testament Ethics. Zondervan.

Kaltner, John "Egypt", n.p. [cited 12 Sep. 2022] https://www.bibleodyssey.org:443/places/main-articles/egypt

Walvoord, John F. "11. Egypt And The King Of The South" | Bible.org. (2008, Jan. 1) https://bible.org/seriespage/11-egypt-and-king-south

Mahoney, Tim; Law, Steve | Investigating Moses Old Testament Authorship Is Important. (2019, Feb. 22) https://patternsofevidence.com/2019/02/22/investigating-moses-old-testament-authorship

Commentary #53/Solunar Siege and Homing Hailstones

Livio, M. "Did Galileo Truly Say, 'And Yet It Moves'?" (2020, May 6)
A Modern Detective Story. SCIENTIFIC AMERICAN, a Division of Springer Nature America, Inc.
https://blogs.scientificamerican.com/observations/did-galileo-truly-say-and-yet-it-moves-a-modern-detective-story

Calahan, Jean L. Jr., "How did the sun stand still in Joshua 10:12-14?" (2017, Jun. 14)
https://www.neverthirsty.org/bible-qa/qa-archives/question/how-did-the-sun-stand-still-in-joshua-10-12-14

Scharping, N. "What would happen if Earth stopped spinning?" Astronomy. (2021, Apr. 15)
https://astronomy.com/news/2021/04/what-would-happen-if-the-earth-stopped-spinning

Fairchild, Mary "How Heavy Was a Talent in the Bible?" (2020, Aug. 28)
https://www.learnreligions.com/what-is-a-talent-700699

Commentary #52/Saint Korah

Altein, Yehuda "Korah: The Rebel of the Bible" (2011, Apr.)
https://www.chabad.org/library/article_cdo/aid/246641/jewish/Korah-The-Rebel-of-the-Bible.htm

Binnie, W. "Korah's Rebellion" (2018, Oct. 23)
https://biblehub.com/sermons/auth/binnie/korah%27s_rebellion.htm

Guzik, David "Numbers Chapter 16" Enduring Word Bible Commentary (2015, Dec. 12)
https://enduringword.com/bible-commentary/numbers-16

Rabbi Gornish, Yitzchak The Laws of a Kosher Mezuzah - Kosher Spirit. (2016, May 2)
https://www.ok.org/article/the-laws-of-a-kosher-mezuzah

Mezuzah - New World Encyclopedia. (2020, Sept. 20)
https://www.newworldencyclopedia.org/entry/Mezuzah

Prof. Ninan, M. "Mezuzah." (2018, Aug. 17) https://www.talentshare.org/~mm9n/articles/mezuzah/7.htm

Commentary #51/Snakes on a Desert Plain

Weliever, Ken The Preacherman "The Gospel in a Nutshell" (2014, Jun. 26) https://thepreachersword.com/2014/06/26/the-gospel-in-a-nutshell

Commentary #50/Rules for a Goring Ox

Exegetical and Hermeneutical Commentary of Exodus 21:28 – Bible Commentary. (2020) https://www.biblia.work/bible-commentary/exegetical-and-hermeneutical-commentary-of-exodus-2128

Exodus 21 - Pulpit Commentary. (2018, Sept. 25) https://biblehub.com/commentaries/pulpit/exodus/21.htm

Rav Mishkin, Jonathan Mishpatim | The Goring Ox | Yeshivat Har Etzion. (2014, Sep. 21) https://www.etzion.org.il/en/tanakh/torah/sefer-shemot/parashat-mishpatim/mishpatim-goring-ox

ALHATORAH.ORG. (2011-2023) https://alhatorah.org/The_Torah_and_Ancient_Near_Eastern_Law_Codes/0

Janowski, Malkie "Is there a difference between the "evil inclination" and the "animal soul"? (2009, Jun.) https://www.chabad.org/library/article_cdo/aid/924915/jewish/Evil-Inclination-vs-Animal-Soul.htm

Leithart, Peter "Israel, the Goring Ox." (2009, Oct. 30) https://www.patheos.com/blogs/leithart/2009/10/israel-the-goring-ox

Commentary #49/New Testament Slaves

Kidd, Thomas S. "Slavery Old and New: Comparing Early America with Biblical Times." (2021, Feb. 23) https://www.desiringgod.org/articles/slavery-old-and-new

Commentary #48/The Scapegoat

Noga Ayali-Darshan, "Scapegoat: The Origins of the Crimson Thread" TheTorah.com (2020, Sep. 23) https://thetorah.com/article/scapegoat-the-origins-of-the-crimson-thread

Rabbi Weisz, Noson "Tzvi - The Scapegoat" Aish.com. Aish. (2022) https://aish.com/149807985

Rabbi Rosenfeld, David "Tzvi - The Cruel Death of the Scapegoat - Aish.com. Aish. (2021) https://aish.com/the-cruel-death-of-the-scapegoat

"Five Afflictions On Yom Kippur." The Book of Our Heritage | Feldheim Publications (2016) https://www.chabad.org/library/article_cdo/aid/4821/jewish/Five-Afflictions.htm

"What can't you do on Yom Kippur?" WhoMadeWhat - Learn Something New Every Day and Stay Smart. (2021, Aug. 27). https://whomadewhat.org/what-cant-you-do-on-yom-kippur

Hunter, Ross and Mary " The year the scarlet thread stopped turning white - the importance of the historical and cultural context." (2017, Jan. 28). http://evbibletalk.blogspot.com/2017/01/the-year-scarlet-thread-stopped-turning.html

Kulp, Dr. Joshua "English Explanation of Mishnah Yoma 5:6:1." (1997-2013). https://www.sefaria.org/English_Explanation_of_Mishnah_Yoma.5.6.1?lang=bi

Commentary #47/Saint Paulradox and the Joys of Circumcision and Exclusivity

Romans 3 - The Pulpit Commentaries - StudyLight.org. (2001-2022) https://www.studylight.org/commentaries/eng/tpc/romans-3.html

Romans 3 - Meyer's NT Commentary. (2018, Sept. 25) https://biblehub.com/commentaries/meyer/romans/3.htm

Commentary #44/Top Picks of Petey the Rock

Prof. Garcia, Jared "The Literary Relationship between Jude and 2 Peter" exegeticaltools.com https://exegeticaltools.com/2020/05/15/the-literary-relationship-between-2-peter-and-jude

Get your very own Brimstone Sulfur Balls From Sodom and Gomorrah City: https://www.ebay.com/itm/283485639428

Commentary #41/Killing vs Injuring a Slave

Biblical literature | Definition, Types, Significance, Survey, & Development. Encyclopedia Britannica. (1998, Oct. 19) https://www.britannica.com/topic/biblical-literature/Exodus

Commentary #40/The Last Triumph of Moses

Guzik, David "Numbers Chapter 31" Enduring Word Bible Commentary (2022) https://enduringword.com/bible-commentary/numbers-31

Commentary #39/Jeremiah's Rotten Underwear

Jeremiah 13 - Benson Commentary. (2018, Sept. 25) https://biblehub.com/commentaries/benson/jeremiah/13.htm

Commentary #37/New Testament Slaves/Goodness Gracious, Great Cloven Tongues of Fire

Stanley, Dr. Charles "What Is the Meaning of Pentecost? What Happened at Pentecost?"

Christianity (2010, May 28) https://www.christianity.com/jesus/early-church-history/pentecost/what-changed-at-pentecost.html

Garrett, Duane A. "Feasts and Festivals of Israel in the Bible - Definition, Meaning and References" (2021) https://www.biblestudytools.com/dictionary/feasts-and-festivals-of-israel/#google_vignette

Commentary #35/Roiders of the Lost Ark

Dr. Dilday "Poole on 1 Samuel 6:4: Golden Hemorrhoids and Mice." (2021, Jan. 18). https://www.fromreformationtoreformation.com/post/poole-on-1-samuel-6-4-golden-hemorrhoids-and-mice

Marcus M. Aquino, MD, FACS, FASCRS Colon and Rectal Surgeon "Biblical references to Hemorrhoids (Emerods)" (2020, Feb 9) https://www.marcusaquinomd.com/blog/biblical-references-to-hemorrhoids-emerods

Brasseaux, Shawn "What are "emerods?" (2017, May 25) https://forwhatsaiththescriptures.org/2017/05/25/emerods

Commentary #34/Familial Cannibalism

Leviticus 26 - Ellicott's Commentary for English Readers (2018, Sept. 25). https://biblehub.com/commentaries/ellicott/leviticus/26.htm

Commentary #33/Ceremonial Purification After Childbirth

Rindner, Sarah "Why Does the Bible Require New Mothers to Atone after Childbirth?" Mosaic (2017, Apr. 27) https://mosaicmagazine.com/observation/religion-holidays/2017/04/why-does-the-bible-require-new-mothers-to-atone-after-childbirth

Leviticus 12:6 Commentaries (2022, Dec. 29) https://biblehub.com/commentaries/leviticus/12-6.htm

Commentary #31/Ass Redemption Rules

Van Popta, George P. "Exodus 13:13a - The Donkey and the Lamb" | Christian Library. Clarion (1997) https://www.christianstudylibrary.org/article/exodus-1313a-donkey-and-lamb

Exodus 13 - Matthew Poole's Commentary (2018, Sept. 25) https://biblehub.com/commentaries/poole/exodus/13.htm

Bumpers, Shawn "Redeeming the Donkey." (2016, Dec. 1) https://www.calvarybirmingham.com/redeeming-the-donkey

Commentary #26/A Fishy Tale

Rosa, S."Polycrates and the Fisherman" | The Art Institute of Chicago. (2019) https://www.artic.edu/artworks/44826/polycrates-and-the-fisherman

SoRelle, Skip "Jesus Tells a Joke" | Medium. (2021 Jul. 10) https://skipsorelle.medium.com/jesus-tells-a-joke-16ab4344c34

Poythress, Vern "The Coin in the Fish's Mouth" - Westminster Theological Seminary. (2016, Nov. 29) https://faculty.wts.edu/posts/the-coin-in-the-fishs-mouth

Bilkes, Gerald M. "The Miracle of Christ: The Coin in the Fish's Mouth" | Christian Library. (2014) https://www.christianstudylibrary.org/article/miracle-christ-coin-fish%E2%80%99s-mouth

Commentary #23/She Will Secretly Eat Her Newborn

Prof. Liebenberg, WA "The Revelation of Y'shua HaMashiach" | HRTI Publishing (2017) https://www.goodreads.com/en/book/show/36179570

Commentary #22/Deviled Ham

Multiple Authors "What's the issue with Noah's son seeing him naked?" | Massachusetts Bible Society. (2021) https://www.massbible.org/exploring-the-bible/ask-a-prof/answers/whats-issue-noahs-son-seeing-him-naked

Commentary #21/Kosher Deli

Cattle Empire "What is cud, and why do cattle chew it?" (2013, Dec. 20)

https://cattle-empire.net/blog/f/what-is-cud-and-why-do-cattle-chew-it

Commentary #20/The First Sacrifice

Genesis 4 - Cambridge Bible for Schools and Colleges. (2018, Sept. 25)

https://biblehub.com/commentaries/cambridge/genesis/4.htm

Cross, John R. "Where in the Scriptures does it say that God told

Cain and Abel to bring a blood sacrifice?" Goodseed (2014, Jan. 2) https://www.goodseed.com/blog/2014/01/02/where-in-the-scriptures-does-it-say-that-god-told-cain-and-abel-to-bring-a-blood-sacrifice

MacCath-Moran, Ceallaigh S. "The Vegan Pagan: The Case Against Animal Sacrifice." (2014, Nov. 2)

https://csmaccath.com/blog/vegan-pagan-case-against-animal-sacrifice

Hoge, Jordan A. "Is the Doctrine of Propitiation Really Biblical?" (2021, Apr. 28)

https://cbaptistc.org/2021/04/28/is-the-doctrine-of-propitiation-really-biblical

St. Catherine of Siena Roman Catholic Church "What is 'the bread of the Presence?'" (2018, May 30)

https://www.stcatherinercc.org/single-post/2018/05/30/what-is-the-bread-of-the-presence

Commentary #19/Sexecutions

Bible.org "Does Jesus in fact say that He is God's Son, not just infer it?" | Bible.org. (2001, Jan. 1)

https://bible.org/question/does-jesus-fact-say-he-god%E2%80%99s-son-not-just-infer-it

Calahan, John "Did Jesus ever say that He was the Son of God?" (2020, Mar. 18)

https://www.neverthirsty.org/bible-qa/qa-archives/question/did-jesus-ever-say-that-he-was-the-son-of-god

Carter, Paul "Did Jesus Ever Talk about Homosexuality?" - The Gospel Coalition | Canada. (2019, May 6)

Retrieved from https://ca.thegospelcoalition.org/columns/ad-fontes/jesus-ever-talk-homosexuality

All Translations Search: "The lord said to Moses." (2022-2023)

https://bible.knowing-jesus.com/search?q=the+lord+said+to+moses&translation=all

Commentary #17/Burn Her to Death and Other Instructions

Stewart, Don "When Paul Said All Scripture Is 'God-Breathed', Was He Also Referring to the New Testament?"

(2 Timothy 3:16). (2018) Blue Letter Bible. https://www.blueletterbible.org/Comm/stewart_don/faq/bible-authoritative-word/question5-paul-said-all-scripture.cfm

Commentary #16/Rest or Die

Stockton, Richard "The Sabbath: How And Why Some Still Observe This Ancient Ritual." All That's Interesting. (2017, May 11) https://allthatsinteresting.com/the-sabbath

List of Sabbath-keeping churches - Wikipedia. Contributors to Wikimedia projects. (2022, Oct. 08). https://en.wikipedia.org/w/index.php?title=List_of_Sabbath-keeping_churches&oldid=1114848672

Commentary #15/The Return of the Shapeshifting Wand of Doom

"What is the significance of Meribah in the Bible?" GotQuestions.org. (2022, Jan. 04) https://www.gotquestions.org/Meribah-in-the-Bible.html

Commentary #14/The Cozbi Show

Carpenter, Melissa "Balak, Pinchas & Mattot: How Moabites Became Midianites." (2015, Jul. 08). https://mtorah.com/2015/07/08/balak-pinchas-mattot-how-moabites-became-midianites

Commentary #13/God's Guide on Hebrew Slaves: ***A Special Loophole***

Prof. Diamond, James A. "The Treatment of Non-Israelite Slaves: From Moses To Moses" - TheTorah.com. (2016, Apr. 19) https://www.thetorah.com/article/the-treatment-of-non-israelite-slaves-from-moses-to-moses

Commentary #12/Zipporah the Zenith Zapper

Carter, Paul "The Strangest Circumcision Story Ever." (2020,

Feb. 21) https://www.thegospelcoalition.org/article/moses-zipporah-strangest-circumcision-story-exodus

Wilson, Dr. Ralph F. "The Circumcision of Moses' Son Gershom (Exodus 4:24-26) in the Moses Bible Study." (2022) https://www.jesuswalk.com/moses/appendix_4.htm

Erickson, Bror "A Bridegroom of Blood." (2016 Dec. 29) https://www.1517.org/articles/a-bridegroom-of-blood

Commentary #10/Lotsa Love

Reaume, J. "The Bloodlines of Jesus" - Trinity Bible Chapel. Reaume, J. (2016) https://trinitybiblechapel.ca/the-bloodlines-of-jesus

Genesis 19:32 Gills Exposition of the Bible | Bible Verse Meaning and Commentary. (2022) https://www.biblestudytools.com/commentaries/gills-exposition-of-the-bible/genesis-19-32.html

Rozy, "Bible Genealogy." Nambian Cornerstone (2021, Sept. 09) https://namibiancornerstone.com/bible-genealogy

Genesis 19 - Ellicott's Commentary for English Readers. (2018, Sept. 25) https://biblehub.com/commentaries/ellicott/genesis/19.htm

Deering, J. "The Ancient Path, Ruth Introduction." AncientPath.net (2012, Nov. 20) https://www.ancientpath.net/Bible/OT/08_ruth/Intro/08_Ruth_intro.htm

Commentary #9/Bloody Sheets

Koller, A. "Sex or power? The crime of the single girl in Deuteronomy 22." Harrassowitz Verlag. (2010) https://repository.yu.edu/handle/20.500.12202/4439

Heath, Nicola "The historic tradition of wedding night-virginity testing." (2018, Jan. 16) https://www.sbs.com.au/topics/voices/relationships/article/2018/01/10/historic-tradition-wedding-night-virginity-testing

All Translations Search: "Decrees" (10 instances) (2022-2023) https://bible.knowing-jesus.com/words/Decrees/book/5

All Translations Search: "Laws" (33 instances) (2022-2023) https://bible.knowing-jesus.com/words/Laws/book/5

All Translations Search: "Commands "(48 instances) (2022-2023) https://bible.knowing-jesus.com/words/Commands/book/5

Guzik, David "Deuteronomy Chapter 22." Enduring Word Bible Commentary (2018, Jul. 07) https://enduringword.com/bible-commentary/deuteronomy-22/#:~:text=bring%20out%20the%20evidence%20of,of%20the%20young%20woman%27s%20virginity

Woolgar, Christine "About that virginity test in Deuteronomy 22: it's not what you think." Light in grey places. (2019, Nov. 25) https://www.workthegreymatter.com/about-that-virginity-test-in-deuteronomy-22-its-not-what-you-think

Prof. Kislev, Itamar "Understanding Deuteronomy on its Own Terms" - TheTorah.com. (2015, Jul. 21) https://www.thetorah.com/article/understanding-deuteronomy-on-its-own-terms

Commentary #8/Baldy & the Bears

James 5:17 [KJV] 17Elias was a man subject to like passions as we are, and he prayed earnestly that it might not rain: and it rained not on the earth by the space of three years and six months.

Luke 4:25 [NLT] 25 "Certainly there were many needy widows in Israel in Elijah's time, when the heavens were closed for three and a half years, and a severe famine devastated the land.

Commentary #7/Covenantal Addicktion

Rabbi Kohn, Daniel "Brit Milah: The Biblical Origins" | My Jewish Learning. (2017, Mar. 07) https://www.myjewishlearning.com/article/brit-milah-the-biblical-origins

Gilad, E. "What is oral suction circumcision and where does it come from?" - Jewish World. Haaretz. (2015)

https://www.haaretz.com/jewish/2015-02-25/ty-article/.premium/what-is-oral-suction-circumcision/0000017f-e663-d97e-a37f-f76764430000

Brit milah - Wikipedia. Contributors to Wikimedia projects. (2023, Feb. 22; *Last Upated*) https://en.wikipedia.org/w/index.php?title=Brit_milah&oldid=1140976360

Commentary #6/Jephthah's Vow

Judges 11:31 Commentaries: (2022, Dec. 29) https://biblehub.com/commentaries/judges/11-31.htm

Commentary #4/Evil Twin, Evil Mother - *A Hallmark Tale*

Karim, Kaleef K. "The Age Of Rebecca When She Married Isaac." – Biblical Perspective. (2016, Oct. 26) https://discover-the-truth.com/2016/10/26/the-age-of-rebecca-when-she-married-isaac-biblical-perceptive

GotQuestions.org. "Why is Jacob called Jacob and Israel alternately in the book of Genesis?" (2022, Jan. 04). https://www.gotquestions.org/Jacob-Israel.html

Commentary #1/The Worst of the Lot

II Peter 2:7-8, [NLT] 7But God also rescued Lot out of Sodom because he was a righteous man who was sick of the shameful immorality of the wicked people around him. 8Yes, Lot was a righteous man who was tormented in his soul by the wickedness he saw and heard day after day.

Additional

Price, Dr. Randall "Did Moses Write the Torah?" – Israel My Glory. (2019, Jul/Aug) https://israelmyglory.org/article/did-moses-write-the-torah

Made in the USA
Columbia, SC
25 January 2025

52541606R00198